**Black Face
Maligned Race**

Black Face
Maligned Race

The Representation of Blacks in English Drama
from Shakespeare to Southerne

ANTHONY GERARD BARTHELEMY

Louisiana State University Press
Baton Rouge and London

Copyright © 1987 by Louisiana State University Press
All rights reserved
Manufactured in the United States of America

Designer: Christopher Wilcox
Typeface: Trump Mediaeval
Typesetter: CSA Press
Printer: Thomson-Shore, Inc.
Binder: John Dekker and Sons, Inc.

Grateful acknowledgment is made to Yale University Press for granting permission to reprint excerpts from Stephen Orgel, ed., *Ben Jonson: The Complete Masques*, copyright © 1969 by Yale University.

Publication of this book has been assisted by a grant from the Andrew W. Mellon Foundation.

10 9 8 7 6 5 4 3 2 1

Library of Congress Cataloging-in-Publication Data

Barthelemy, Anthony Gerard, 1949–
  Black face, maligned race.

  Bibliography: p.
  Includes index.
  1. English drama—17th century—History and criticism. 2. Africans in literature. 3. Blacks in literature. 4. English drama—Early modern and Elizabethan, 1500–1600—History and criticism. 5. English drama—Restoration, 1660–1700—History and criticism. 6. Racism in literature.   I. Title.
PR678.A4B37 1987   822'.3'093520396   86-27716
ISBN 0-8071-1331-X   ISBN 0-8071-2485-0

To my mother
Ruth Fernandez Barthelemy

Contents

Preface and Acknowledgments   ix

I   Satan's Livery: Blackness and the Western Tradition   1
II   Beauty's Beasts: Blacks in the Court Masque   18
III   Words of the Sponsors: Blacks in Lord Mayors' Pageants   42
IV   Princes of Darkness: Black Villains on the Mimetic Stage   72
V   Ethiops Washed White: Moors of the Nonvillainous Type   147
VI   White Men Burdened: White Moors on the English Stage   182

Conclusion   200
Bibliography   203
Index   211

Preface and Acknowledgments

This work is primarily a study of black characters on the English stage from 1589 to 1695, from George Peele's *The Battle of Alcazar* to Thomas Southerne's *Oroonoko*. The two plays establish the boundaries of this study because they identify important changes in the dramatic representation of blacks. Peele's *Alcazar* put on the mimetic stage the first black Moor of any dramatic significance; *Oroonoko* was the first play to have an African slave as its hero. Although the central focus of this study is on black characters in mimetic drama of that period, two nonmimetic dramatic subgenres, court masques and Lord Mayors' Pageants, are included here because they reflected prevailing popular notions about black people and helped to propagate notions about blackness.

Attitudes toward black people in the seventeenth century were formulated in an environment that had not distinguished between the traditional Christian view of black people as devils and the then not entirely familiar African. In fact, the very word that was frequently used to identify Africans, *Moor*, reflects the conflation of the older views of blackness with newly acquired though not completely accurate information about Africans and their origins. Because *Moor* is so common and powerful an appellation, I begin the book with an extended discussion of the etymology of that word. Since seventeenth-century Englishmen had available other words with which to identify black men, including *Negro* and *African, Moor* may have been chosen because it helped to distinguish in a more precise way something supposed to be essential about blacks that *Negro* and *African* did not.

Readers of seventeenth-century literature know that while blacks were called "Moors," all Moors were not black. In fact, almost anyone who was not Christian, European, or Jewish could have been called a Moor; this includes Asians, Native Americans, Africans, Arabs, and all Muslims regardless of ethnicity. Of the other Moors, I limit my discussion to Native Americans and North Africans to whom the term *Moor* is applied. The Native Americans are discussed exclusively in Chapter III and the North Africans in Chapter VI. These two groups are included because they were portrayed in a manner similar to the way blacks were portrayed and because they share the perceived "otherness" that so clearly identifies blacks on the stage.

Throughout this study, I attempt to keep in balance the three greatest influences on the representation of blacks: English political, social, and theatrical history. It is impossible to imagine that political and social events did not influence the way Englishmen saw Africans. In fact, I suggest that the word used to identify Africans in some fundamental way reflects those historical influences. The Moors of Africa's Mediterranean coast had proved how threatening they were to Christendom, and they remained a threat to commerce well beyond the seventeenth century. At the same time, Africans from the interior confronted Christians with a vision of humanity and the world that was full of wonder. But Englishmen had witnessed black characters on the stage long before they saw real black men. This theatrical history of blackness was not lost when Englishmen became familiar with Africans. Indeed, earlier representations of blackness seemed to receive reconfirmation and validation from the tales with which explorers returned home. The theatrical past combined with knowledge of the world beyond Christendom to give us Aaron and Othello and other black Moors. But these Moors helped to create a new theatrical convention with its own history, and that convention has long needed examination and explication. This is the task I undertake.

x

Preface and Acknowledgments

Of course there are many other Moors in addition to Aaron and Othello. I have made every effort to locate all the plays, court masques, Lord Mayors' Pageants, and other dramatic works in which black characters appear. I have also attempted to find in sixteenth- and seventeenth-century dramatic literature any character who is identified as a Moor whether that character is Native American, Asian, or North African. Although for safety's sake I will not claim absolute success, I feel confident that I have found nearly all the Moorish characters in dramatic literature and surely all those of any dramatic significance.

I have also made every effort to use reliable modern scholarly editions of dramatic texts and secondary sources when possible. Some of these editions, it should be noted, do not use modern spellings. I have not modernized the spelling in a quotation except for the use of "th" in place of "edh" and "thorn" in the quotations from "Rouland and Vernagu" and *Mandeville's Travels*. Because there are so many variant spellings, I have not used *sic* to identify any. To have done so would have burdened the text.

At last I have the opportunity to thank those who have offered me assistance, encouragement, and friendship while this project was underway. My special thanks go to Henry Louis Gates. I dare not begin to measure his assistance or my gratitude for fear that any accounting or expression of them would appear to be hyperbole when in fact it would actually be litotes. I am also especially grateful to G. K. Hunter for sharing his inexhaustible and indefatigable knowledge of sixteenth- and seventeenth-century English drama. I am a beneficiary of that knowledge and of incalculable other good offices. I wish also to thank Kim Benston, Margie Ferguson, Carl Freedman, John Guillory, Richard Halpern, Lanny Hammer, Tony O'Keefe, Ethan Nasredden, Jack Opel, and Margie Waller. They all know what they did, and to them I am grateful.

xi

**Black Face
Maligned Race**

I

Satan's Livery
Blackness and the Western Tradition

> Alas, alas, and wele-wo!
> lucifer, whi fell thou so?
> We, that were angels so fare,
> and sat so hie aboue the ayere,
> Now ar we waxen blak as any coyll,
> And vgly, tatyrd as a foyll.
>
> —*The Towneley Plays*

Black Africans probably first arrived in England in 1554. Long before those real black men reached English shores, however, black faces had been seen on English stages. The dramatic representation of black characters on the English stage in the sixteenth and seventeenth centuries obviously reflected English attitudes toward blackness and English experiences with black men, both real and imagined. Reflected too in English responses to blackness were attitudes that were common throughout Christian Western Europe, attitudes derived in part from shared historical experiences with Africans and Muslims and from a common ancient literary tradition. Much of this collective European experience with blacks and blackness is synopsized in the history of the word *Moor*. For this reason, an etymological examination of that word provides a useful starting point for a study of the representation of black characters on the English stage during the sixteenth and seventeenth centuries. As we learn how and why *Moor* became synonymous with *black African*, we will also begin to understand the origins of the stereotypical black villain whose villainy is frequently summarized in that very word. However, before we look at *Moor*, it is important to comment briefly on the significance of blackness in the Western tradition.

Black Face, Maligned Race

The association of evil with blackness is so much a part of Western tradition that to catalog it would belabor the point.[1] In the ancient world, black was the color of evil. The following line from Horace serves as an example of the antiquity of the tradition, as well as its power and simplicity: "Hic niger est, hunc tu, romane, caveto" ("This is a black, Roman; beware this"). A poem from the sixth century A.D. found in the Codex Salmasianus exemplifies still further the power of evil that blackness was believed to possess:

Filius Aurorae, Phoebi nascentis alumnus,
    Producit gentis milia tetra suae.
Succurrens fessis faustio non omine Teucris
    Pergit Pelidae protinus ense mori.
Iam tunc monstratur, maneat qui Pergama casus,
    Cum nigrum Priamus suscipit auxilium.
(The son of Dawn, foster son of rising Phoebus,
    Produced black thousands of his race.
Running to aid the exhausted Trojans with inauspicious omen,
    He proceeded to die at once by the sword of the descendant of Pelius.
Already then it is shown how Troy awaits her fall,
    When Priam accepts black help.)[2]

Borrowing from this tradition, the church fathers linked blackness directly to sin. Augustine wrote that Ethiopians were "the remotest and foulest of mankind." Jerome in a letter on sin and purity wrote:

"You are of your father the devil, and the lust of your father it is your will to do." So it was said to the Jews. And in another place, "He that committeth sin is of the devil." Born, in the first instance, of such parentage we are naturally black, and even when we have repented, so long as we have not scaled the heights of virtue, we may still say:

---

1. See Winthrop Jordan, *White over Black: American Attitudes toward the Negro, 1550-1812* (Chapel Hill, N.C., 1968), 4-11. See also George K. Hunter, "Othello and Colour Prejudice," in *Dramatic Identities and Cultural Tradition: Studies in Shakespeare and His Contemporaries: Critical Essays* (New York, 1978), 33-39.

2. Horace, *Satires, Epistles, Ars Poetic* (1926; rpr. Cambridge, Mass., 1970), I, iv, 85; "De Memnone," in *Anthologia Latina*, ed. Alexander Riese (Leipzig, 1869), I, 132-33.

Satan's Livery

"I am black but comely, O ye daughters of Jerusalem." But you will say to me, "I have left the home of my childhood; I have forgotten my father, I am born anew in Christ. What reward do I receive for this? ... Your bridegroom [Christ] is not haughty or disdainful; He has married an Ethiopian woman." He will miraculously change your complexion so that it shall be said of you, "Who is this that goeth up and hath been made white?"[3]

In the Christian tradition, whiteness is desired, blackness is condemned. White is the color of the regenerated, of the saved; black is the color of the damned, the lost. This allegorical reading of white and black finds repeated expression from the earliest of Christian exegeses to the present.

Accommodated within this allegorical reading of blackness is a theory of the origin of Africans that makes them and all other blacks the heirs of Noah's sinful son Ham. Winthrop Jordan writes in *White Over Black* that Jerome and Augustine "casually accepted the assumption that Africans were descended from one or several of Ham's four sons, an assumption which became universal in Christendom despite the obscurity of its origins."[4] Leo Africanus and Samuel Purchas, to name just two authors, carried this tradition into the seventeenth century. By linking the cause of Africans' blackness to the sin of their mythic progenitor, the Christian tradition with remarkable economy attached to all people of African ancestry an irrevocable bond to a sinful past. In a theological system that believes that sinfulness is the inheritance of all and that employs the trope of ablution through Baptism, the mark of sin on blacks is uniquely severe because the sign of their sinfulness is indelible.

The association of blackness with evil has a long history on the English stage as well. There the tradition goes back at least to early medieval drama. In many medieval miracle plays, the souls of the

---

3. Augustine, "Psalm 72," in *Expositions on the Book of Psalms*. Vol. III of *A Select Library of the Nicene and Post Nicene Fathers of the Christian Church*, trans. A. Cleveland Coxe, ed. Philip Schaff (New York, 1893), 331; Jerome, *Letters and Works*. Vol. VI of *A Select Library of the Nicene and Post Nicene Fathers of the Christian Church*, trans. W. H. Fremantle, ed. Philip Schaff (New York, 1893), 22–23.
4. Jordan, *White over Black*, 18.

damned were represented by actors painted black or in black costumes.[5] However, the prevalence of the tradition can be clearly seen in the mystery plays. In the play of the Fall in the Towneley, York, Coventry, and Chester cycles, Lucifer and his confederate rebels, after having sinned, turn black. In the Towneley play, a newly fallen angel, looking on their blackness, laments this metamorphosis:

> Alas, alas, and wele-wo!
> lucifer, whi fell thou so?
> We, that were angels so fare,
> and sat so hie aboue the ayere,
> Now ar we waxen blak as any coyll,
> And vgly, tatyrd as a foyll.[6]

As blackness identifies the sons of Ham, so too it identifies Lucifer and his minions, their blackness the external manifestation of their sinfulness.

The English iconographic tradition also uses blackness as an emblem of sin and evil. W. L. Hildburgh writes about medieval English alabaster sculpture: "The very dark faces of the torturers and other iniquitous persons are black." He speculates that these sculptures reflect the actual staging of certain scenes from the mystery plays.[7] If he is correct, then the number of black or nonwhite characters in these plays may have been far greater than the number that can be documented through textual references. What is certain, however, is that on the stage, in iconography, and in the literary and religious traditions, the face of evil is frequently black.

Blacks, in addition to being thought sinful, were also thought to be bestial. This view goes back to the earliest days of English exploration in Africa.[8] In 1554, the chronicler of John Lok's voyage to Guinea reported: "It is to be understood, that the people which

---

5. See E. K. Chambers, *The Medieval Stage* (Oxford, 1903), II, 142; and Chambers, *The Early English Folk Play* (Oxford, 1933), 164. See also M. Lyle Spencer, *Corpus Christi Pageants in England* (New York, 1911), 226.

6. *The Creation*, in *The Towneley Plays*, ed. George England (London, 1897), ll. 132-37.

7. W. L. Hildburgh, "Medieval English Alabasters," *Archaeologia*, XCIII (1949), 76.

8. See Jordan, *White over Black*, 24-32.

now inhabite the regions of the coast of Guinea, and the middle parts of Africa, as Libya the inner, and Nubia, with divers other great & large regions about the same, were in old time called AEthiopes and Nigritae, which we now call Moores, Moorens, or Negroes, a people of beastly living, without a God, lawe, religion, or common wealth, and so scorched and vexed with the heat of the sunne, that in many places they curse it when it riseth."[9]

Leo Africanus, the single most authoritative source on Africa until the age of modern exploration, wrote similarly of black Africans: "The Negros likewise leade a beastly kinde of life, being vtterly destitute of the vse of reason, of dexteritie of wit, and of all artes." This idea received further dissemination when in 1613 Samuel Purchas in *Purchas, His Pilgrimage* quoted Leo directly. Purchas wrote: "They [Africans] lived, saith *Leo*, like beasts, without King, Lord, Commonwealth, or any government, scarse knowing to sowe their grounds: cladde in skinnes of beasts: not having any peculiar wife; but lie ten or twelve men and women together, each man chusing which he best liked."[10] Purchas' unqualified repetition of Leo's assertions demonstrates the pervasiveness and endurance of those allegations.

Concupiscence stands prominently amongst the bestial characteristics of Africans. In fact, the very word *bestial* as it was used in the sixteenth and seventeenth centuries strongly implies lascivious conduct. Winthrop Jordan writes: "Indeed the sexual connotations embodied in the terms *bestial* and *beastly* were considerably stronger in Elizabethan English than they are today, and when the Elizabethan traveler pinned these epithets upon the behavior of Negroes he was frequently as much registering a sense of sexual shock as describing swinish manners."[11] This sense of shock perhaps served as the catalyst for a wide range of observations and characterizations that focus on the sexual behavior of

---

9. Richard Hakluyt, *The Principal Navigations, Voyages, Traffiques and Discoveries of the English Nation* (1554; rpr. London, 1927), IV, 57.

10. Leo Africanus, *The History and Description of Africa*, trans. John Pory, ed. Robert Brown (1600; rpr. New York, 1896), I, 187; Samuel Purchas, *Purchas, His Pilgrimage* (London, 1613), 537.

11. Jordan, *White over Black*, 33. See also pp. 32–40 and 136–179 for Jordan's discussion of English opinions on the libidinous nature of blacks. See also Elliot H. Tokson, *The Popular Image of the Black Man in English Drama, 1550–1688* (Boston, 1982), 82–105.

Africans. Some commentators go so far as to discourse on the anatomy and genitalia of Africans. Purchas, as we have seen, claims that the alleged bestiality of Africans found expression in their licentiousness. He also reports: "The Moore may have foure wives, & as many co[n]cubines as he can purchase." Leo says of "Negros": "Yet is there no nation vnder heauen more prone to venerie." Having still more to say on the subject of lechery in "Negros," Leo writes: "They have great swarmes of harlots among them; whereupon a man may easily coniecture their manner of living."[12]

Blacks, then, came to be seen as creatures beyond the realm of grace and civil society. Viewed in this manner, every aspect of their being was touched by their strangeness, their otherness. Because the legendary origin of their blackness is part of a myth of sin and exclusion, blacks were never able to separate the physical reality of their color from their alleged spiritual state. This linkage of their blackness to sin, seeing blackness as an outward manifestation of that sin, condemned blacks and their blackness to a symbolic role, one from which even today they are not entirely free. We shall see in defining the word *Moor* that these views of blacks and blackness were so pervasive that they inform the meaning of the word.

Like the words *Turk, Saracen, Oriental,* and *Indian, Moor* is difficult to define precisely. In the fifteenth, sixteenth, and seventeenth centuries, the word meant different things to different people. All these words, however, shared a common connotation: alien, or foreigner. Because these words were used so imprecisely—frequently they were used simply to identify any non-Christian—they came to denote a rather general category of alien. On the imprecise use of *Indian* and its nonspecific denotation, the erudite Samuel Purchas writes:

> This confusion of names, I thinke, did first grow from the confusion of nations. For as is before observed out of *Eusebius*, the Ethiopians arose from the River *Indus*, & setled their habitation neere to Egypt. Perhaps they brought the Indian name also to these parts. Or else the ignorance of those remote countries might doe it: in which respect, not only a third part of the olde world, but another new-found world, is named India. Therefore *Acosta* esteemeth India to be a generall

12. Purchas, *Purchas, His Pilgrimage,* 518; Leo Africanus, *History and Description of Africa,* I, 180, 187.

name to all countries which are far off, and strange to vs, although it be properly attributed to the East Indies.[13]

Similarly, *Moor* denotes a variety of things, some general, some specific, as illustrated by the breadth of the first definition for the word in the *Oxford English Dictionary*:

> In *Ancient* History, a native of *Mauretania*, a region of Northern Africa corresponding to parts of Morocco and Algeria. In later times, one belonging to the people of mixed Berber and Arab race, Mohammedan in religion, who constitute the bulk of the population of North-western Africa, and who in the 8th c. conquered Spain. In the Middle Ages, and as late as the 17th c., the Moors were commonly supposed to be mostly black or very swarthy (though the existence of 'white Moors' was recognized), and hence the word was often used for 'negro;' cf. BLACKAMOOR.

The *OED* cites the 1390 *Confessio Amantis* of Gower as the earliest example of *Moor* meaning Negro. The second meaning of *Moor* offered by the *OED* focuses on religion, while it identifies yet another ethnic group: "A Mohammedan, esp. a Mohammedan inhabitant of India." 1588 is cited as the earliest example of this meaning, although evidence in *Mandeville's Travels* suggests this is somewhat late.[14] The layers of qualifications given in the first definition allow us to include under the word *Moor* many people who are neither Berbers nor Arabs, as well as to exclude many who are Negroes. If we consider the second meaning, we can identify by the word *Moor* people of many different races and different religions. *Moor* can mean, then, non-black Muslim, black Christian, or black Muslim. The only certainty a reader has when he sees the word is that the person referred to is not a European Christian.

---

13. Purchas, *Purchas, His Pilgrimage*, 559.

14. In the Cotton Manuscript of *Mandeville's Travels* (ed. P. Hamelius [London, 1919], 29), we find: "And men of Nubye ben cristen but thei ben blacke as the Mowres for gret hete of the sonne." This description of the Nubians also appears in the fourteenth-century Paris Manuscript of *Mandeville's Travels*. The above reference to "Mowres," however, is found in what is called the "Egyptian Gap," and does not appear in print until 1725. The distinction made here between Muslims and Christians, while not explicit, seems clear since the Nubians share blackness with the "Mowres." We know at the very least from the author's observation that "Mowres" are non-Christian.

Black Face, Maligned Race

Moor is most probably derived from the Greek Μαῦpos, a proper noun that identifies the inhabitants of ancient Mauretania, the area that now makes up Morocco and Algeria. Ernest Klein, in *A Comprehensive Etymological Dictionary of the English Language*, suggests that Μαῦpos is related to ἀμαυpós, dark, or dim. Whether these two words spring from the same root (*Liddell and Scott* says the origin of the root μαυp is unknown) is less important than the fact that μαῦpos was used as a synonym for black. *The Thesaurus Graecae Linguae* locates examples of this usage in Byzantine Greek. It also cites several compounds in which the μαυp root means black; among these are μαυpοθpiξ, which translates as black hair, and μαυpοφpυs, meaning black eyebrows. *The Dictionnaire Etymologique de la Langue Grecque* also cites several examples of μαῦpos meaning black. One such example is found in the sixth or seventh century apocryphal Acts of Peter and Paul. Many other such examples can be gleaned from the lexicons and etymological dictionaries of the Greek language.

The Greek Μαῦpos became *Maurus* in Latin, a proper noun that identified a particular ethnic group and that, like its Greek predecessor, came to mean black. *Novum Glossarium Mediae Latinitatis Ab Anno DCCC Usque Ad Annum MCC* lists several such examples. The most interesting example is found in the first entry for *Maurus*. Defining the word as *maure* (the French translation of the Latin), *Novum Glossarium* cites the definition found in the twelfth-century *Liber Derivationum* of Pisanus Ugutio. Ugutio writes of *maurus*: "quidam populus qui estivo calore combustus speciem nigri coloris atraxit" ("a certain people burnt black with summer heat").[15] *Novum Glossarium* also offers earlier examples of derivatives of *Maurus* that express some idea of blackness. *Maura*, meaning "habit noir" (black clothes), occurs in the ninth-century *Chronographia* of Anastasius. Anastasius also uses *maurophorus* which means "qui porte un habit noir" (the one who wears black clothes).

The widespread use of *maurus* and its various derivatives in the Middle Ages as synonyms for black is clearly documented by the above examples. However, it must not be forgotten that the orig-

---

15. *Novum Glossarium Mediae Latinitatis Ab Anno DCCC Usque Ad Annum MCC* (Copenhagen, 1959), 276.

inal definition of *Moor* is a person from Mauretania. The conflation of these two meanings led to a confusion about the color of the natives of this North African region:

> The ethnic term *Maurus* has been semantically influenced by the greek words "amaυpos" and "maυpos" meaning "dark," and the latin adjective *morus* which designates the blackberry. In medieval France as in Rome, *maurus* is synonymous with *niger*. The gallo-roman term *Maurus* like the French *moreau* is used as a nickname and alludes more to the black color of the hair than a dark complexion since the inhabitants of the African shores of the Mediterranean have roughly the same complexion as the Italians from Camparia and Latium. It was, therefore, not possible to mistake a Negro and a Mauretanian. That confusion, however, becomes general in the early centuries of the Middle Ages. In France, the adjective *more* is then used in many cases synonymously with the word *noir*.[16]

This confusion reached England in the fourteenth century when the author of *Mandeville's Travels* spoke of the Moors as black. In his description of Ethiopia, he reported that "Moretane" was a part of Ethiopia and described its inhabitants as black: "Ethiope is departed in .ij. parties princypall. And that is in the est partie + in the meridionall partie, The which partie meridionall is clept Moretane. And the folk of that contree ben blacke ynow + more blacke than in the tother partie + thei ben clept mowres."[17]

While the numerous manuscripts of *Mandeville's Travels* were making their way around England, the Spanish were struggling to expel their foreign conquerors from the Iberian Peninsula. From the eighth century until the fifteenth, Spain was dominated by Islamic invaders who came north from Mauretania. Using the word passed on from ancient Greece, the Spanish called their Muslim conquerors "Moros." The *Diccionario Critico Etimologico de la Lengua Castellana* gives as its first definition of *Moro*: "'habitante de Mauretania." *A Medieval Spanish Word List* dates the first documented use of *Moro* in 1091. *Diccionario Critico Etimologico* defines *Moro* as follows: "In Spain *moro* was used to refer to all Muslims and came to mean 'gentile,' 'pagan,' 'unbaptized.' It is still common to say of a child not yet baptized that he

---

16. M. Roblin, "Mauritania," *Bulletin de la Société Nationale des Antiquaires de France*, 1949, p. 172.
17. *Mandeville's Travels*, 103-104.

is a *'moro'*. And thus Berceo [c1190-1264] applied the term to the Romans of antiquity to distinguish them from Jews."[18]

Not long after *Moro* was documented as meaning "mahomentanos" and "pagano," it picked up the meaning Negro: "The term *'Maurus,'* first used to allude to the dark skin of the Mauritanians, was used to refer to black or dark horses . . . and also other animals and eventually was applied to people."[19] *Moredo*, another word that seems related to *Moro* and its Latin antecedents, appeared in 996 according to *A Medieval Spanish Word List*. It means "de color oscuro." However, none of the standard Spanish etymological dictionaries mention *moredo*; therefore, its relationship to *Moro* cannot be definitely established. The similarities, though, are worth noting. More importantly, we find in Spain the earliest example of a form of *Moor* used to distinguish Christian from non-Christian, particularly Christian from Muslim.

European attitudes toward Islam in the Middle Ages were characterized by ignorance and fear: ignorance of the origins and doctrines of this religion and fear of the military might of its adherents. The Islamic threat was real. By the twelfth century, Europe had mounted three unsuccessful crusades against the Muslims of the Middle East. North African Muslims still possessed a large portion of Spain. European Christians, as a result of their fear and ignorance, came to portray their non-Christian adversaries in stereotypical terms. Adopting the traditional view that enemies of Christianity were demonically inspired, European Christians endowed Muslims—Moors, Saracens, and, later, Turks—with the characteristics of the devil, and as we have seen, one of the devil's most important and common characteristics is his supposed blackness.

Consistent with this tradition is the twelfth-century *Chanson de Roland*, which portrays Roland's Saracen attackers as blacks:

> What does it matter? If Marsilie is fled,
> His uncle Marganice has stayed behind,

18. Victor R. B. Oelschlager, *A Medieval Spanish Word List: A Preliminary Dated Vocabulary of First Appearances up to Berceo* (Madison, Wisc., 1940), 137; Joan Corominas and José A. Pascual, *Diccionario Critico Etimologico de la Lengua Castellana e Hispanico* (Madrid, 1981), IV, 151.

19. Corominas and Pascual, *Diccionario Critico Etimologico*, IV, 151.

Satan's Livery

> The lord of Carthage, Alfrere, Garmalie,
> And Ethiopia, a cursed land
> Whose black-skinned people are beneath his sway;
> They have large noses and great outstretched ears;
> Together they are more than fifty thousand.
> Fiercely, with angry zeal they ride along
> And shout aloud the pagan battle cry.
> . . . .
> When Roland sees that race of infidels
> —Each one of them is blacker far than ink,
> Their teeth the only feature that shows white—
> The count concludes, 'Now do I know in truth
> That we shall die today; I know it well.'

The Saracens of the French epic are not exceptional; in fact, they are stereotypical and have many other black kinsmen. C. M. Jones has noted that Saracens "are frequently presented as physical monstrosities, many of them are giants, whole tribes have horns on their heads, others are black as devils." Such a Saracen can be found in the fourteenth-century English poem "Rouland and Vernagu":

> He [Vernagu] loked lotheliche,
> & was swart as pich,
> of him men might adrede.[20]

Dorotheé Metlitzki, elaborating on the association of blackness and Islam, cites several romances in which a black Muslim turns white when he receives the sacrament of Baptism.[21] This association and its ramifications, as we have seen above, are fully within the patristic tradition. Blackness is a sign of sin; baptism washes sin away. Saracens are sinful; therefore, they are black. Yet, the simplest consequences of presenting Saracens as blacks cannot be ignored. When the word *Moor* came into currency as a term to describe Muslims, those very Muslims had already been misrep-

---

20. *The Song of Roland*, trans. Howard S. Robertson (London, 1972), 1913-21, 1932-36; C. M. Jones, "The Conventional Saracen of the Songs of Geste," *Speculum*, XVII (1942), 205; "Rouland and Vernagu," in *The English Charlemagne Romances*, ed. Sidney Herrtage (London, 1882), Part IV, 11. 482-84.

21. Dorotheé Metlitzki, *The Matter of Araby in Medieval England* (New Haven, Conn., 1977), 137-40.

resented as blacks. As we have seen, in Spain *Moro* and *moredo* appeared almost simultaneously. Perhaps the physical blackness of Moors was originally meant only as a metaphor for their alleged spiritual blackness. On the other hand, if we consider the etymology of *Moor*, particularly the fact that its classical antecedents came to denote blackness, it becomes clear that *Moor* provided a more economical way of rendering the blackness of these Islamic enemies of Christianity. Whatever the circumstances—though it seems likely that it was a combination of both—the inevitable occurred: Moors came to be thought of as black. The consolidation of sign and sinner was complete. And because *Moor* could not be disassociated from its classical antecedents, it became the word to describe all black peoples. Moreover, the state in which white Europeans first witnessed black Africans on the African continent confirmed European attitudes about the sinful and bestial nature of these black people. In the minds of Christian Europeans, there seemed little distinction between Muslim and non-Muslim: the only relevant categories were Christian and non-Christian, and black and white. Not until the seventeenth century was *Moor* slightly freed of the connotation of blackness, and this came about with the popularity of the term *white Moor*.

John Pory's 1600 translation of Leo Africanus' *The History and Description of Africa* provides us with important information in understanding the degree to which the word *Moor* is associated with blacks. In the 1559 Latin translation of Leo's Italian text, the translator, Joannes Florianus, made several critical changes in the text, not to mention many errors in translation. Where Leo wrote "Affricani bianchi," Florianus wrote "subfusci" (somewhat brown, or brownish). In place of Leo's "bruni" (brown), Florianus substituted "fusci" (dark, or swarthy). These alterations by Florianus betray some degree of prejudice toward nonblack Africans. In translating, John Pory chose to disregard Leo's terminology, and following Florianus' lead, the English translator darkened the people of North Africa.[22] This can be seen in the following comparison

22. In his introduction to the Hakluyt Society edition of Leo Africanus' *History and Description of Africa*, Robert Brown suggests that in spite of Pory's references to Ramusio's Italian edition of Leo Africanus' book, Pory relied more heavily on the Latin text of Florianus.

Satan's Livery

of the original Italian sentence with the Latin and English translations:

> Questa è la più nobile parte dell'Affrica [Barberia], nella quale sono le citta degli uomini bianchi, che per ordine de ragione e di legge si governano.

> Haec est nobilissima totius Africae regio, hanc, homines subfusci coloris inhabitant, qui & ratione, & praescriptis quibusdam vtuntur legibus.

> This [Barbary] is the most noble and worthie region of all Africa, the inhabitants whereof are of a browne or tawnie color, being civill people, and prescribe wholesome lawes and constitutions vnto themselves.[23]

In addition to darkening the nonblack peoples of Africa, Pory made a significant innovation; he introduced the word *Moor*. Pory published along with his translation of Leo's text an original contribution entitled: "A General description of all Africa, *togither with a comparison of all the ancient and new names of all the principall countries and prouinces therein.*" In this long section prefixed to the translated text, Pory described the various peoples of Africa: "Moreover this part of the worlde is inhabited especially by five principall nations, to wit, by the people called Cafrior Cafates, that is to say outlaws, or lawlesse, by the Abassins, the Egyptians, the Arabians, and the Africans or Moores, properly so called; which last are of two kinds, namely white or tawnie Moores, and Negros or blacke Moores.[24]

Pory chose *Moor* rather than *African* as the common name for a large group of diverse peoples who inhabited the African continent. While it may be impossible to determine his purpose in so doing, we can recognize the results of his choice. He endowed these peoples with the common heritage contained in the word *Moor*. They no longer simply shared a land mass; they shared the traditional prejudices and characterizations belonging to *Moor*.

---

23. Leo Africanus, *Il Viaggio di Giovan Leone, e Le Navigazioni*, ed. Giovanbattista Ramusio (Venezia, 1837), I, 13; *Ioannis Leonis Africani de Totivs Africae Descriptione*, trans. Ioannes Florianus (Zurich, 1559), 2; *History and Description of Africa*, I, 123.

24. Leo Africanus, *History and Description of Africa*, I, 20.

While the above quotation acknowledges the possibility of white Moors, the actual sentence does not allow for an unqualified endorsement of that idea. If we consider that "uomini bianchi" was replaced by "inhabitants whereof are of a browne or tawnie color," it is not rash to conclude that Pory misrepresented the people of North Africa. And the introduction of *Moor* permitted, if indeed it did not encourage, a continuation of that misrepresentation.[25]

The full effect of Pory's innovation is seen in his translation of the passage that treats the origin of Africans. Leo's Italian reads:

> Gli Affricani veramente della Terranegra dipendono tutti dalla origine di Cus, figliuolo di Cam che figliuolo fu di Noe. Adunque, qualsia la differenza tra gli Affricani bianchi e tra i neri, eglino tuttavia discendono quasi da una medesima origine.

Florianus' and Pory's translations read:

> Nam Nigrite omnes aborigine Chusi dependent, qui patrem habuit Chamum filium Noae. Attamen qualecunque habeant subfusci & Nigritae inter se discrimen, certum est idem omnes habuisse principium.

> For all the Negros or blacke Moores take their descent from *Chus*, who was the sonne of *Noe*. But what soever difference there be betweene the Negros and the tawnie Moores, certaine it is that they had all one beginning.[26]

The Italian "Affricani neri" became "Negros or blacke Moores," and "Affricani bianchi" became "tawnie Moores." Besides following Florianus's error in darkening the "Affricani bianchi," Pory compounded it with his introduction of *Moor*. *Moor* is simply not the equivalent of African. For at least two centuries prior to Pory's translation, *Moor* had carried meanings that are not limited to describing the people of the area of Mauretania. Because *Moor* can mean Muslim, *Moor* is subject to the pejorative meanings associated with Muslim or Mohammedan. *African* never acquired any

---

25. Eldred Jones in his book *Othello's Countrymen: The African in English Renaissance Drama* (Oxford, 1965), 22, expresses the opinion that Pory's translation is quite clear on the point of distinguishing black Moors from white. Lois Whitney in an article entitled "Did Shakespeare know Leo Africanus?" expresses an opinion similar to mine. (*PMLA*, XXXVII (1922), 477.)

26. Leo Africanus, *Il Viaggio*, 15; *De Totivs Africae Descriptione*, 8; *History and Description of Africa*, I, 130.

meaning beyond that of Negro or of or pertaining to Africa. And although *African* may be affected by hostile attitudes toward Negroes and Africa, this hostility was not formalized in a definition, nor does the word reflect in any way the inimical attitude of Christians toward Muslims.[27]

Pory's persistent use of *Moor* where it does not appear in either Leo's own Italian text or Florianus' Latin compounded the confusion enveloping the word. Inaccurately representing "Affricani bianchi" as Moors—whether "tawnie" or not—gave the word *Moor* an air of authority and accuracy that it did not possess. If Leo himself, described as a "Moor" on the title page of Pory's translation, appeared to be calling these North Africans "Moors," this very imprecise term was mistakenly perceived as having authorial validity. Leo, however, tended to be very precise about nationality and ethnicity. When we read of the "Affricani bianchi" or the "Affricani neri," we know exactly whom he meant.

A comparison of Leo and Pory will demonstrate clearly the confusion that followed as a result of Pory's use of *Moor*, and the inaccuracy of his representation. When speaking of a bazaar in a section of Egypt, Leo wrote: "nel qual vi sono assaissimi artigiani e mercatanti, e massime della Barberia." Pory translated this in the following manner: "Here dwell also great store of Merchants, and artificers, especially such as are Moores of Barbarie."[28] In Leo we know who the Berbers are; they are "Affricani bianchi" who inhabit the Barbary coast. In Pory, we need to know what he meant by the "Moores of Barbarie." Are these Moors "tawnie Moores" or "blacke Moores"? We are certain only of the fact that they are not Christians. Careful reading of Pory will tell us that the people of Barbary are "tawnie people," but this information about the Berbers is in Book One of *The History and Description of Africa*.

---

27. The religious situation in Africa is much too complex to treat fully here. As we have seen above, the existence of African Christians was known throughout Europe at least as early as *Mandeville's Travels*. By 1600, the time of Pory's translation, Europeans were fully aware of the existence of the Ethiopian Church. Knowledge of the missionary work of the Portuguese in Africa was also available through Francisco Alvaras's book, published in Portuguese in 1540 and in Italian in 1550, a section of which Pory himself translates and includes in *History and Description of Africa*.

28. Leo Africanus, *Il Viaggio*, 149; *History and Description of Africa*, III, 874.

The sentence quoted above is found in Book Eight. Whether Pory fully *intended* to further the stereotypical representation of North Africans or simply used the ambiguous terminology of his contemporaries is not germane to this discussion at present. What is certain is that he passed on a woefully imprecise term already overwrought with hostile connotations and contributed both to the confusion and to those connotations. The popularity of Pory's translation in the seventeenth century—it served many writers as an authoritative source on Africa—helped to continue a tradition of misrepresentation and confusion in a time when Englishmen could have accurately differentiated between black Africans and white Africans, and blacks and Muslims.

An attempt to use precise ethnic terms was made by Samuel Purchas in 1613, in *Purchas, His Pilgrimage*. The scholarly Purchas for the most part distinguished between blacks and whites by employing the words *Aethiopian* or *Negro* when he spoke of the black people of Africa. As for the word *Moor*, he attempted to reduce it to a general term for all Muslims: "They which dwell in Townes and Cities observing a more civill life, are called Moores, the other Arabians, in a more proper appellation. The name Moores was given them of the Spaniards, because out of Mauritania they invaded Spaine, and now is taken vsually, not so much for the inhabitants of the Arabian Cities, as for all of the Arabian and Mahumetane Superstition."[29] However, when he gave what he believes to be the etymology of *Moor*, Purchas unwittingly continued the previous association of the word with dark people. He wrote that North Africa "was by the Romans called Mauritania Caesariensis: the name came of the Inhabitants called Mauri, and of the Greeks μαυροσιοι: some say of the colour, because it is obscure and darke. They were supposed to come hither first with *Hercules* out of India. More likely it is that they descended of *Phut*, the sonne of *Cham, Gen.* 10. 6."[30] The earlier reference to Moors as being adherents to the "Mahumetane Superstition" affixed to the term the general meaning of Muslim. Yet by "documenting"

29. Purchas, *Purchas, His Pilgrimage*, 188. Purchas' use of *Arabian* in the above quotation is of some interest because he uses it inconsistently. He seems to use it as a geographic term, meaning North Africa and the Arabian Peninsula. However, at times he also uses *Arabian* as a synonym for *Moor* and *Mahumetane*.
30. Purchas, *Purchas, His Pilgrimage*, 503.

that *Moor* originally derived from the dark color of the North Africans who invaded Spain, Purchas also fused the two meanings.

The slightly more precise definition of *Moor* given by Purchas did not abate the confusion surrounding the word, nor did it establish one unambiguous and indisputable meaning. Neither did the definition attempt to erase any of the pejorative connotations—Purchas actually assigned it a pejorative denotation. While a complete etymological study of *Moor* would require more time than can be devoted to it in this study, there is an observable consistency in the history of the word in Spanish, French, Italian, and English. What we see is the continuous use of *Moor* to serve as a general term for those who were strange. This strangeness may have been religious, ethnic, or national, though frequently it was a combination of the three. At no time was the strangeness of those who were identified as Moors viewed neutrally or benignly. Thus when new peoples came to be called "Moors," particularly Native Americans and Asian Indians, none of whom were Muslims, they also inherited the centuries of hostilities that characterized the previous relationship of English and European Christians with those exotic humans called "Moors."

Similarly, when Moors came to be impersonated on the stage either by masked royalty or by actors, they too inherited a legacy of several centuries of prejudice. At the simplest level, they were the Other, the non-English, the non-Christian. But the history of the word *Moor* is far too complex to allow Moors to escape untainted by that name. If a stage Moor, therefore, was other than Muslim or black, he had to identify himself as such by denying his kinship with his kind. If he was not black of spirit, he had to declare himself so. Yet, while the stage Moor may have been able to divest himself of several of his inherited traits, never was he able to cast off his strangeness. Other he would always be.

II

Beauty's Beasts
Blacks in the Court Masque

> The ugly clashes with all that is divine
> while beauty is in harmony with it.
> —Plato, *The Symposium*

Masques and pageants offer a particularly useful starting point for a study of black characters on the stage. Unlike the popular drama of the late sixteenth and seventeenth centuries that aspires to mimesis, masques and pageants primarily seek to advance or to endorse religious, moral, cultural, or political ideas. This goal is frequently achieved through the enactment of an allegory, usually by personifications or type characters. The appearance of a recognizable type character or personification on stage evokes certain expectations in an audience. When a black character appears on stage, a variety of responses is possible, all of which correspond to the audience's expectations of such a character. Like the *miles gloriosus* or the *senex* of the classical stage, the stereotypical Moor is confined within the boundaries of his type. Yet, type characters are not characters devoid of all human characteristics. To the contrary, they are intended to be believable as people. What Angus Fletcher says about personifications also applies, with one qualification, to type characters. Fletcher writes: ''Such personified agents are of course intended to represent ideas, not real people; they could not, like characters in a young author's first novel, be traced to their particular 'originals.' This point can be easily misunderstood—allegorical agents are *real enough*, however ideal their referents may be, however 'unlike ourselves' they may appear. They have what might be called an 'adequate representational power.' . . . The main point here is that we should make no automatic assumptions about the 'unreality' of allegorical personifications."[1]

Type characters, unlike personifications, are intended to be "real people" even as they sometimes personify certain ideas or traits associated with their types. Yet it is their credibility as "real people" that enables type characters to represent some race, group, nation, or religion, and to animate certain characteristics that group supposedly embodies. Thus we shall see in *Tempe Restor'd* that Indians are meant to represent uncivilized and bestial behavior. Such roles mute distinctions between individuals and a group and between attributed characteristics and actual personality. In the allegorical universe of masques and pageants, the type characterization of blacks reveals the station that they are assigned in the family of man, in the structure of the universe, and in relationship to God. Ultimately such characterization placed blacks into a single camp in the great moral conflict between good and evil. In allegorical and nonmimetic drama, we are able to see the type characterization of blacks in its purest, most abstract form. By starting with masques and pageants, we have an opportunity to assess the degree to which these type characterizations are relied upon in the characterization of blacks in the more mimetic popular drama.

Courtiers masquerading as Moors has a long history in England.[2] The earliest documented instance occurred in 1510 at the court of Henry VIII. Between 1510 and 1605, there were at least six documented masques in which courtiers appeared as blacks.[3] The maskers usually wore Moorish garb, black stockings, gloves, and

1. Angus Fletcher, *Allegory: The Theory of a Symbolic Mode* (Ithaca, N.Y., 1964), 32.
2. There were at least two masques with Moors at the Scottish Court: George Buchanan's *Pompae Deorum* and the anonymous masque performed on August 30, 1594, to celebrate the baptism of Prince Henry of Scotland. It is doubtful that the Turma Aethiopium in *Pompae Deorum* were played by courtiers. In the baptism masque, a Moor pulls a triumphant chariot; he was clearly not a courtier. See Anna Jean Mill, *Mediaeval Plays in Scotland* (New York, 1924), 50.
3. Edward Hall, *Henry VIII*, ed. Charles Whibley (London, 1904), I, 15–16. See also Jones, *Othello's Countrymen*, 28, 145–46.

a black mask. In these early masques the appeal of masquerading as Moors was in the Moor's exotic nature. Since masques were celebrations that sanctioned behavior outside the usual boundaries of decorum, Moors, as well as other exotics such as Turks, Russians, or mythological figures, served well as symbols of the extravagance of these events. By masking as a recognizable Other, as one who is beyond the boundaries of court protocol, national custom, and civil and religious law, maskers too placed themselves outside the demands of custom and protocol. That is, the maskers inscribed a circle within society in which unusual behavior was temporarily expected and accepted. Since masking occurred on days that were in themselves unusual and extraordinary, all aspects of these events could be extraordinary. It is not surprising, then, that even polite maskers became known for their risqué conversation and overt flirtations.[4] Such behavior was, after all, the expected behavior of lustful Moors, bloody Turks, and godless Saracens. Later, when the masque was used by Charles I to justify his policies, royal maskers ceased to impersonate these indecorous creatures and confined them to the other world of the antimasque. These royal maskers then chose to personate deities and virtues. However, when in 1605 Queen Anne, consort to James I, asked Ben Jonson to devise a masque in which she and certain of her ladies could mask as "Black-mores," she requested nothing extraordinary.[5] The resulting *The Masque of Blackness*, written by Jonson with costumes and sets designed by Inigo Jones, however, was.

Jonson's *The Masque of Blackness* is the earliest English court masque in which royal maskers appeared as Moors for which there is an existing text. There are many other firsts connected with *The Masque of Blackness*. It was the first court masque written by Jonson, the first collaboration between Jonson and Jones, the first recorded use of perspective scenery in England, and the first recorded use of blackening to actually darken the skin of the royal maskers. The story of the masque seems deceptively simple and

---

4. See Enid Welsford, *The Court Masque: A Study in the Relationship between Poetry and the Revels* (Cambridge, England, 1927), for a complete discussion of the origins of the masque, especially pp. 8–16 and 134–41.

5. According to Hall, the Lady Mary, sister of Henry VIII and later Queen of France, was one of six ladies who, in 1510, "seemed to be a nigrost or black Mores" (Hall, *Henry VIII*, I, 17).

innocent, yet it is far more complicated than a rudimentary plot synopsis reveals. Essentially the masque dramatizes the River Niger's search for a solution to his problem: how his black daughters, personated by the queen and several other ladies, may be returned to their original whiteness. Arriving on the British shores, he is told by Oceanus, his father, that in Great Britain, the sun, in the personage of the king, possesses the power "To blanch an Ethiop and revive a corse."[6] So informed, Niger happily leaves his daughters to the power that will make them again white and, consequently, beautiful. But the masque is really a story of redemption that employs traditional Christian allegorical readings of blackness and whiteness, beauteousness and ugliness, and foulness and fairness. The seriousness of the masque and of Jonson's intentions should not be underestimated; the poet undertook the task of writing masques with great earnestness, as his learned annotations to the text and his defense of masques attest.

The premise of *Blackness* presented Jonson with a unique problem, the solution of which required some of the thematic complexities of the masque. Jonson had to devise a method of presenting the Queen of England and other ladies of the court in blackface, while he acknowledged the traditional attitudes toward black skin in a manner that was neither uncomplimentary to his royal maskers nor to their beauty. He solved this problem by alluding to the Song of Songs and Plato's *Symposium*, two popular texts that deal directly with ideas of beauty and ugliness.

An echo of the biblical text is heard when three sea creatures sing greetings to Niger:

> Fair Niger, son of great Oceanus,
> Now honored thus,
> With all his beauteous race,
> Who, though but black in face,
> Yet are they bright,
> And full of life and light,
> To prove that beauty best
> Which not the color but the feature
> Assures unto the creature. (ll. 79–87)

---

6. Ben Jonson, *The Masque of Blackness*, in *Ben Jonson: The Complete Masques*, ed. Stephen Orgel (New Haven, 1969), line 225. (All citations of Jonson's masques, unless otherwise noted, are from this edition.)

The oxymoronic direct address, "Fair Niger," immediately reveals Jonson's solution to one of his challenges. Niger, obviously not fair in color, must therefore be fair of feature, of form, and of spirit, or at least one of these. The reader (and obviously that first audience) is invited, however momentarily, to ignore the color value of the word *fair*, and to focus his attention on other meanings of the word and other aspects of Niger's personality. By proclaiming Niger and his daughters "bright" and "full of life and light," the song continues to emphasize other aspects of their personality that are unobscured by their blackness.

The first several lines of the poem, particularly the phrase "Fair Niger," seem clearly to allude to a verse from the Song of Songs: "Nigra sum sed formosa." The English translation of this line found in the Bishops' Bible of 1568, "I am blacke (O ye daughters of hierusalem) but yet fayre and well fauoured," reads like a paraphrase of this opening song. Ironically, the allusion to this verse gives it a literal reading though it is usually given an allegorical one. Like the biblical verse, the song says that Niger and his race are black, "yet are they bright." The reader is invited to accept, with no less than biblical authority, the idea that these are beautiful women in spite of their blackness. Such a realization, therefore, isolates their blackness for contempt. Yet, the traditional allegorical reading of this verse focuses on the spiritual beauty that those who are ugly through sin and imperfection can attain through Christ. The gloss of this line in the 1568 Bishops' Bible reads: "Blacke, thorowe the spottes of sinne and persecution. Fayre, thorowe fayth in the blood of Christe." The gloss of this line in the more popular Geneva Bible of 1592 reads: "Consider not the Church by the outwarde appearance." Jonson emphasizes both the physical and spiritual beauty of the maskers through this allusion. In addition, he also alludes to the salvific powers of the king who will remove the black spots from the maskers' faces.

The concluding lines of the song offer reassurance that these women are truly beautiful because "not the color but the feature / Assures [beauty] unto the creature." The idea that there is more to beauty than the mere physical accident of color literally stated in these lines and underscored by the allusion to the Song of Songs, recalls the discussion of beauty in Plato's *Symposium*.

Beauty's Beasts

The seeker of true beauty, Socrates is warned, should live

> in the contemplation of beauty absolute; a beauty which if you once beheld, you would see into to be after the measure of gold, and garments, and fair boys and youths, whose presence now entrances you; and you and many a one would be content to live seeing them only and conversing with them without meat or drink, if that were possible—you only want to look at them and to be with them. But what if a man had eyes to see the true beauty—the divine beauty, I mean, pure and clear and unalloyed, not infected with the pollutions of the flesh and all the colors and vanities of mortal life—thither looking, and holding converse with the true beauty simple and divine? Remember how in that communion only, beholding beauty with that by which it can be beheld, he will be enabled to bring forth not images of beauty, but realities (for he has hold not of an image but of a reality), and bringing forth and nourishing true virtue will properly become the friend of God and be immortal, if mortal man may.[7]

Even though the word *feature* emphasizes physical appearance, Platonic ideals are called to mind by this song. These daughters of Niger, we are to believe, are distinguished in body and soul, disfigured only by their scorched complexions.

Following the opening song, Niger tells his father Oceanus of the quest that brought him so far west and recounts his unsuccessful attempts to convince his recently blackened daughters that they were indeed beautiful: "That in their black the perfect'st beauty grows" (l. 119). Niger offered to his daughters

> . . . arguments to prove how far
> Their beauties conquer in great beauty's war,
> And more, how near divinity they be
> That stand from passion or decay as free. (ll. 126–29)

But Niger's daughters, unconvinced by his arguments, do not desire such perfection or divinity. They know that they will only be truly beautiful when they are white. And they will be proven correct, as the greater authority and wisdom of poets refute Niger's complaints and arguments:

---

7. Plato, *The Symposium*, in *The Dialogues of Plato*, trans. B. Jowett, (Oxford, 1953), I, 543.

> Yet since the fabulous voices of some few
> Poor brainsick men, styled poets here with you,
> Have with such envy of their graces sung
> The painted beauties other empires sprung,
> Letting their loose and winged fictions fly
> To infect all climates, yea, our purity;
> As of one Phaeton, that fired the world,
> And that before his heedless flames were hurled
> About the globe, the Ethiops were as fair
> As other dames, now black with black despair. (ll. 130-39)

Niger's efforts to question poetic authority, of course, fail. Had they succeeded, he and his daughters would not have traveled so far; in their voyage, poetic authority receives confirmation, as does the legitimacy of the daughters' complaint. Even Niger unconsciously reaffirms the authority of poets when he describes his dilemma in a poetic language that employs double entendres and traditional black/white and dark/light imagery.

From the moon, who appears in the shape of the goddess Aethiopia (and it is important to note that Aethiopia is not black but is instead light and bright), Niger learns that it is he who is brainsick and wrong. She tells him to seek a climate where the sun is more temperate and will help to beautify his daughters. Oceanus congratulates Niger for having found that "temperate air" in "Albion the fair" (ll. 179-80). To approve this, the goddess Aethiopia appears to the unhappy father who seeks her continued aid:

> O see, our silver star!
> Whose pure, auspicious light greets us thus far!
> Great Aethiopia, goddess of our shore,
> Since with particular worship we adore
> Thy general brightness, let particular grace
> Shine on my zealous daughters: show the place
> Which long their longings urged their eyes to see.
> Beautify them, which long have deified thee. (ll. 194-201)

Niger's plea to Aethiopia confirms what the double entendres and traditional black/white and dark/light imagery of his language have revealed all along: it is better to be white than black. His simple request, "Beautify them," denies all of his previous arguments and renders true the opinions of blackness espoused by poets, Oceanus, and Aethiopia. Aethiopia's reply to Niger underscores his earlier mistake in asserting that his black daughters were beautiful. To Niger's request the goddess replies:

> Niger, be glad; resume thy native cheer.
> Thy daughters' labors have their period here,
> And so thy errors. (ll. 202-204)

The pun on "errors" lays to rest any further arguments or assertions that the blackened nymphs are beautiful. For recognizing the truth and laboring to attain it, the daughters will be rewarded with the return of their beauty. They will be made white; they will be saved.

The allusions to Christian theology and redemption find completion when Aethiopia describes the perfect world to which Niger and his daughters have come at the cessation of his "errors." This new land is "*A world divided from the world*, and tried / The abstract of it in his general pride" (ll. 218-19). It is the antithesis of their Ethiopian homeland. And here too is that glorious sun that rules beneficently:

> . . . a sun that to this height doth grace it [England],
> Whose beams shine day and night, and are of force
> To blanch an Ethiop, and revive a corse.
> His light sciential is, and past mere nature
> Can solve the rude defects of every creature. (ll. 223-27)

The sun, the King of England, seems to possess the powers of baptismal waters. He can make white those who are black. He can make perfect those who are defective.

It is essential for the reader to remember who personated the daughters of Niger; this masque was acted by the queen and other ladies of the court. The audience at Whitehall that January evening in 1605 needed no such reminder. Nor could any number of compliments or learned allusions remove from their sight the vision of the queen in blackface, obscured by the mark of Ham. With the arrival of the maskers, the audience could recognize the essential truth of the masque's fiction because, ironically, the fictive world that unfolded before the audience paralleled exactly the real world. The audience saw twelve women who were perceived as ugly because of their blackness. The women could only be made truly beautiful by returning to their natural, white complexions. We need only turn to Dudley Carleton's comment on the masque to understand fully the truth of this. Carleton writes: "Instead of Vizzards, their Faces [the Queen's and other maskers'] and Arms up to the Elbows, were painted black, which was Disguise sufficient for they were hard to be known; *but it became them nothing so well as their red and white, and you cannot imagine a more ugly Sight, then a Troop of lean-cheek'd Moors.*"[8]

Carleton's comments point to an interesting conundrum in *Blackness*. Initially it seems that blackness itself is the evil of the masque, and it is blackness from which Niger's daughters are saved. None of the usual evils signified by blackness seems to contaminate the issues here. The daughters, like the woman in the Song of Songs, are "nigra sum sed formosa." It is their blackness that is contemptible because blackness is ugliness. Yet in the world of the mask and in the new Jerusalem in which the daughters arrive, blackness signifies imperfection, just as it signifies sin in allegorical readings of the Song of Songs. The daughters are redeemed from more than ugliness, which is to say blackness; they are redeemed from imperfection. *The Masque of Blackness* really is a play about salvation (remember Niger's "errors"), and blackness really does signify separation from grace, in this case the saving grace of James I. These issues receive a fuller and more political treatment in the companion piece to *Blackness*, *The Masque of Beauty*.

Although there was a three-year lapse between *The Masque of Blackness* and *The Masque of Beauty*, *Beauty* was clearly conceived as a conclusion to the former. *Blackness* ends only in promise; *Beauty* renders the promise true. *Beauty* heightens the dialectic between blackness and beauty that exists in the earlier masque by explicitly assigning blackness its traditional significance while emphasizing beauty's importance in a Neoplatonic universe. Published together in 1608 in quarto form, the title page of that edition reveals the dialectic that characterizes the two masques: "*The Characters of Two royall Masques. The one of Blackness, the Other of Beautie.*"

8. Dudley Carleton to Sir Ralph Winwood, January, 1605, cited in C. H. Herford and Percy Simpson (eds.), *Ben Jonson* (Oxford, 1925), X, 448.

Beauty's Beasts

The synopsis of the earlier masque offered by Boreas in *Beauty* also makes clear the contest between blackness and beauty. He reports of the "twelve Ethiop dames" who "were in the waves to leave / Their blackness, and true beauty to receive" (ll. 46–47). But *Beauty* dramatizes more than the simple return of the twelve Ethiopian nymphs who are now washed white. Complicating this tale are the introductions of four new nymphs who also desire to be made white and of a jealous Night who fears that her blackness, now the very emblem of ugliness, will be little esteemed. The quest of these new nymphs immediately reaffirms the value of being white and the despair of being black. The introduction of Night, however, focuses our attention on more than the ugliness and imperfection of blackness; Night reveals the evil and danger of blackness.

The subplot of the four black sisters is quite simple. Having heard of the transformation of the original twelve, these four nymphs seek the same favor. That four more Ethiopians wish to be made white is certainly not startling since true beauty is held to be incompatible with blackness in both the fictive world of *Blackness* and the real world of the court. The desire to be white, therefore, is only reasonable; the alternative is to be "black with black despair" (*Blackness*, l. 139). No lesser authorities than the "sacred muses' sons" acclaim and verify the superior beauty of white women and lament the blackening of Ethiopian women (*Blackness*, ll. 131–41, 212–14). Augmenting the arguments of the fictive world, the audience of this play had the parallel reality to support its view. The audience had seen the queen and her ladies in blackface. Reinforced one by the other, the fictive world and the court world both agree with these four new nymphs; they can only have perfection after they are washed white.

The abduction of the sixteen nymphs by Night introduces into the masque a cross reference that reaffirms traditional prejudices against darkness through fear of night. Believing the original twelve turned white in her "despite" (*Beauty*, ll. 66–67), Night seizes the four unchanged nymphs in a misguided effort to maintain whatever fame blackness yet has. Reporting Night's rage, Boreas says:

... [Night] mad to see an Ethiop washed white,
Thought to prevent in these [the four], lest men should deem

Her color, if thus changed, of small esteem;
And so by malice and her magic, tossed
The nymphs at sea, as they were almost lost
Till on an island they by chance arrived,
That floated in the main, where yet she'd gyved
Them so in charms of darkness as no might
Should loose them thence, but their changed sisters' sight. (ll. 67-75)

Black in color and malicious of spirit, Night employs herself with her usual tasks, confounding light, goodness, and truth. Nor can there be much esteem for her or her color so long as she herself works "charms of darkness."

Night proves herself more nefarious when she demands that the virtuous sisters rescue their beleaguered siblings. By appealing to the virtue of the twelve bright sisters, Night hopes to capture them. As the antithesis of good, she will not reward virtue; rather, she hopes to punish it. This insidious plan, however, does not succeed. The bright moon, Aethiopia, she who tames the darkness of the night with her light, breaks the dark charms of Night:

> The Night's black charms are thrown.
> For, being made unto their goddess known,
> Bright Aethiopia, the silver moon,
> As she was Hecate, she brake them soon;
> The glorious isle wherein they rest takes place
> Of all the earth for beauty. (ll. 104-10)

The defeat of Night represents more than the victory of daylight over darkness. It is the victory of virtue over vice, with each assuming its traditional emblematic colors.

With the spell of darkness broken by light, we are again ushered into a world of beauty with which blackness is incompatible. Accompanied by chaste Loves, the sixteen nymphs appear enthroned on an island that is emblematic of the perfection of creation and antithetical to the island ruled by Night:

> There their queen [Beauty]
> Hath raised them a throne that still is seen
> To turn unto the motion of the world,
> Wherein they sit, and are, like heaven, whirled
> About the earth; whilest to them contrary,
> Following those nobler torches of the sky,

> A wor[l]d of little loves and chaste desires
> Do light their beauties with still moving fires.
> And who to heaven's consent can better move
> Than those that are so like it, beauty and love?
> Hither, as to their new Elysium
> The spirits of the antique Greeks are come
> . . . .
> They live again these beauties to behold,
> And thence in flowery mazes walking forth,
> Sing hymns in celebration of their worth. (ll. 110-21, 125-27)

The center of this Elysium is the "Throne of Beauty," but the beauty of which Jonson speaks here is not simply physical beauty. Virtue triumphs on Beauty's island. To demonstrate this, Jonson seats the maskers in couples between personifications of Splendor, Serenitas, Germinatio, Laetitia, Temperies, Venustas, Dignitas, Perfectio. Crowning these virtues is Harmonia, a "personage whose dressing had something of all the others" (l. 195). Virtue's triumph in the form of beauty expresses again those Platonic ideals found in the *Symposium* and their continued vitality for Neoplatonists. Donald Gordon sees the very design of this Elysium as "a translation into visual terms of certain ideas about love and beauty held by Ficino and the Florentine Platonists."[9]

In such an Elysium, blackness, as a version of ugliness, opposes beauty and virtue, and because blackness is irreconcilable with beauty, it must be banished entirely. Just before songs are sung in praise of love and beauty, a song is sung that once and for all dispels blackness:

> When Love at first did move
> From out of chaos, brightened
> So was the world and lightened
> As now !
> . . . .
> Yield, night, then, to the light,
> As blackness hath to beauty,
> Which is but the same duty.

---

9. Donald Gordon, "The Imagery of Ben Jonson's *Masques of Blacknesse and Beautie*," in *The Renaissance Imagination*, ed. Stephen Orgel (Berkeley, Calif., 1975), 144.

> It was for beauty that the world was made,
> And where she reigns Love's lights admit no shade. (ll. 236-44)

This world of light and beauty and love expels Night and with her darkness, and here the ban on blackness is total. Yet not only is physical blackness expelled—night and darkness—but clearly what is felt to be the spiritual darkness embodied in Night; even the black messenger Vulturus, the warm eastern wind, must depart before the nymphs alight, and with him goes Boreas, the cold northern wind, because extremes and discord are not possible in this Elysium. Like the initial act of creation that brought forth light and beauty out of Chaos, the masque crushes the forces of darkness and chaos and brings forth an ideal world. Thus when Night is utterly routed and the triumph of beauty complete, songs may be sung of beauty and love, because their opposites, embodied in the blackness of Night, no longer exist. Night has yielded to the light, as blackness has to beauty.

In *The Masque of Beauty*, Night or blackness is more than an emblem of ugliness; she is also undeniably an emblem of evil. And since Night cannot be separated from her blackness, blackness too is an emblem of evil. Triumphant over evil, therefore, is Beauty. As we have seen in Plato's *Symposium*, the contemplation of true beauty brings forth and nourishes "true virtue," and "the ugly clashes with all that is divine." Evil, therefore, wishes to do battle with beauty as surely as it wishes to conquer virtue. Evil and ugliness, now firmly linked, can no longer be distinguished from blackness, nor blackness from them. The now transformed nymphs, by being restored to their former beauty (that is, having been made white), are now not only freed from a mark of ugliness, but more importantly, they are freed from a mark of evil. At the conclusion of this masque, to be black is to be evil, and therefore necessarily to be denied entrance into the Neoplatonic world that appears triumphantly in place where "night was painted" (l. 144).

Jonson again employs blackness as an emblem of evil in *The Masque of Queens*. Like *The Masque of Beauty*, *The Masque of Queens* puts two worlds in conflict. One world is hell, a place of darkness and night presided over by hags; the other is a world of beauty and light presided over by queens. Unlike *Beauty*, in *Queens* both worlds are presented on the stage; the first made all the uglier

Beauty's Beasts

by the beauty of the second. Although there is no evidence that the hags themselves are portrayed as physically black people, they clearly belong to an ideological and spiritual realm that is characterized by blackness.

Queens begins with the hags dancing perverted dances and reporting on their activities and necromancies. These rites of the night are performed especially to defeat the glory of the House of Fame and the bright queens. The Dame of the Hags commands her cohorts:

> Join now our hearts, we faithful opposites
> To Fame and Glory. Let not these bright nights
> Of honor blaze thus to offend our eyes:
> Show ourselves truly envious, and let rise
> Our wonted rages; do what may beseem
> Such names and natures. Virtue else will deem
> Our powers decreased, and think us banished earth,
> No less than heaven.
> . . . .
> Ill lives not but in us.
> I hate to see these fruits of a soft peace,
> And curse the piety gives it such increase.
> Let us disturb it then, and blast the light;
> Mix hell with heaven. (ll. 120-27, 131-35)

To assist them in their efforts to "blast the light," the hags attempt to conjure other "fiends and furies." These are summoned in the name of hell, darkness, and night:

> Bark dogs, wolves howl,
> Sea roar, woods roll,
> Clouds crack and all be black
> But the light our charms do make. (ll. 275-78)

When the charm fails to produce more fiends or furies, the Dame of the Hags complains:

> Not yet? My rage begins to swell;
> Darkness, devils, night and hell,
> Do not thus delay my spell. (ll. 279-81)

These conjurations still do not succeed, and all the cries for a darker, blacker world fail.

As the hags later perform a "magical dance," doing "all things contrary to the custom of men" (l. 329), a "loud music" is heard. Like the blast or sounding of trumpets that heralds the destruction of Jericho and the earth in the Bible, so does this blast proclaim the destruction of the hell of the hags: "In the heat of their dance on the sudden was heard a sound of loud music, as if many instruments had made one blast; with which not only the hags themselves but the hell into which they ran quite vanished, and the whole face of the scene altered, scarce suffering the memory of such a thing" (ll. 334-37). Like the enemies of God, the hags disappear utterly, leaving nothing but the memory of their existence. The following lines from *Beauty* seem appropriate to describe this scene as well:

> Yield, night, then to the light
> As blackness hath to beauty,
> Which is but the same duty. (ll. 240-42)

As in the two earlier masques, *Blackness* and *Beauty*, the world of darkness can never be compatible with the world of light. Light totally obliterates darkness in the Jonsonian masque. In hell's stead, we find the House of Fame: "But in the place of it [hell] appeared a glorious and magnificent building figuring the House of Fame, in the top of which were discovered the twelve maskers sitting upon a throne triumphal erected in form of a pyramid and circled with all store of light" (ll. 337-41).

With hell conquered, Heroic Virtue, in the "furniture of Perseus," proclaims the new order and sings praises of Fame and Virtue, and of the power of light:

> So should, at Fame's loud sound and Virtue's sight,
> All dark and envious witchcraft fly the light.
> . . . .
> When virtue cut off Terror, he gat Fame.
> And if when Fame was gotten Terror died,
> What black Erinyes or more hellish pride
> Durst arm these hags now she [Fame] is grown and great,
> To think they could her glories once defeat? (ll. 344-45, 351-55)

The power of light and virtue is greater than the "black Erinyes," and they must yield completely to the right. The "black Erinyes" mentioned here seem to be spirits of evil who are the superiors of the hags. Since the "black Erinyes" do not appear on stage, we do not know if they have black complexions. Black, though, is obviously used synonymously with evil and is the color of their souls.

To display the triumph of good and light, Heroic Virtue then introduces to the audience twelve queens, a "bright bevy," who stand in direct opposition to the twelve hags. Eleven of the twelve queens are queens renowned from antiquity; the twelfth and greatest queen is Queen Anne. So great is their virtue that the queens defeat their opposites by simply appearing. To demonstrate their complete domination of the hags, and thus the supremacy of virtue over vice, the queens ride in a triumphant procession with the vanquished hags bound to the victresses' chariots. It is interesting to note that one of the twelve queens is Candace, "the pride of Ethiopia" (1. 381). From all the documentary evidence that exists for this masque, including Jones's sketches for costumes, there is nothing to indicate that Candace was portrayed in the "color of an Ethiop." Her costume, as elaborate as the others', is in no way Ethiopian. It is certainly hard to imagine that amongst a host of women one would be singled out to appear in blackface. And the appearance of a black queen in the "bright bevy" would conflict with the prevailing dark/light imagery of the masque. If we are to believe the notions of beauty espoused in *Blackness*, *Beauty*, and *Queens* itself, there is clearly no place for a black queen in the ideological structure of this masque. Black is the color of the hags, perhaps not the color of their skin, but certainly the color of their souls.

Tawny is the word the gypsies in *The Gypsies Metamorphosed* use to describe themselves. In this masque, a favorite of James I, who saw it performed on three separate occasions, a group of gypsies, portrayed by noblemen, tell the fortunes of the assembled guests. These gypsies, however, distinguish themselves from real gypsies, whom they describe as vagabonds, lechers, and thieves. Jackman, the first of the maskers to appear, leads five gypsy boys onto the stage. Of them, he mockingly says: "Room for the five princes of Egypt. . . . Gaze upon them, as on the offspring of Ptolemy, begotten upon several Cleopatras in their several counties; especially on this brave spark struck out of Flintshire upon Justice Jug's daughter . . . who running away with a kinsman of our captain's, and her father pursuing her to the marches, he great with justice, she great with juggling, they were both for the time turned stone upon the sight of each other in Chester" (ll. 52–61).

Jackman is then joined by his colleagues, the four other noble maskers; these gypsies reassure the audience that it has nothing to fear of them:

> Knacks we have that will delight you,
> Slights of hand that will invite you
> To endure our tawny faces,
> And not cause you cut your laces. (ll. 119–22)

One wonders whether the ladies are expected to faint because they see gypsies or because they see "tawny faces." Whatever the cause, the ladies are again reassured that they are safe in the company of these gypsies. Unlike other gypsies, these are neither rogues nor thieves, and other than some palm reading, their activities remain totally uncharacteristic of gypsies. So obviously unique are the maskers that a simple local proclaims them "the finest olive-colored spirits" (l. 691), and later he expresses doubt about their actually being gypsies: "One shall hardly see such gentlemanlike gypsies though, under a hedge, in a whole summer's day, if they be gypsies" (ll. 706–707).

At the close of the masque, the gypsies reveal what the audience already knows: "we are gypsies of no common kind" (l. 1380). They also disclose how they are "transformed" from gypsies to white courtiers:

> But lest it prove like wonder to the sight
> To see a gypsy, as an Ethiop, white,
> Know that what dyed our faces was an ointment
> Made and laid on by Master Wolf's appointment,
> The court lycanthropos, yet without spells,
> By a mere barber, and no magic else. (ll. 1385–90)

By disclosing the method of transformation, the maskers deny totally any possible relationship with gypsies. They are not magicians; they are civilized men creating illusions with the tools of civilization: poetry, a barber, and a tailor. The maskers identify their behavior that is uncharacteristic of gypsies as being the behavior of the nobility. The illusory world gives way to the real. Nobles behave nobly and gypsies roguishly. And now that the masque is over, the audience should again beware of "tawny faces."

These four Jonsonian masques, *The Masque of Blackness*, *The Masque of Beauty*, *The Masque of Queens*, and *The Gypsies Metamorphosed*, express similar attitudes toward skin color and masking. In the masques in which the courtiers darken their skin, the maskers are merely "supposing" to be outside of society, playing at being the Other. As in Gascoigne's *Supposes*, the maskers and the audiences playfully accept the notion of supposing: "But understand, this our Suppose is nothing else but a mystaking or imagination of one thing for an other."[10] The queen and her ladies are simply supposed to be Moors, as the courtiers in *Gypsies* are supposed to be gypsies. Even in these supposings, however, the maskers always seek to return to their proper position. The daughters of Niger want not to be Moors, as those "finest olive-colored spirits" want not to be gypsies. There is an explicit understanding in these masques of the fact that to be black is to be Other. Those who are Other remain black, either physically or spiritually. They are, after all, *supposed* to be black, and so they are. In these masques, those who wish to conform, those who wish to be white, are good and noble; those who, like Night and the hags, are content with their blackness, their otherness, are evil and, therefore, properly colored.

Three other masques with black characters were performed before the court; however, in none of these masques does a courtier portray a black character. In Thomas Campion's *The Squire's Masque*, performed in 1613, four squires come before the king and queen to tell how the knights whom they serve have been enchanted by Error, Rumor, Curiosity, and Credulity. An antimasque follows their narrative, in which the confusion loosed upon the world by the enchanters and enchantresses comes to life. Participating in this antimasque is "Africa, *like* a Queen of *the Moores*, with a crown," who dances with the "foure parts of the earth in a confused measure."[11] Queen Anne, interceding, dispels the chaos and frees the enchanted knights. Africa, whose only role is to

---

10. George Gascoigne, *The Supposes*, in *The Complete Works of George Gascoigne*, ed. John W. Cunliffe (1907; rpr. New York, 1969), 188.
11. Thomas Campion, *The Squire's Masque*, in *The Complete Poems of Thomas Campion*, ed. Walter R. Davis (New York, 1976), 271.

represent one of the four parts of the world that is tossed into general chaos, disappears with the antimasque.

In Aurelian Townshend's *Tempe Restor'd*, performed in 1632, a knight escapes the captivity of the lustful Circe and begs the protection of the king. Circe and her kind, in pursuit of the fugitive, unleash an antimasque of beasts, Indians, barbarians, and other creatures, all of whom partake in the sinful pleasures of the flesh. As in *The Squire's Masque*, order is restored, this time through the offices of Harmony and the queen who, representing Divine Beauty, enters to offer an example of righteous love and beauty.

The Indians and barbarians in *Tempe Restor'd* represent the bestial nature of Circe's realm. Townshend introduces them in this manner: "Her [Circe's] song ended, she sits, and before her are presented all the Antimasques, consisting of Indians, and Barbarians, who naturally are bestial, and others which are voluntaries, and but halfe transformed into beasts."[12] There exists no textual evidence that these barbarians are black, but drawings of them among Inigo Jones's designs for the masque show them to be so.[13] If we can trust this evidence, these barbarians and their Indian counterparts are portrayed as no more than beasts in the company of other beasts, their skin color perhaps making any transformation into demi-beasts redundant.

In *Tempe Restor'd* the same ideological distinction exists between blacks and whites that is observed by Jonson in his masques. Black characters represent the Other, those outside the mythical, orderly world that is supposed to be the Stuart court, and in *Tempe Restor'd* they are restricted to the antimasque. Their exclusion from the part of the masque that is identified with the glories of the court and that is actually ruled over by the king and queen only

12. Aurelian Townshend, *Tempe Restor'd*, in *Aurelian Townshend's Poems and Masks*, ed. E. K. Chambers (Oxford, 1912), 87.

13. Orgel and Strong believe the drawings of the barbarians that show them colored black were not tinted by Jones himself. These drawings, however, are contemporaneous with Jones's other drawings for the masque, and except for the addition of skin color to the barbarians, the tinted drawings duplicate Jones's in every other way. See Stephen Orgel and Roy Strong, *Inigo Jones: The Theatre of the Stuart Court* (Berkeley, Calif., 1973), II, 490–91, and Percy Simpson and C. F. Bell, *Designs by Inigo Jones for Masques and Plays at Court* (Oxford, 1924), 72.

further emphasizes their condition of strangeness and their separation from the source of truth and virtue. Their dark complexions preclude them from the possibility of redemption, as the states of their souls must correspond to the colors of their faces.

The beasts, both human and nonhuman, must be vanquished and the antimasque dispatched before Divine Beauty and the Influences, personated by the queen and her ladies, are free to enter and to dance. And as in the Jonsonian masque, the victory of Beauty over evil is complete. Recognizing the superior virtue of Divine Beauty and her spouse Heiroicke Vertue, Circe retires, leaving Tempe to be ruled by them. Summing up the meaning of the masque, Townshend writes of the couple portrayed by Charles and Henrietta Maria:

> That divine *Beauty* accompan'ed with a troope of Stars of a happy Constellation ioyning with Heiroicke vertue should dissolve the enchantments, and *Circe* voluntarily deliver her golden rod to *Minerva*, is meant that a divine Beame comming from above, with a good inclination, and a perfect habit of vertue made, by the *Harmony* of the Irascible and concupiscible parts obedient to the rationall and highest part of the soul. Making man onely a mind vsing the body and affections as instruments, which being his true perfection brings him to all the happinesse which can bee inioyed heere below.[14]

Townshend intends for the barbarians to represent those whose "irascible and concupiscible parts" are uncontrolled. These beings stand outside the realm where the "rationall and highest part of the soul" has sway.

The reputed ugliness of blacks is a theme that resurfaces in John Crowne's *Calisto*. Acted by the Princesses Anne and Mary before their father, the Duke of York, and their uncle, James II, in 1675, *Calisto* is a long and undistinguished masque based on a classical story. The two princesses play Calisto and Nyphe, two nymphs who are dear to the goddess Diana and who are the embodiment of chastity and innocence. Calisto, in order to preserve her virtue, flees Jupiter and his lust. Later, believing Diana to be Jupiter metamorphosed into the goddess' form, Calisto and Nyphe wound Diana. In punishment for their crime, they must die. But Jupiter,

14. Townshend, *Tempe Restor'd*, 98-99.

out of love and respect for virtue, commutes the sentence and instead places the nymphs as stars in the heavens.

Before the actual story of Calisto is acted, there is a thoroughly conventional prologue designed to praise the king and the accomplishments of the Stuarts. In the prologue, two nymphs, Peace and Plenty, accompany the four parts of the world, all of whom have come to offer their gifts to the nymph Thames. Africa says: "Thou for thy slaves, shalt have these / Scorched sons of mine."[15] While this is no unusual gift, in the context of this masque the offer will prove significant, for it provides the reader with a criterion against which to judge the claims of the black women who appear later in the masque.

The actual story of Calisto requires "Two African Women or Blacks" who appear in the last fifty lines of the masque.[16] These African women seem to be kindred sisters to the nymphs in Jonson's earlier *The Masque of Blackness*; they too search for their lost beauty. In their quest, the African nymphs encounter and frighten some shepherds and shepherdesses who await the night to hide their sexual antics. A shepherd, apparently startled by the sight of these black women, says: "What vision's this come to greet us?" A fellow shepherd responds: "See! the night is come to meet us." Attempting to prevent the shepherds from fleeing in terror, a black nymph speaks: "Stay gentle swains be not afraid, / To see our faces hid in shade" (p. 321). The shepherds obviously have never seen any people as dark as these in Arcadia, so the black nymph explains to them how she and her companion arrived at this unnatural state of darkness:

> We, but lately were as fair,
> As your shepherdesses are.
> Did not a frantic youth of late
> O'erset the chariot of the sun?
> . . . .

---

15. John Crowne, *Calisto*, in *The Dramatic Works of John Crowne*, ed. James Maidment and W. H. Logan (Edinburgh, 1873–74), I, 242.

16. The masque actually requires more than these two women; there are three African nymphs in the scene at the end of the play. Several other Black women appear to carry the canopy under which Calisto and Nyphe walk at the conclusion of the masque. At least two of the "Africans" are actually white women masquerading as Africans.

Beauty's Beasts

> It is he that hath undone us:
> > He pour'd whole streams
> > > Of melting beams,
> >
> > Red, and glowing hot upon us.
> > And now we range the world around,
> > To see if our lost beauty can be found. (p. 321)

Unfortunate indeed are these women. The other nymphs and shepherdesses know to avoid the sun's heat and thereby avoid becoming black. Earlier in the masque, when Mercury and Jupiter are searching for their beloved nymphs, Mercury knows where to look:

> In the cool groves our Nymphs we now shall find,
> Wading in shades, and bathing in the wind;
> > Whilest Phoebus shoots his arrows round,
> > And vainly seeks the Nymphs to wound,
> > The grove he vainly does invade;
> > His fiery darts are quenched in shade. (p. 263)

The black nymphs are not so lucky or so wise, and now they suffer, grievously wounded by Phaeton.

Like the Ethiopian nymphs in *Blackness*, also victims of Phaeton's ill-fated round, these black nymphs now hope to recover their lost beauty. However, they do not fare as well as their earlier sisters. They cannot be restored to their former beauty—that is, to their former whiteness. Instead they are called upon to sacrifice it to Calisto and Nyphe. This discovery is joyously reported by a third black nymph who races in to tell the others her news:

> > Rejoice, rejoice! our beauty's found,
> > > Our lovely white and red,
> >
> > To two chaste Nymphs of Cynthia's train is fled,
> > And they must stars be crown'd:
> > And now instead of what we sought
> > Our black with us must fair be thought. (p. 321)

The only recourse for these irreversibly darkened nymphs now seems to be self-delusion. But they willingly practice self-deception and as willingly sacrifice their beauty: "This happy fate, who could divine? / Our beauty then in heav'n must shine" (p. 321). Yet, such acceptance does not alter the magnitude of their loss. We understand the real loss of the Africans by such words as *fair* and *shine*, words that indicate the true state of affairs. Their loss is made all the greater and sadder as one of them contemplates her future:

> No losers we shall prove,
>   By parting with our red and white;
> If black will serve the turn of love;
>   For beauty's made for love's delight. (pp. 321-22)

One wonders whether these women will find love; after all, their countrymen, the frightened Arcadians, attempted to flee the nymphs. In Crowne's Arcadia, beauty remains firmly associated with "red and white." This Neoplatonic hope seems not to take into account the idea expressed in the *Symposium* that "the ugly clashes with all that is divine while beauty is in harmony with it."[17] Moreover, it seems particularly unreasonable for these women to hope for love, when Africa has earlier offered his "scorched sons" as slaves to Thames. It would be better for them to anticipate a life of slavery and sorrow, or perhaps even worse, a life as a meretrix, rather than one of love and happiness. Nor should it be forgotten that it is Calisto's "bright" physical beauty that leads Jupiter to a more spiritual love of her. He seems to follow the advice given to Socrates in the *Symposium*. Reporting the course of his love, Jupiter says:

> Rapt with her beauties, but her virtues more:
> I tarry here her virtues to adore.
> They us'd that force upon my vanquish'd mind,
> Which once on her bright beauties I design'd.
> The fire these kindled th'other did put out. (p. 283)

The beauty of light and the love of beauty that are honored in this masque deny the Africans both beauty and love. And the conclusion, which installs the two nymphs as heavenly lights, endorses the idea that beauty is light.

In Arcadia, where beauty is found only in the "red and white," the scorched nymphs have no hope. Neither thinking their blackness "fair" nor willingly sacrificing their "red and white" can alter the fact that they are outside the Arcadian norm, that they are other than Arcadians. Bereft of beauty, they must redeem them-

---

17. Plato, *The Symposium*, 543.

selves from the condition of otherness and spiritual disgrace that their color signifies; they must distinguish themselves from other stereotypical blacks who both know and relish evil. They achieve this by sacrificing themselves for the good of others even as they desire not to be black. Explicit in the acceptance of their loss is the recognition that whites are beautiful and that they, the black nymphs, are not, but they redeem themselves by acknowledging the superiority of whites. Niger's daughters knew these things too. They were more fortunate; they were blanched and admitted into the pale.

In these masques, blacks are consistently assigned the role of the Other. The desire of so many women (nineteen in three masques) to be freed of the sign of their otherness, the sign of their type, can be neither overlooked nor underestimated. They, the gypsies, and most of all the audience understand exactly what it means to be black. In the world of the masque, to be black is to be denied everything that the learned tradition has canonized. It is to be outside an imitation heaven, outside the Elysian Fields.[18] To be included requires being washed white, but that is impossible except for those who can invoke the privileges of masking, those who can enter the circle of "supposes." Those who cannot enter that circle, those for whom color is a sign of condition, can never be washed white. They too are what they are supposed to be.

18. Jonson, *The Masque of Beauty*, in *Ben Jonson: The Complete Masques*, ll. 336 and 344.

III

Words of the Sponsors
Blacks in Lord Mayors' Pageants

This laden Camel, bears part of your Trade,
Which back'd by an Indian Sallies from the Fort;
To express their Plenty and to shew you Sport.
—Thomas Jordan, *The Triumphs of London*

If the politics of otherness and exclusion are the primary forces in determining the portrayal of blacks in the masque, the economics of colonialism play an essential role in creating the black stereotypes found in Lord Mayors' Pageants. Between 1585 and 1692, there were at least nineteen such pageants with black characters. Produced by trade guilds, the pageants obviously reflect some of the trade and economic interests of these groups. Many of the pageants call attention to the benefits of global trade acquired by England. In some Restoration-era pageants, plantation and slave economics are justified and endorsed. During this period, expanded trade with both the East and West Indies was producing new wealth for noblemen and guildsmen alike, and it is impossible to ignore the nature of the organizations that sponsored these pageants.

While trade guilds in other parts of England were in decline in the sixteenth and seventeenth centuries, the London guilds suffered no such decline. In fact, in London, guild membership included some of the city's most powerful and wealthy merchants. D. C. Coleman writes:

Words of the Sponsors

In London, craft guilds came under the domination of mercantile guilds whose members, richer and thus economically more powerful, controlled either the markets or the raw materials of the craftsmen. . . . The big London companies—Grocers, Merchant Tailors, Haberdashers, Goldsmiths, and the like, the majority of them incorporated by royal charter in the later fifteenth century, itself an expensive process, dependent on a wealthy group in the guild—survived to typify the guild structure of the capital and to mark out the paths of power in the government of the City, dominated as it was by the richest merchants of the land.[1]

In pageants that celebrate the guild membership's wealth and power, one would expect to find favorable commentary on guild views and enterprises. And even in those pageants in which economic issues are not always in the forefront, the demands of trade and guild interests are never completely overlooked. However, before we look at these specific pageants, it will be useful to discuss briefly some of the conventions of pageants, so that we might better understand the demands of characterization and the framework within which the various pageant writers worked.

Held in London on the twenty-ninth of October of every year, the Lord Mayors' Pageants celebrate the inauguration of the city's new lord mayor. Consisting of several splendid pageant wagons, troops of marchers in their guild or office livery, and speeches organized, however loosely, around a central theme, these pageants were not unlike other civic pageants and royal entries in the sixteenth and seventeenth centuries. After the main procession, there was a banquet, fireworks, and music at the guild hall of the new lord mayor. The pageants are still held today, although they are now somewhat less sumptuous.

These annual events were very popular in the sixteenth and seventeenth centuries, if the comments found in contemporary diaries are any indication, and the enormous expenses incurred by the guilds in producing the pageants further indicate their importance.[2] The Merchant-Taylors' Guild, for example, spent five times

1. D. C. Coleman, *The Economy of England, 1450-1750* (Oxford, 1977), 74-75.
2. See Frederick W. Fairholt, *Lord Mayors' Pageants: Being Collections Towards a History of these Annual Celebrations* (London, 1843-44), 20-24; and Henry

more to produce its 1602 pageant than it spent for its 1561 pageant. This leap in expenditures demonstrates the willingness of the guilds to present ever more elaborate shows to maintain public approval and to demonstrate their own political and economic power. The clearest indication of the popularity of these pageants, however, lies in the fact that their texts were published annually beginning in 1585. Certain guild records specifically mention the amount that was spent on publishing the pamphlets; others record the number of copies published. For example, the records of the Ironmongers' Guild show that five hundred copies of that year's pageant text were published in 1609.[3] Such a relatively large printing apparently was not unusual, since copies of almost all the pageants from 1585 onward still exist today.

The publication of the texts of the pageants indicates more than their popularity. It also reflects the seriousness with which these projects were undertaken by both the poet-playwrights and the sponsoring guilds. In the introduction to the text of his 1613 pageant, *The Triumphs of Truth*, Middleton writes: "But to speak truth, which many besides myself can affirm upon knowledge, a care that hath been seldom equalled, and not easily imitated, hath been faithfully shown in the whole course of this business, both by the wardens and committees, men of much understanding, industry, and carefulness, little weighing the greatness of expense, so the cost might purchase perfection, so fervent hath been their desire to excel in that, which is a learned and virtuous ambition, and so unfeignedly pure, the loves and affections of the whole Company to his lordship [the new lord mayor]."[4]

Some sixty years later the same seriousness of purpose is expressed by Thomas Jordan in his 1674 pageant, *The Goldsmiths Jubile*: "When by your own Indulgence more than my desert, I was preferr'd to the Honour of this Imployment, you were frequently

---

Machyn, *The Diary of Henry Machyn, Citizen and Merchant Taylor of London, From A.D. 1550 to A.D. 1563*, ed. John Gough Nichols (London, 1848) 47–48.

3. David M. Bergeron, *English Civic Pageantry, 1558-1642* (London, 1971), 138, 131; Malone Society, *Collections III: A Calendar of Dramatic Records in the Books of the Livery Companies of London, 1485–1640*, ed. Jean Robertson and D. J. Gordon (Oxford, England, 1954), 82.

4. Thomas Middleton, *The Triumphs of Truth*, in *The Works of Thomas Middleton*, ed. A. H. Bullen (New York, 1964), VII, 234.

pleased to Admonish me, that I should be careful in my Studies, and rally up all my Abillities, in the performance of this Duty, from a consideration, that the great and good object of my Addresses would deservedly require my choicest Thoughts, and accutest Contemplations."[5] While there is a certain amount of naked flattery and bold self-congratulation in both quotations, it is easy to see why the author of a pageant had to approach his task with earnestness. The lord mayor must be pleased; royal spectators were frequently present; the guild was spending large sums of money; and the pageant writer's reputation, not to mention future profitable commissions, was at stake.

In addition to protecting his reputation and future commissions, the author had to meet the didactic requirements of the guilds, which wanted more than frivolous festivals and pageantry; the sponsors wanted a moral lesson as well. An entry made in 1568 in the *Merchant-Taylors' Books* records some verses that emphatically state what the members of this guild felt to be important in pageants: "These verses or p'ceptes to be written aboute the Pageant if it shalbe thoughte good/viz: ffeare god/be wyse/be true/accepte no bribes." As it turns out, the verses that follow the above quotation "were not written aboute the pageant nor in no other place elles/at that tyme." Their absence, however, does not reflect a desire to abandon the "inherent didacticism" of the pageants. "Inherent didacticism," writes David Bergeron, is "a characteristic of all such civic entertainment." And throughout the period under discussion, the pageants did not swerve from their sponsors' demands for moral instruction. Interspersed amidst their praise of London or the mayor or monarch, the playwrights include moral exempla or instructions to the lord mayor in honesty, good government, and other such related virtues. Frequently themes grander than practical moral lessons were dramatized in the streets of London. Bergeron states: "Indeed occupying a vast portion of the thematic concern [of civic pageants] is the eternal conflict between virtue and vice, the ancient psychomachia between good and evil. Owing a debt to medieval morality drama, almost all pageants

---

5. Thomas Jordan, *The Goldsmiths Jubile, or, Londons Triumphs* (London, 1674) sig. A2a.

contain some sort of reference to the moral struggle, and one need only view the pageants to see the theme in action."[6]

Like the court masques of the period, civic pageants tend to rely on personifications and type characters to animate the moral or lesson of the pageant. However, unlike the masque in which there is usually some dramatic action, the pageant is more often a tableau vivant, its characters almost never involved in any action or dialogue. Instead, characters deliver panegyrics, or monologues or lectures on moral themes. To augment this moralism, the major characters in these tableaux generally are personages drawn from emblem books. The pageants' texts frequently provide descriptions of the costumes of characters as well as explications of their dress and devices. Middleton's description of Truth in *The Triumphs of Truth* exemplifies this:

> Zeal . . . makes way for the chariot wherein Truth his mistress sits, in a close garment of white satin, which makes her appear thin and naked, figuring thereby her simplicity and nearness of heart to those that embrace her; a robe of white silk cast over it, filled with the eyes of eagles, showing her deep insight and height of wisdom; over her thrice-sanctified head a mild-white dove, and on each shoulder one, the sacred emblems of purity, meekness, and innocency; under her feet serpents, in that she treads down all subtlety and fraud; her forehead empaled with a diadem of stars, the witness of her eternal descent; on her breast a pure round crystal, showing the brightness of her thoughts and actions; a sun in her right hand than which nothing is truer; a fan, filled all with stars, in her left, with which she parts darkness and strikes away the vapors of ignorance.[7]

On other occasions, the author may have believed that certain of the emblems employed were commonly known, and therefore, he provides some scant description and little or no explication. Such an example is found in Anthony Munday's 1616 pageant, *Chrysanaleia*: "All the forefront is beautified with Royall Vertues, as Truth, Vertue, Honor, Temperance, Fortitude, Zeale, Equity, Conscience, beating down Treason and Mutinie. Behind, and on the sides, sits Justice, Authority, Lawe, Vigilancy, Peace, Plentie and Discipline, as best props and pillars to any kingly estate.

---

6. Malone Society, *Collections III*, 49, 50; Bergeron, *English Civic Pageantry*, 128, 306–307.
7. Middleton, *The Triumphs of Truth*, 244.

These, as all the rest, are best obserued by their seuerall Emblems and properties, borne by each one, and their adornments answerable to them in like manner." A similarly vague description is found in Thomas Jordan's *London's Joy* of 1681: "On these two Stages are Eight figures, *viz.* one at each Corner, called *Power, Prudence, Fate, Fame, Fertility, Integrity, Agility,* and *Alacrity,* properly attired."[8] The readers' imaginations and experiences with emblems and emblem books are required here in order to visualize such common personifications as Honor, Peace, Virtue, and the like. Surely spectators on London's streets had to rely on their personal knowledge and experiences to recognize all the emblems and their accoutrements.

In many civic pageants, the emblematic role assigned to black characters is very simple. They more often than not seem to be exotic paraphernalia, used essentially to increase the air of extravagance surrounding a particular pageant car. Blacks also serve as visible reminders of British success in trade and exploration, as do Indians. In fact, a few pageant writers, particularly Thomas Jordan, make no distinction at all between Indians and blacks. This sentence from Jordan's 1674 pageant, *The Goldsmiths Jubile,* illustrates that common failure: "This Chariot is drawn by two Golden *Unicorns* . . . on whose backs are mounted two beautiful Raven-black *Negroes,* attired according to the dress of India."[9]

In Jordan's 1672 pageant, there is a character identified as an "Indian Emperour" who claims to be the Emperor of Mexico. He is described as follows:

> And in the reer of the Camel, highly exalted on a silver throne and under a Canopy of Silver fringed, sitteth an Imperial person alone, in Royal habit; his face black, and likewise his Neck and Arms,[10] which

---

8. Anthony Munday, *Chrysanaleia: The Golden Fishing, or Honour of Fishmongers* (London, 1616), sig. B4-5; Thomas Jordan, *London's Joy, or, the Lord Mayors Show* (London, 1681), 9.

9. Jordan, *The Goldsmiths Jubile,* 3.

10. A description such as this of the color of the neck, arms, and face of speaking characters seems to indicate that this is an actor in blackface. Likewise, when a nonspeaking character is simply identified as a Negro, this person is probably a black person. Jordan makes such a distinction later in this same passage. After identifying the speaker, Jordan describes the scene as follows: "and on a descent gradually next under him sitteth two Negroes, attired properly in diverse colour'd Silks, with Silver or Gold Wreaths or Coronets upon their Heads, as Princes of

are naked to the Elbows; on his head a Crown of various coloured Feathers, a rope of Pearl about his Neck, Pendants in his Ears, short curl'd black wool-like-Hair, a Coat of several painted Feathers, a silver Mantle cross him, from the right shoulder to the left side; in his right hand he holdeth a Scepter of Silver with a bright Golden Sun on the top of it, Carnation Silk Stockings and on them Silver Buskins laced before and surfled with Gold Ribon.[11]

This is quite obviously a hybrid character, black but dressed in a West Indian or Mexican manner. Similarly, a black goddess named Opulenta in John Tatham's 1661 pageant *London's Tryumphs* is dressed as an Indian. In most of the nineteen pageants with black characters, their costumes and sometimes the characters themselves are described as "Indians." The use of the single word *Indian* to describe three distinct peoples is neither unusual nor surprising. As Purchas speculates, *Indian* is simply a word that came to be synonymous with exotic. Yet there are historical reasons for the conflation of two separate nations and peoples into the same term. The imprecise use of *India*, attested to by the appellations "East Indies" and "West Indies" used by explorers, traders, and geographers, surely eases the way of this imprecision into common parlance. And certainly not all playwrights desired to be as precise with geographical names as Marlowe is in *Tamburlaine*. For some, the exotic was distinction enough.

To add exotic color is the primary function of the Moor in George Peele's 1585 pageant. This pageant, published under the title *The Device of the Pageant Borne before Woolstone Dixi Lord Maior of the Citie of London* is the first pageant for which there is an extant text. The Moor in *Woolstone Dixi* therefore serves as a point of comparison for many of the Moors who follow in later pageants. Like so many of his descendants, this Moor arrives riding an exotic beast. In the text, he is introduced in this manner: "A Speech spoken by him that rid on a Luzarne [lynx] before the Pageant apparelled like a Moore."[12]

West-India." Jordan later uses the word "Black-a-moores" to describe other attendants to the "Indian Emperour."

11. Thomas Jordan, *London Triumphant, or, The City in Jollity and Splendour* (London, 1672), 4.

12. George Peele, *The Device of the Pageant Borne before Woolstone Dixi Lord*

Words of the Sponsors

Unfortunately, Peele provides no further description of the scene or costume. But we learn in the Moor's speech of his distant homeland:

> From where the Sun doth settle in his wagon
> And yoakes his Horses to his fiery Carte,
> And in his way gives life to Ceres Corne,
> Even from the parching Zone behold I come
> A straunger straungely mounted as you see,
> Seated upon a lusty Luzerns back. (ll. 1-6)

The rest of his speech is rather conventional; it includes praises for London, her lord mayor, and her sovereign. London the Moor proclaims to be "riche and fortunate, / Famed through the Worlde for peace and happinesse" (ll. 9-12). He then proceeds to catalog the city's many fortunes, not least of which is its queen, Elizabeth, "renowned through the world" (l. 39). The Moor continues, proclaiming the English queen

> Stall'd and annointed by the highest powre,
> The God of Kings that with his holy hand,
> Hath long defended her and her England. (ll. 40-42)

A non-European, come from the East and presumably from beyond Christendom, the Moor's very presence provides credibility to his reports of London's and Elizabeth's fame. Thus along with his exoticness, the Moor lends an air of cosmopolitan sophistication to the proceedings. His presence there also acknowledges the success of British traders and explorers who are capable of bringing exotic men and strange beasts to London for the pleasure of its citizens. The fact that the Moor actually speaks in praise of London only makes explicit what is implicit in his presence. The Moor, in this context, becomes an emblem of London's, and consequently England's, global renown, power, and superiority.

The Moor in Peele's 1585 pageant is prototypical. In some eleven other pageants, Moors or Indians appear riding exotic beasts. Riding two griffins are a "Neggarr" and an "Indian" in Tatham's 1659 pageant. Heywood's 1639 pageant has two Indians riding camels.

Maior of the Citie of London, in *The Minor Works of George Peele*, ed. Charles Tyler Prouty (New Haven, Conn., 1952), 209.

In the pageants of 1672, 1673, 1674, 1678, 1679, 1680, 1681, 1691, and 1692, "Negro-boys" appear astride lions, griffins, camels, or unicorns. In a few of these pageants, most notably the pageants of 1672 and 1681, black characters appear in another tableau, but in most of these pageants, the black characters only serve as emblems of British achievements in trade.

In the pageants of 1672, 1673, 1678, 1681, and 1692, years in which the new lord mayor was a member of the Grocers' or Merchant-Taylors' Guilds, the black youths seem to be explicit reminders of the distance and difficulty these tradesmen conquered to provide London with fruits and spices. In Thomas Jordan's 1678 pageant, *The Triumphs of London*, two black youths throw dates and raisins and other fruits from the baskets borne by artificial camels. An emblem of Fidelity says of the youths:

> This laden Camel, bears part of your Trade,
> Which back'd by an Indian Sallies from the Fort;
> To express their Plenty and to shew you Sport.[13]

Surely, this scene makes manifest the benefits of trade to citizen and merchant.

Africa itself, represented by personifications, appears in three pageants. Modeled after emblems found in emblem books or on maps, the personifications of Africa are usually accompanied by personifications of America, Asia, and Europe; these too closely resemble emblems in books or on maps.[14] In each of these pageants, Africa has a nonspeaking role; like the "Negro boys" in other pageants, Africa personified serves as exotic decoration. However, in two of the pageants in which Africa appears, she is directly linked to trade and commerce. In Jordan's 1674 pageant, Africa

---

13. Thomas Jordan, *The Triumphs of London* (London, 1678), 6–7.
14. Some examples of personifications of Africa found on maps may be seen in Ronald Vere Tooley, *Collectors' Guide to Maps of the African Continent and Southern Africa* (London, 1969). Personifications and maps that may be of interest to the reader are: Allard's *Africae Descriptio*, 1690, plate 5; Blaeu's *Africae Nova Descriptio*, 1630, plate 18; Hondius' *Africae Nova Tabula*, 1606, plate 40; Ogilby's *Aethiopia Interior*, 1670, plate 69; and de Wit's *Africa Tabula*, 1680, plate 94. For illustrations of Africa in popular emblem books, the reader should see Cesare Ripa, *Iconologia* (Facsim.; New York, 1976), 358; and Ripa, *Iconologie*, trans. Jean Baudouin (Facsim.; New York, 1976), pt. II, 6.

Words of the Sponsors

arrives accompanied by the other three continents. Her dress is similar to the dress of other black characters in these pageants: "Affrica. A tall Person, with a Face, Shoulders, Breast and Neck, all black, with Ropes of large round Pearl, about it, and also about her Arms . . . a black woolly-curl'd Hair . ... an *Indian* Gown very rich of divers Colours; a Girdle of Feathers about her middle . . . A Quiver of Arrows at her Back, an *Indian* Bow in her left hand and a Banner of my Lords [the new mayor's] in her right." Together with America and Asia, Africa represents the riches available to those willing to conquer the distances. None of the three speaks; only Europe does, saying to the Lord Mayor:

> May both the Indies furnish you with Gold:
> That as your Place of Office is of Trust,
> You may have Power and Treasure to be Just.[15]

The personification of Africa in Matthew Taubman's 1686 pageant again merely represents the wealth of the continent that can be Europe's through commerce. Although the description of Africa given by Taubman is not as detailed as that offered by Tatham, Taubman's composition of the tableau and interpretation of the emblems show the extent to which Africa and the non-European world is viewed as a place of great wealth that is Europe's for the taking: "On each Horse is mounted a person of a different Name and Country, properly apparell'd, alluding to the support of the *Virgin* or Mystery of the Company. On the second three [horses], *Peace* and *Plenty, Europe* riding the middle: And on the last three, *Africa, Asia* and *America,* representing Merchandize, Traffick, and other Dealings, both at home and abroad, appertaining to the Right Worshipful the Company of *Mercers.*"[16]

Though John Tatham makes no explicit connection between trade and Africa in his 1658 pageant (the earliest pageant in which I have found a personification of Africa), so clearly do the 1674 and 1687 pageants link Africa to trade that an analogy becomes inevitable. In Tatham's pageant Africa, accompanied by Asia, arrives astride a griffin: "A Carriot drawn by two Griffins (being the Supporters of the Companies Arms) on each of which is set a

15. Jordan, *The Goldsmiths Jubile*, 8, 10.
16. Matthew Taubman, *London's Yearly Jubilee,* (London, 1686), 12.

Figure, representing Affrica and Asia; each having a Pendant in their hands."[17] Tatham provides neither a description of their dress nor an explication of the figures' meaning; however, the implied meaning is impossible to ignore. At the very least, Africa and Asia are viewed in the same way that the "Negro-boys" are in so many of these pageants.

Of a much more complex nature is the representation of blacks and Indians in the Grocers' Guild's pageants of 1672, 1673, 1678, and 1681, all of which were written by Thomas Jordan. In these pageants, Jordan includes a droll (a comic scene) of planters. In all but the 1673 pageant, the planters sing a song about their toil, but they never complain because they have managed to remain in a pastoral world that is as near paradise as any in the postlapsarian era. In the 1681 pageant, a black planter sings:

> We are Jolly Planters that live in the East,
> And furnish the World with Delights when they Feast,
> For by our Endeavours this country presumes
> To fit them with Physic, Food, Gold and Perfumes.
> . . . .
> From Torments or Troubles of Body and Mind,
> Your Bonny brisk Planters are free as the Wind,
> We eat well to Labour, and Labour to eat,
> Our planting doth get us both Stomach and Meat;
>   There's no better Physic
>   To vanquish the Phthific,
> And when we're at Leisure our Voices are Music:
> And now we are come with a brick-drolling Ditty,
> To honour my Lord; and to humor the City,
> We Sing, Dance, and trip it as Frolick and Ranters;
> Such are the sweet Lives of your bonny brave Planters.[18]

The song obviously follows some conventions of the pageants we have seen earlier. There is praise for London and the new lord mayor. There is also a certain amount of inaccuracy in the placement of these black planters in "East-India." This droll, however, also contains important political ideas, ideas that are made to seem benign by invoking the pastoral convention. The planters are

17. John Tatham, *London's Tryumph, Presented by Industry and Honour: with Other Delightful Scaenes* (London, 1658), 9.
18. Jordan, *London's Joy*, 13.

"jolly" as well as trouble-free in body and mind. Their work keeps them happy and healthy; they find contentment in working hard to provide pleasures for others.

The fact that the toilers are black and the feasters white should not be overlooked. This song subtly offers justification for slavery as well as for colonialism and the consequent notions of racial superiority. These happy planters refer to themselves as "Your Bonny Planters" throughout. If one considers that the English royal family had been involved in the slave trade since 1663, it becomes clear that the planters are not simply being courteous when they use the genitive pronoun.[19] In another stanza the planter sings: "Our weighty Endeavours have Drams of Delight, / We slave it all day, but we sleep well at night." The use of the verb *slave* emphatically evokes the condition of the planters. Yet they are presented as pleased with their "Drams of Delight" in spite of their lot.

So too are the "Tawny Moors" of America who sing the planters' droll in Jordan's 1672 pageant. In a scene similar to the one above, these planters sing and dance in their distant paradise:

> This Wilderness is
>   A place full of Bliss,
>   For caring and sparing
> We know not what 'tis:
> By the sweat of our brows
>   We do purchase our meat:
> What we pluck from the boughs
>   We do lye down and eat.
> . . . .
> Of Fruits that are ripe
>   We all freely can take,
> With Tongues and Bag-Pipe

---

19. In that year, the Duke of York, later James II, launched the Company of Royal Adventurers Trading to Africa; the King himself was a shareholder. (See David Brion Davis, *The Problem of Slavery in Western Culture* [Ithaca, N.Y., 1966], 131.) The first Englishman to make a voyage to Africa expressly to capture slaves was John Hawkins in 1562. His three voyages to Africa are recorded in Hakluyt's *Principal Navigations, Voyages, Traffiques and Discoveries*. Queen Elizabeth invested in Hawkins' second voyage. (See Hakluyt, IV, 58–59; and Michael Craton, *Sinews of Empire: A Short History of British Slavery* [Garden City, N.Y., 1974], 34–35.)

Black Face, Maligned Race

> Jolly Musick we make:
> In our Perricraniums no mischief doth lurk;
> We are happier than they that do set us a work.
> We never are lofers
> What ever wind drive;
> Then God Bless the Grocers,
> And send them to thrive.
> CHORUS
> *We labour all Day, yet we frollick at Night,*
> *With smoaking and joking, and tricks of Delight.*[20]

These blissful "Tawny Moors" are quite happy to be set to work, so long as they are free to frolic during the night. The song goes so far as to have the workers claim to be happier than their masters. As in the portrayal of blacks, this one of Indians overlooks the realities of Indian slavery even as it justifies the continuation of that slavery and colonial policies.

The portrayal of Indian planters in 1678 has the same result. Save for the necessity to work, the planters claim to live in a postlapsarian paradise. Sings the "stout Planter with a voice like a Trumpet":

> With Mattock, Spade, Pruning-Hook, Shovel, & Sieve,
> What a Life of Delight do we Labourers live?
> The bonny brisk Planter (for delving design'd)
> Hath Health in his Body, and Peace in his Mind.
> Though this as a Curse in the Scripture we read,
> In the sweat of thy brows thou shalt purchase thy Bread.
> Chorus. Yet by Patience and Labour, in Digging and Dressing
> Th'old Curse is Converted into a new Blessing.
>
> II
>
> With Cinamon, Cloves, mace and all other Spice,
> We Planters have planted a New Paradise.
> We feel no Effects of the Faults that was Adam's,
> Here's Pepper for Gallants, and Nutmegs for Madams.
> We work, and we Sweat, yet are never the worse;
> At the most we have but a Spice of the Curse.[21]

The lyrics of this particular song, which is reminiscent of the planter's song in Jordan's 1681 pageant, emphasize the new par-

20. Jordan, *London Triumphant*, 11–12.
21. Jordan, *The Triumphs of London*, 13.

adise in which the "bonny planters" happily live and work; the song also makes the bold proposition that what is a curse to white Christians—servile labor—is an unmitigated blessing for the Indian planters.

In the 1673 pageant, the drollers are "Black and Tawny." Though the text does not preserve the lyrics of the song, it gives Jordan's description of the scene:

> Near St. *Lawrence* Lane[']s end he [the lord mayor] is intercepted by another Scene of Drolls, in a Garden of Fruits and Spices, where the Black and Tawny Inhabitants are very actively imployed, some in Working and Planting, others Carrying and recarrying; some are Drolling, Piping, Dancing and Singing; there are three Pipers, which, together with the Tongs, Keg, Frying-pan, Gridiron and Salt-Box, make very mel-odious Musick, which, the worse it is performed, the better it is accepted. But (upon an Eminent Promontory richly Embroydered with the Native Bravery of Flowers) on the extreme height sits a Lady of comely Proportion and pleasant Complexion, representing POMONA Goddess of Plantations.

This lady with a "pleasant Complexion" is later described as having "a long fair Hair." The obvious correlation between color and station is hardly surprising, as the goddess of plantations clearly must rule over those lesser creatures. Proclaiming her supremacy she says: "I am the Pregnant Goddess of these Brutes, / That Plant and Gather all delicious Fruits."[22] That is her sole reference to the "Brutes," although it seems safe to assume that they too were quite happy with "Drolling, Piping, Dancing and Singing" between their work.

Such portrayals of blacks and Indians as happy with their lot are not uncommon. The supposed happiness of African slaves was one of the strongest defenses offered by apologists for slavery. In 1613, Purchas wrote: "Here [in Jago] the Negro's were wont to bring slaves to sell to the Portugalls for beads, and other trifles, and cottons, with other base commodities; and them not such alone as they took in war, but their fathers and mothers, thinking they did them a benefit, to cause them thus to bee convayed into better Countries." Richard Ligon in his 1657 book, *A True and Exact History of the Island of Barbados*, describes the African slaves as

22. Jordan, *London in its Splendor* (London, 1673), 11-12.

"happy people, whom so little contents, very good servants, if they be not spoyled by the English." To demonstrate the willingness of these "happy people" to serve their master, Ligon reports the extraordinary—and clearly unbelievable—efforts certain slaves made to extinguish a fire in a sugar cane field: "And I have seen some Negros so earnest to stop this fire as with their naked feet to tread, and with their naked bodies to tumble, and roll upon it, so little they regard their own smart or safety in respect of their masters benefit."[23]

Similar statements about Indians exist too. A long poem in Edmund Hickeringill's *Jamaica Viewed* (1661) praises the devotion of Indian slaves:

> Under the line that equal's night and day
> *Guiana* stands, part of America . . .
> Whose Native *Indian* hath not, nor needs Art
> To clothe himselfe, Nature Supplies that Part.
> They're true Philosophers, not much they have,
> Nor do they want much, nor much do they crave.
> They care not for to morrow; nor supply,
> But just from hand to mouth, nor Granary.
> . . . .
> Thus much I'le say: I would not wish to have
> A better friend, or foe, or better slave
> Than is an *Indian* where he once affects,
> In love and service shall be no neglects.
> Command him as your slave, his life his All,
> If he do once you but *Bone-aree* call;
> And who would wish an easier foe than he,
> That (like a Buck) at noise of Guns will flie,
> But then your slave if that an *Indian* be,
> No other Caterer you need but he.[24]

Like black slaves, Indians, at least according to Hickeringill, are willing to give their "all" to their masters.

Of course, there were alternative views available, particularly about the brutal enslavement of Indians. In 1583, the first English translation of Las Casas' *Destruccion de las Indias* (first published

---

23. Purchas, *Purchas, His Pilgrimage*, 597; Richard Ligon, *A True and Exact History of the Island of Barbados* (London, 1657), 44, 45.
24. Edmund Hickeringill, *Jamaica Viewed* (2nd ed.; London, 1661), 56-61.

in 1552), appeared under the title, *The Spanish Colonies*. In 1656, a translation of the same work, embellished with illustrations of the carnage, including depictions of dismembered bodies, rapes, and tortures, was published with the title *The Tears of the Indians*. Thirty-three years later, yet another translation was published; this one was entitled *Popery Truly display'd in its Bloody Colours*. While it is undeniable that these translations were meant to be to some degree anti-Spanish propaganda, they neither deny the severity of nor English participation in Indian enslavement.[25] Each translation reports in a chilling manner both the deception employed by the Spanish to lure the Indians into slavery and the barbarous treatment they received at Spanish hands.

Similarly frank seventeenth-century evaluations about black slavery also exist. Even slave apologists could not ignore the harsh reality of slavery. Richard Ligon, who writes of the devoted slaves who incinerate themselves for their masters, also reports some of the means used to prevent slave uprisings:

> They [enslaved Africans] are not suffered to touch or handle any weapons . . . they are held in such awe and slavery, as they are fearfull to appear in any daring act; and seeing the mustering of our men, and hearing their Gun-shot (then which nothing is more terrible to them) their spirits are subjugated to so low a condition, as they dare not look up to any bold attempt. Besides these, there is a third reason, which stops all designes of that kind, and that is, they are fetched from several languages, and by that means, one of these understands not another.[26]

Ligon describes a severe and conscious subjugation of one people by another. This acknowledgment and the candid recognition that slaves would and did revolt against their enslavement clearly contradicts Ligon's earlier declaration that these are "happy people" who care not but for "their masters benefit." In addition to statements such as this by Ligon, several books treat extensively the abuse of African slaves. Morgan Godwyn's *The Negro's + Indians Advocate Suing for Their Admission into the Church* (1680) and Thomas Tryon's *Friendly Advice to the Gentlemen-Planters of the*

---

25. For a fuller discussion of Indian slavery, see Davis, *The Problem of Slavery in Western Culture*, 167–73 and 176–80.
26. Ligon, *History of Barbados*, 46.

East and West Indies (1684) are two of the most powerful and direct. The latter of these two books appeared only twelve years after the earliest of Jordan's pageants that has a planters' droll.

The employment of this happy slave type in the pageants of 1672, 1673, 1678, and 1681 demonstrates the extent to which types can be developed and employed in spite of enormous amounts of evidence to the contrary. The needs of the pageant, both dramatic and ideological, are paramount in Jordan's mind, and misrepresenting the conditions of enslavement and oppression of blacks and Indians is obviously of little or no consequence. Even an apologist for slavery such as Ligon could not completely ignore the true nature of slavery. However, essential to the theme and ideology of these pageants is the picture of happy planters gleefully surrendering their freedom in exchange for a few songs and dances in order that London's grocers might provide the population with exotic fruits and spices and, of course, reap the financial benefits of plantation and slave economics. Here we see that even if the employment of the type was unconsciously political, the results are the same: the pageants endorse racial slavery and foster an unrealistic and damaging stereotype.

Perhaps a further political purpose, and one far more subtle, is effected by these pastoral drolls. William Empson writes that "the feeling that life is essentially inadequate to the human spirit, and yet that a good life must avoid saying so, is naturally at home with most versions of pastoral; in pastoral you take a limited life and pretend it is the full and normal one, and a suggestion that one must do this with all life, because the normal is itself limited, is easily put into the trick though not necessary to its power."[27] Much of the public audience could apply to their personal lives this important lesson of the pastoral, and the economic and class distinctions between the pageants' sponsors and the vast street audiences suggest the legitimacy of such a reading. The poor can rejoice in the alleged superiority of a life uncomplicated by luxuries and comforts. But all of this receives further complication by the irony of having merchants who, while busily peddling their wares and boasting of their acquisitiveness, allow this anti-materialist view to be so positively articulated. True, no Englishman could

27. William Empson, *English Pastoral Poetry*, (1938; rpr. Freeport, N.Y., 1972), 114–15.

ever believe that *he* would be happier as a slave, but there were multitudes of poor Englishmen in personal circumstances almost as dire as the planters'. For that portion of the audience able to afford the merchandise from the Indies, the acquisition of such goods helps to elevate and distinguish them from the brutes who labor to produce the goods; for that portion unable to afford the spices and other luxuries, consolation comes in the example of the "planters" who report themselves "happier than they that do set us a work." But, of course, the greatest consolation for those of the lower economic and social classes comes through recognizing themselves as English and therefore members of the race and nation that enjoy this materialistic civilization. Those who cannot afford the riches of the Indies are at least English enough to covet those riches. As we all know, racism all too frequently flourishes among victims of class oppression, and victims of one or the other or both are all too willing to view the propaganda of their oppressors with a divided consciousness.

The comments on the music in the planters' drolls of the 1672, 1673, and 1678 pageants also allege the inferiority of the planters. In the quotation above from the 1673 pageant, we are told that the "Black and Tawny Inhabitants" of the garden "make very melodious Music, which, the worse it is performed, the better it is accepted." One cannot help but wonder if the orthography of "melodious" is not meant as a pun on the final three syllables. "Confused musick" is also made by the "Tawny Moors" in Jordan's 1672 pageant. In the 1678 pageant, *The Triumphs of London*, the garden scene is described in this manner: "The front part of the Stage is planted with variety of Trees, bearing all sorts of Spices and Fruits, as Oranges and Lemons, Citrons and Pomegrantes; with several Planters and Labourers at work, some Digging, some Planting; others Prunning, Dressing and Gathering; with divers Drolls, Piping, Dancing, Tumbling; and sundry kinds of Mimical Gestures, Antick Motions, Ingenious Confusion and Studious Disorder."[28]

Jordan's impression that the music of blacks and Indians is but so much confusion echoes the testimony of many travelers to Africa and America. "Full ill to our eares," is how William

28. Jordan, *London Triumphant*, 9; Jordan, *The Triumphs of London*, 12.

Townson, in 1555, describes the singing of African women. Ligon describes the music of African slaves with disdainful amusement: "The drum all men know, has but one tone; and therefore varietie of tones have little to do in this [African] musick, and yet so strangely they varie their time, as 'tis a pleasure to the most curious eares, and it was to me one of the strangest noyses that ever I heard made of one tone . . . for time without tone, is not an eight part of the science of Musick."[29]

These negative appraisals of the music of Africans are more than comments on the skill of African musicians. From classical antiquity to the Enlightenment, music was believed to be more than a simple art form or an expression of man's creativity. At its best, music connects man to God.[30] The praise of music offered by Lorenzo in *The Merchant of Venice* reflects the popular attitude toward music in Shakespeare's day and beyond:

> . . . soft stillness and the night
> Become the touches of sweet harmony.
> Sit Jessica. Look how the floor of heaven
> Is thick inlaid with patens of bright gold.
> There's not the smallest orb which thou behold'st
> But in his motion like an angel sings,
> Still quiring to the young-eyed cherubins;
> Such harmony is in immortal souls,
> But whilst this muddy vesture of decay
> Doth grossly close it in, we cannot hear it.

Lorenzo continues by telling Jessica of the power of the music that man can hear:

> For do but note a wild and wanton herd
> Or race of youthful and undandled colts
> Fetching mad bounds, bellowing and neighing loud,
> Which is the hot condition of their blood:
> If they but hear perchance a trumpet sound,
> Or any air of music touch their ears,
> You shall perceive them make a mutual stand,

---

29. Hakluyt, *Principal Navigations, Voyages, Traffiques and Discoveries*, IV, 73; Ligon, *History of Barbados*, 48.

30. See Gretchen Ludke Finny, *Musical Backgrounds for English Literature, 1580–1650* (New Brunswick, N.J., 1961); and Kathi Meyer-Baer, *Music of the Spheres and the Dance of Death: Studies in Musical Iconology* (Princeton, 1970).

Words of the Sponsors

> Their savage eyes turned to a modest gaze
> By the sweet power of music. Therefore the poet
> Did feign that Orpheus drew trees, stones and floods;
> Since naught so stockish, hard and full of rage
> But music for the time doth change his nature.
> The man that hath no music in himself,
> Nor is not moved with concord of sweet sounds,
> Is fit for treasons, stratagems and spoils,
> The motions of his spirit are dull as night,
> And his affections dark as Erebus.
> Let no such man be trusted.[31]

Music is a universal measure of the glory of God's creation and of the souls of men and beasts. Such assessments of the spiritual and cosmic value of music are neither unique nor hyperbolic. Some ninety years later in "A Song for St. Cecilia's Day, 1687," Dryden attributes the same powers to music. What then is to be thought of these people who are capable of only "confused musick" and know only "an eight part of the science of musick"? Culturally they must be of an inferior nature. Spiritually they seem not to enjoy that correspondence with God enjoyed by those who know the value of harmony. Politically they are but fit for "treasons, stratagems and spoils." Africans "not moved with a concord of sweet sounds" seem but fit for Erebus. The esteem accorded music by sixteenth- and seventeenth-century Englishmen underscores the seriousness of Jordan's comments on the music of Africans. While the comic nature of the droll gives the performance of "confused musick" a lighthearted touch, the spiritual, cultural, and political importance of music is neither undermined nor refuted. And the laughter that the scene provokes only serves to emphasize the musical and hence cultural, political, and spiritual bankruptcy of these blacks and Indians.

Not all black characters in the pageants are so humble as planters or managers of exotic beasts. Mention has already been made of an "Indian Emperour" in Jordan's 1672 pageant. In addition to this royal Moor, the 1613 and 1616 pageants have characters who are

---

31. William Shakespeare, *The Merchant of Venice*, V, i, 56–65 and 71–88. This and all future citations of Shakespeare's works except when otherwise noted come from *The Complete Signet Classic Shakespeare*, ed. Sylvan Barnet (New York, 1972).

Black Face, Maligned Race

described as "Kings of the Moors." In all three of these pageants, the monarchs come to offer homage to London, the lord mayor, and the king, and like their less regal Moorish brothers the planters, the Moorish kings too are happy with their inferior condition. Speaking to the lord mayor in 1672, the Indian Emperor says:

> To fill your Triumphs, and compleat this Show,
> The Princes of *Peru* and *Mexico*
> With our Imperial Train appear in State,
> Your Royal Revellings to Celebrate:
> Especially to be received a Guest
> By those [the Grocers] that bear this *Camel* in their crest;
> Because it is reported (as Fame saith,)
> That *England's* great Defender of the faith,
> Head of four Thrones, doth not disdain to be
> A Member of the *Grocers* Companie
> If their indulgent Soveraign be so good
> As to consociate in Brotherhood,
> And be concorporated well may I
> (That furnish them with Fruits and Spicery)
> Give them a visit.[32]

In his praise of Charles II, the Indian Emperor happily acknowledges both his inferiority to the English king and his kinship to other Moors who represent British overseas trade.

No speech is recorded for the King of the Moors in Anthony Munday's 1616 pageant, *Chrysanaleia*, but the text preserves a description of the Moors' pageant: "Then commeth the King of Moores, gallantly mounted on a golden Leopard, he hurling gold and silver every way about him. Before, on either side, and behinde him, ride six other his tributarie Kings on horse-back, gorgeously attired in faire guilt Armours, and apt furniture there to belonging. They carry Ingots of golde and silver, and each one his dart, and in this order they attend on him: shewing thereby that the Fishmongers are not vnmindfull of their combined brethren, the worthy Company of Golde-Smithes." Later, in a speech that focuses on the league between the Fishmongers and Goldsmiths, the speaker explains the significance of the Moor to the lord mayor: "His

32. Jordan, *London Triumphant*, 4.

62

Indian treasure liberally is throwne: / To make his bounteous heart better knowne."[33]

The belief that gold and riches of untold worth abound in the Indies is, of course, commonplace at this time. The three English translations of Las Casas' *Destruccion de las Indias* provide ample descriptions of the wealth and treasures of Indians. And even though Las Casas condemns the greed of the Spanish and their barbarous behavior, the first English translation attempts to justify these cruelties and ultimately to justify the rapine. Saying that tyrants are the "Axe in the Lordes hands and executioners of his justice," the translator in his introduction continues:

> But here may expresse reasons be alleadged for such iudgements of God, which seeming seuere to man are neuerthelesse, in that they proceeded from God, meere iustice. Moses saith, when the Lord thy God had reiected them before thy face, think not in thine hearte, saying: The Lorde for my righteousnesse hath caused mee to enter possession of this land, seeing he hath for their wickednesse rooted out these nations before thy face. For thou art not through thy righteousnesse and vprightnesse of heart come to inherite their land, But it is for the abhominatio[n]s of these people, whom the Lord thy god hath expelled before thy face.[34]

While the author clearly condemns the "wickednesse" of the Spanish, he also emphasizes the "abhominations" of the Indians, therefore making it only just to expropriate the wealth.[35]

The riches of Africa were also cataloged by explorers and voyagers. The records of the voyages to Africa found in Hakluyt frequently mention the gold and ivory taken by the explorers. One such account, after noting the beastliness of the Africans, com-

---

33. Munday, *Chrysanaleia*, sig. B2, sig. C3.
34. Las Casas, Bartolome, *The Spanish Colonie*, trans. M. M. S. (London, 1583), sig. ¶3v and ¶4r.
35. The translator later warns against self-righteousness while performing these acts. He writes: "But Gods iudgements being in the meantime such, that by the wicked he punisheth those that be wicked: not withstanding their wickednes be somwhat lesse, as also the good be chastined by the cruell and blood thirstie: it is certaine that wee are not there by to iudge that our selves, shall have the victorie ouer our enemies, because our cause is the better, for we are replenished with vice enough, where by to leaue vnto [G]od sufficient matter to punish us" (*Ibid.*, sig. ¶4v).

ments with surprise on the great wealth of these same Africans:

> Among other things therefore, touching the manners and nature of the people, this may seeme strange, that their princes & noble men use to pounce and rase their skinnes with pretie knots in divers formes, as it were branched damaske, thinking that to be a decent ornament. And albeit they goe in maner all naked, yet are many of them, & especialy their women, in maner laden with collars, bracelets, hoopes, and chaines either of gold, copper, or ivory. I my selfe have one of their braslets of Ivory, weighing two pounds a sixe ounces of Troy weight, which make eight and thirtie ounces: this one of their women did weare upon her arme.[36]

This description of otherwise naked and "beastly" people laden with gold and ivory creates a startling image for the reader. Surely a people so excessively wealthy have much to spare; and the success of the voyagers as reported in Hakluyt indicated that the Africans really did. While there was some price to pay in getting the gold, the gold was believed to be there in abundance. The profligate Kings of the Moors who tossed their wealth on to London's streets were just another indication of the riches and an invitation to it. At least those who financed the trade and profited from it were happy to foster this impression.

The realm over which the King of the Moors in Middleton's *Triumphs of Truth* reigns is also probably a gold- and treasure-rich place. This king, however, is Christian, and he comes to commend "English merchants, factors, and travellers, / Whose Truth did with our spirits hold commerce."[37] Before he is free to profess and praise his faith, however, the Moor must dispel the expectations of the spectators. Thus he begins:

> I see amazement set upon the faces
> Of these white people, wonderings and strange gazes;
> Is it at me? does my complexion draw
> So many Christian eyes, that never saw
> A king so black before?
> . . . .
> I must confess, many wild thoughts may rise,
> Opinions, common murmurs, and fix'd eyes,
> At my so strange arrival in a land

36. Hakluyt, *Principal Navigations, Voyages, Traffiques and Discoveries,* IV, 62.
37. Middleton, *The Triumphs of Truth,* 248.

> Where true religion and her temple stand;
> I being a Moor, then in opinion's lightness,
> As far from sanctity as my face from whiteness,
> But I forgive the judgings of th'unwise,
> Whose censures ever quicken in their eyes,
> Only begot of outward form and show;
> And I think meet to let such censurers know,
> However darkness dwells upon my face,
> Truth in my soul sets up the light of grace. (pp. 247-48)

Recognizing the traditional association of blackness with sinfulness, the king reveals that he has the light of Truth in his soul, a light planted by distant-traveling Christian merchants. For their gift of Christianity, the king praises their virtue and example. The unspoken yet clear implication of his words, though, is an endorsement of continued trade. According to this king, the Moors (and that includes all Africans and Indians), are the greatest beneficiaries of such trade, through which they have been rescued from damnation.

The king's proclamation that he and his queen have converted to Christianity provokes an interesting dramatic situation. A raging Error suddenly appears in the street and threatens to win back her Moors with necromancy: "What, have my sweet-fac'd devils forsook me too? / Nay, then my charms will have enough to do" (249). Error's response to the loss of two of her natural partisans simply acknowledges what is supposed to be. Moors, as is well known, are supposed to be devils in Error's train, not Christians and compatriots of Truth. Truth, however, champions the Moors and her cause and defeats Error in the streets.

Because it is extraordinary for Moors to be Christians, Christian Moors offer valuable testimony of the salvific powers of Christianity, testimony that confirms for a Christian audience the truths of the faith. In three other pageants there is some discussion of religion as it concerns blacks. In the 1678 pageant, there is a black goddess, Opulenta, who is accompanied by three "Black Indian Princesses," Animalia, Mineralia, and Vegetablia. All four black women are opulently dressed. The emphasis on earthly riches underscores the obvious absence of any spiritual values in any of the four. The rites offered to Opulenta also demonstrate the idol's separation from real spiritual values. Jordan describes the temple and rites: "This Temple-like Fabrick in front [of the pageant cart] stands so open, that with easy perspicuity every Common eye may discharge it's sight up to the high Altar, on which an *East-Indian* Deity called OPULENTA, a Representative of all the Intrinsic Treasure in the Oriental *Indies,* and is their Tutelary Goddess, before whose Shrine the Idolatrous Natives after the preparation of a long feast) with Pagan Piety, and diabolical Devotion prostrate themselves with all the adoration imaginable."[38]

Neither innocent nor harmless, Opulenta's rites are diabolical. The goddess herself, however, knows of her real importance both to Christians and to Christianity. After offering the customary homage to London, the mayor, and the king, Opulenta says:

> May you prove prosperous, and (when you please)
> You shall command my Cities and my Keys;
> My Deity it self: But I divine
> You do adore a Power greater than Mine,
> A God, that doth all other Gods excell,
> Imitate Him, and you will Govern well.[39]

Through this speech Opulenta confesses herself to be a charlatan who accepts the homage and offerings of the "Idolatrous Natives" though she fully understands her own inferiority and duplicity. She also recognizes the superiority of the English to herself and her devotees. By acknowledging the superiority of the God of the English, Opulenta also recognizes the supremacy of spiritual values over earthly riches. Her invitation to the Christian English to "command my Cities and my Keys" justifies emphatically their moral right to her wealth. The establishment of Christianity in place of this idolatry becomes a moral obligation for the English. Ironically, the reward for dismantling the worship of the "Intrinsic Treasure of the Oriental *Indies*" is that very treasure. Missionary efforts reap material benefits. Commerce and Christianity are made compatible.

A black Christian serves as the spokeswoman for Christianity in Jordan's 1681 pageant. This pageant, written to honor the new lord mayor, John Moore, proposes that during his tenure London will

38. Jordan, *The Triumphs of London,* 8.
39. *Ibid.,* 9.

be like a fruitful plantation ruled by a beneficent Moor. Fructifera, the Moorish governess with "a Raven black Face," rules wisely over her plantation, attended by "four other Delightful Ladies . . . who sit about her, viz *Fragra, Florida, Delicia and Placentia.*" Significantly, these four are later identified as "European." However, like John Moore, Fructifera is no ordinary Moor; she shares with him his Christian faith, a fact that she reveals at the conclusion of her conventional speech of praise:

> Perhaps you think it strange, my Lord, that I
> An Indian Moor, should talk of Piety,
> Of the Creation, and the Deity.
> I have been Baptiz'd in the Christian Faith,
> And do believe in all the Scripture saith!
> I am a Moor, yet a good Christian too,
> With Reverence to your Lordship, so are You.[40]

The first verse quoted above reveals Fructifera's awareness of the audience's expectations of her. She too is not supposed to be a Christian or versed in the Scriptures; she does, after all, wear the mark of the devil on her face. Her awareness of the contemporary opinion of Moors prompts her to beg the indulgence of John Moore for punning on his name. Not only are Moors held in low esteem, later in this pageant, they are characterized as the "bonny planters" who "slave it all day." What Fructifera and John Moore have in common is their calling from the ordinary and their righteousness and faith, not a shared history of contempt.

Jordan raises the issue of the morality and religion of blacks twice in his 1672 pageant. The Indian Emperor mentioned earlier admonishes the lord mayor to temper justice with mercy and to avoid hypocrisy; failure to do so, the emperor implies, would cast the English to a moral level lower than the one held by Indians:

> *Justice* supports the World, for without that
> No man hath title to his own Estate;
> Which mixed with *Mercy*, gives mankind new birth,
> And may be fitly styl'd Heaven upon Earth,
> Which there's no question, but you will dispense
> To punish Guilt, and cherish Innocence;

---

40. Jordan, *London's Joy*, 11.

> And with your Eagles eyes to search out those
> That are your God's your King's and Country's foes.
> . . . .
> You bear the Sword of Government (my Lord)
> In such a peevish Age,[41] that (I may say)
> Many are studious how to Disobey,
> And yet Speak well, but if they Act not so,
> We are better Moralists in *Mexico*.[42]

As Error and all contemporary Christians knew, blacks bear the mark of the devil upon their faces. To fall to a spiritual and moral level below this black emperor and his subjects, would condemn Englishmen to diabolical company.

Later in this pageant, America, "A proper Masculine Woman, with a tawny Face,"[43] makes a long speech comparing some other European Christians unfavorably to both the Indians and the English:

> (Unknownt to Christendom) I liv'd at ease,
> Enrich'd with Gold, Tranquility and Peace;
> But when by fierce Invasions, they did know
> The treasures of *Peru* and Mexico,
> (My two great Empires) I became a Prey
> To divers Nations, who did rob and flay
> My naked Natives, such as knew no Art
> In War-like Weapons, but the Bow and Dart.
> Then came the winged Ship, with thundring Gun,
> Which dimm'd the Eyes of our great God, the Sun,
> The only Deity we worship'd, and
> Ransack'd my Riches, over-ran my Land,
> Ruin'd my Princes, (my sad Fate was such)
> The haughty *Spaniard* and the cruel *Dutch*[44]
> (Than which the Devil is not worse) did Build

---

41. This is obviously an allusion to the political troubles of the time, including the recent English reversals in the Third Dutch War (Summer, 1672), the unpopularity of the Declaration of Indulgence (March 15, 1672), and the growing unhappiness with Charles II's alliances with Louis XIV of France.

42. Jordan, *London Triumphant*, 4.

43. Jordan, *London Triumphant*, 9.

44. As was noted above, the English were at war with the Dutch in 1672. Also in *Destruccion de las Indias*, Las Casas writes of the horrible way the Dutch treated Indians. The English translation entitled The *Tears of the Indians* was published in 1656.

> Fortifications, rout me in the Field,
> Brought over Priest, and Monks with Holy Hoods,
> To teach Religion, whilst they stole my Goods.[45]

The Dutch and Spanish, found wanting when subjected to the moral criteria established earlier by the Indian emperor, are placed in the company of the devil. America declares the simple natives, victims of the duplicity and greed of these Europeans, to be morally superior to their conquerors. Obviously, the point of this comparison is to attack the Dutch and the Spanish, but it is the assumption that Indians lack any moral or ethical standards that makes the comparison so damning and so effective.

America continues, however, with praise for the English:

> Only the *English* Nation I did find
> Amongst the rest more peaceable and kind,
> Full of Humanity, who did perswade
> Me to a generous and fair way of Trade;
> Faithful in Word and Deed, which makes me come
> To this Celestial Part of *Christendome*,
> And bear my share in the Triumphant Glory.[46]

Like the king in Middleton's pageant, America proclaims the English to be model Christians and implies that their religion, being the true religion, is superior to the sun worship of her "naked Natives." As in the earlier pageants, the natives are grateful partners in trade with the English because they receive something which is of greater value in return; they receive the truth of Christianity.

Of course, many people did set out to convert the non-Christian peoples of Africa and the Indies. But the sole motive of many who professed Christian zeal, some English included, was commercial profit. In *Destruccion de las Indias*, Las Casas condemns the Spanish conquistadores and traders for failing to convert the Indians, one of the declared goals of their mission. And English translators make good use of this failure, using it as yet another example of Spanish duplicity and Catholic hypocrisy. Yet, for the English and all others involved in the slave trade, the issue of conversion becomes more and more important as trade and plantation econ-

---

45. Jordan, *London Triumphant*, 9.
46. *Ibid.*

omies come to depend upon slavery and the slave trade. Europeans had questioned since the Middle Ages the justice of Christian enslaving Christian, and by the seventeenth century, the debate was particularly strident.[47] Many proslavery, anticonversion spokesmen had gone so far as to deny the very humanity of Africans—something not even the earliest explorers had done—in an effort to put an end to the debate. Morgan Godwyn in *The Negro's + Indians Advocate* has to refute the assertion that Africans were not human before he can commence his arguments for conversion.[48] Appeals for conversion of slaves were made by others, including the Englishmen Richard Ligon in 1657 and Thomas Tryon in 1684.[49] Efforts by the Quakers began in the 1670s. These prolonged and numerous efforts point out the strength of opposition to missionary work among Africans, as well as the continued reluctance of some Englishmen to propagate the faith. Middleton's Moorish king and these few others in Jordan's pageants are the fortunate ones, for many merchants struggled to deny Christianity to the Moors.

The overriding importance of commercial considerations, even in the discussions of religion in these pageants, cannot be ignored. The pageants were mounted to praise merchants and trade. Thus the employment of these type characters serve more than a purely dramatic or even emblematic function. The characters endorse ideas upon which British colonialism was founded and expanded. Not only are cultural and national values invoked or praised in the treatment of black and tawny Moors in these pageants, but the growing economic strength of the nation becomes involved. Just as financial interests play an unambiguous role in the development of some type characterizations seen in these pageants, most notably the happy slave, there is a *real* monetary value in the continuation of particular stereotypes. To deny this is to deny the very reason for global exploration.

Although this chapter discusses material which covers nearly a hundred years, the common themes remain constant. The pageant

47. See Davis, *The Problem of Slavery in Western Culture*, 98–102.
48. Morgan Godwyn, *The Negro's + Indians Advocate, Suing for Their Admission into the Church* (London, 1680), 12–14.
49. See Ligon, *History of Barbados*, 53–54; and Thomas Tryon, *Friendly Advice to the Gentlemen-Planters of the East and West Indies* (N.p., 1684), 120, 146–221.

writers always portray blacks as inferiors, either cultural or spiritual. Their aspirations, or alleged lack thereof, remove them from the realm of normally ambitious men. As Christians, they merely serve as exceptions to the rule. Some few are blessed, but the majority of their unregenerate kind is rightfully damned. These types, we shall see, are not confined to these nonmimetic pageants; they cross freely into the popular mimetic drama of the period. It is this crossover and its ramifications, including the near-failure of English drama to produce anything but stereotypical black characters, that we shall take up next.

IV

Princes of Darkness
Black Villains on the Mimetic Stage

<blockquote>Seeing your face, we thought of hell.
—Thomas Dekker, Lust's Dominion</blockquote>

It is no exaggeration to say that the overwhelming majority of black Moors who appeared on the popular English stage between 1589 and 1695 endorsed, represented, or were evil. Understanding why blacks were so consistently portrayed in this manner requires some knowledge of developments on the stage between the appearance of the black-faced Prince of Darkness and of his agent, the dark Prince Muly Mahamet, some centuries later in Peele's 1589 play, *The Battle of Alcazar*.

Writers of the medieval mysteries would have us believe that long before the creation of man, the face of evil was frequently black. The black faces of the fallen angels signify their fall from grace and make visible the color of their damned souls. Black demons also appeared in morality plays, "Belial the blake" in *The Castle of Perseverance* being perhaps the most famous example. Relying on the simplest opposition between black and white, medieval playwrights employed this centuries-old allegory of color. However, for reasons we shall investigate, Satan and lesser demons disappeared from the morality play, and in their stead appeared a new kind of character, one who acts as Satan's agent on earth. This character is the vice.

Charged with securing the damnation of the soul of the figure of mankind, the vice operates under a cloak of secrecy, hiding his true nature from his dupe. "As for the Vice's method in his stratagem, it is first, last, and always deceit," Bernard Spivack writes. "In the arsenal of his deceit," Spivack continues, "the chief weapon is dissimulation in the form of moral, abetted often by physical, disguise." In other words, in order to dissemble and to deceive, the vice must look like a man. Were he to appear indistinguishable from Satan—though he too relied on disguises from the start—the vice would be unable to achieve his desired end; few men, after all, are willing to believe the devil in his own guise. Accordingly, Avarice, "the vice of the plaie" *Respublica* (1553), presents himself to the widow Respublica as Policie, making sure he is unrecognized as Avarice; his cohorts Insolence, Oppression, and Adulation disguised respectively as Authoritie, Reformation, and Honestie also beguile the widow.[1]

From dramatic necessity, the face of evil changes, and the Vice's face, rather than looking very different from the faces in the audience, comes to resemble them. The agent of Satan learns to distinguish himself from the other characters by other means. Primary among these is the vice's monologue, in which he confesses to the audience or for its benefit his true identity and true purpose while he keeps them secret from his victims. In *Respublica*, Avarice tells the audience:

> Therefore, to worke my feate I will my name disguise,
> And call my Name 'polycie' in stede of Covetise.
> . . . .
> The Name of 'polycie' is of none suspected:
> Polycye is ner of any cryme Detected.
> So that vnder the Name and cloke of policie,
> Avaryce maie weorke factes & scape all Ialousie.[2]

In addition to exposing himself as a "contriver and manipulator," the vice's monologues reveal another very important trait: his arrogant braggadoccio. Indeed, the vice takes great pride in his ability to deceive and to seduce the innocent and the righteous, and

---

1. Bernard Spivack, *Shakespeare and the Allegory of Evil: The History of a Metaphor in Relation to His Major Villains* (New York, 1958), 155.
2. *Respublica*, ed. Leonard A. Magnus (1553; rpr. London, 1905), I, i, 79-80 and 83-86.

as he reveals his methods to the audience, he haughtily boasts of his skill. Witness Ill Report in *The Commedy of the Moste Vertuous and Godlye Susanna* (1569), bragging of his ability to ruin Susanna:

And when that they haue got their wils, and so haue wrought her shame
Myselfe will blow the leaden Trumpe of cruell slaunderous fame,
Lo thus my Dad I please I trow, and thus my nature showe,
Thus shall ech man my power and might in every corner blow,
And say that though the Devil himself, could not tempt Susans grace
The wit of Mayster *Ill Report* hath her and it deface,
Oh goodly wit, oh noble brayne, whence commeth this deuyce.[3]

Such pride is common to the vice in general, as any reader of medieval moralities knows. And once the vice becomes recognizable by his methods, manners, and goals, distinguishing physical features prove redundant or unnecessary. Satan and his black face become a hindrance to the dramatic action, blackface obsolete in the characterization of evil. Without it, the vice is able to move freely through the community showing the human face of sin through his deceit, dissimulation, and bold vaunts.[4]

The vice, however, is not a human character in a mimetic play. At work in an uncompromisingly allegorical world, he personifies a particular evil or particular human flaw, and his career stood in jeopardy with the triumph of secular mimetic drama at the end of the sixteenth century. Therefore, the vice had either to yield the stage or to adapt. By evolving from vice to villain, from personification to type character, the vice assured his survival. There was, of course, a long period in which to adapt, for the break from allegorical drama to mimetic drama was not decisively achieved at once, and that long period of contact between the developing secular drama and the declining allegorical play facilitated the evolution of vice to villain.[5] Yet as he acquired the necessary

---

3. Thomas Garter, *The Commedy of the Moste Vertuous and Godlye Susanna* (1569; rpr. Oxford, 1936), ll. 179-85.

4. Spivack catalogs a fuller list of conventional behavior in the vice. The three traits that I discuss seem to be the most significant. See also F. P. Wilson, *The English Drama, 1485-1585*, ed. G. K. Hunter (Oxford, 1969), 59-66.

5. F. P. Wilson writes on the waning moralities: "Medwall's *Fulgens and Lucrece* [1497], the interludes of Heywood, *Calisto and Melibea* [1527], and *Gentleness and Nobility* [1527], these may suggest that the tradition was decaying and was being supplanted by a secular drama, yet unless our records are even more fragmentary

human characteristics to make him more suitable for the mimetic stage, the vice did not alter his histrionic style or dramatic purpose; these passed unchanged into the villain:

> But whereas metaphor sustained his tragic intrigues on the allegorical stage, in the literal drama they are sustained by fusion with the character and behavior of some person of serious stature, whose evil career has come to the attention of the dramatist out of literature or life. Such a villain and his history wrap the perennial role in the surface texture of human passion and appetite, beneath which it goes its ancient bravura way in the homiletic dimension and out of the organic compulsion with which we are familiar.... The Vice's exposition of his name, experience and "property" survives, converted to villainy's exposition of its name, experience, and "property." And the Vice's unique intimacy with the audience survives, although progressively modified by an evolving sense of theatrical naturalism.[6]

The point of this discussion of vices and villains is not to convince the reader of their obvious relationship. I wish instead to emphasize the evolution of the villain into a more visibly human character, one who could participate in that "evolving sense of theatrical naturalism" of which Spivack writes. For only when we understand this can we begin to understand what occurred sometime around 1589, when Barabas in *The Jew of Malta* and Muly Mahamet in Peele's *The Battle of Alcazar* mounted the stage. At that time, evil characters could be recognized by their histrionics; distinctive physical characteristics or dress was unnecessary.[7] This is underscored by the very fact that the histrionics were transmitted to the mimetic stage unchanged, while the character himself had to adapt to that stage. The vice had no symbol of office to hand down to the villain, so the villain received instead the vice's characteristic dissembling and ranting. Neither blackface nor bot-

---

and deceptive than we suppose, we have to wait for a quarter of a century before we find such another group of non-academic secular plays. It is as if the Reformation killed the secular play for a time or alternately gave the morality drama a new lease of life. Even as late as the eighties and early nineties, when the tradition seems at its last gasp, banished from London for the most part and acted by amateurs ... in nooks and corners of the kingdom, morality elements appear without seeming archaic in *Doctor Faustus* and *Summer's Last Will and Testament*" (Wilson, *The English Drama*, 74).

6. Spivack, *Shakespeare and the Allegory of Evil*, 339.
7. See *Ibid.*, 161–62.

tle nose was required to know which characters were good and which were evil. The villain made himself known by his histrionic style.

By 1589, even black-faced devils had virtually disappeared from the stage; the mystery plays, performed irregularly from the start of Elizabeth's reign, were by that time long since dead in most places.[8] Why then does Muly Mahamet, the first Moor of any dramatic significance on the popular stage, seem to follow in the footsteps of his ancient theatrical ancestors?[9] To answer this we must examine the historical and dramatic circumstances that rendered this Moor the archetype for most black Moors for over a century.

The arrival of Muly Mahamet on the stage in 1589 was largely the result of several historical accidents. The popularity of Marlowe's *Tamburlaine* and other "heroical romances" certainly influenced Peele's choice of subject, as did the unflagging interest in the historical events surrounding the Battle of El Ksar et Kebir in 1578 and its principal participants. Perhaps the greatest catalyst to the animation of Muly Mahamet was the publication in 1587 of John Polemon's *The Second Part of the Book of Battailes, Fought in Our Age* in which could be found a section entitled: "The Battaile of Alcazar, fought in Barbarie, betwene Sebastian King of Portugall, and Abdelmelec the King of Marocco, the fourth of August 1578. Taken out of a namelesse Portugall auctor, Translated into Latine by Thomas Freigius."[10] From this source Peele retrieved all the

---

8. Harold C. Gardiner, S.J., *Mysteries' End: An Investigation of the Last Days of the Medieval Religious Stage* (New Haven, Conn., 1946), 92.

9. Muly Mahamet in *The Battle of Alcazar* was not the first Moor to appear on the popular stage. In *Tamburlaine*, Parts I and II, the Kings of Fez, Morocco, and Argier appear as tributaries to Tamburlaine. They, like the Moors in Greene's *Alphonsus, King of Aragon*, are of no dramatic significance. They seem to be there as exotic personages to give substance to the exotic names the conquering kings like to bandy about. It is uncertain whether the Moors in *Alphonsus* were black, but it seems likely that those in *Tamburlaine* were. See Jones, *Othello's Countrymen*, 37–40.

10. For discussions of Polemon's book as the source of Peele's play see Warner G. Rice, "A Principal Source of *The Battle of Alcazar*," *Modern Language Notes*, LVIII (1943), 428–31, and John Yoklavich, "Introduction to *The Battle of Alcazar*,"

elements, characters, battles, details, and motives necessary for dramatizing this historical event. Peele also learned from Polemon of Muly's blackness and his corresponding evil genius.

In his moralistic account of the battle, Polemon tells of an evil usurper "who was the author of so many evils and slaughters." Polemon further describes this villain as being

> of stature meane, of bodie weake, of colour so blacke, that he was accompted of many for a Negro or black *Moore*. He was of a peruerse nature, he would neuer speak the truth, he did all things subtelly and deceitfully. He was not delighted in armes, but as he shewed in all battailes, of a nature cowardly and effeminate. But he so cruelly hated Christians, that he would kil either with famine or nakednesse, those that he caught. If that in these warres he being constrained by necessitie, gave any signification of good will towards them, he did it against the heart, + in a maner unwillingly that he might make more readie and chierfull to endaunger themselues for him.[11]

Of Muly Mahamet's adversary, Abdelmelec, the rightful and righteous heir to the throne, Polemon writes: "He was of a meane stature, of a fine proportion of bodie, with brode shoulders, white face, but intermixed with red, which did gallantlie garnish his cheekes, a black berd thicke and curled, great eies and graie." Much to Abdelmelec's credit, he was "well affected towards men of the Christian Religion," a trait that clearly distinguishes him from the rest of his misbelieving kind who "doe desire no warres more, than those that are kept against the Christians."[12]

In addition to these starkly drawn combatants, Polemon includes the young, misguided Christian King, Sebastian of Portugal, who became embroiled in the battle between good and evil for a noble cause: he was "studious to enlarge his empire and Religion." And although Sebastian fought on the wrong side, "chieflie because he trusted the promises of Mahamet, which he beleeved to be verie true," the young king earns praise for his valor: "Yet the king of Portugal ceased not to indanger the enimie, now in this

---

in *The Dramatic Works of George Peele* (New Haven, Conn., 1961), 226-79. Vol. II of Charles Tyler Prouty, ed., *The Life and Works of George Peele* , 3 vols.

11. John Polemon, *The Second Part of the Book of Battailes, Fought in Our Age* (London, 1587), sigs. Yi r and Yiii r.

12. *Ibid.*, sigs. Yii v, Ti v-r, and Siii v.

quarter, now in that. . . . Yet king *Sebastian* forsaketh not his people: thinking it dishonorable to seek safetie by flight, and with those few that followed him, he behaved himselfe valiantly."[13]

Peele surely recognized the dramatic value of his source as clearly as we do. Delineated for him in the story of the battle was the classic confrontation between good and evil. There was his "Belial the blake" and Belial's adversary, Righteousness. Moreover, the old psychomachia was literalized for Peele in Polemon's historical account, in which actual historical facts confirmed the validity of the metaphor. Making the psychomachia all the more theatrical, history provided a misguided Juventus for the evil Muly Mahamet to seduce and to corrupt and for the virtuous Abdelmelec to admonish and to summon. That Renaissance historians saw themselves as moralists only saved Peele the trouble of making allegorical that which, ironically, offered itself readily as allegory. From *Wolston Dixi* we learn that Peele was not predisposed to allegorizing all Moors as partisans of the devil. Because it is uncertain whether that Moor was black (since he proclaims himself "from the parching Zone," I treat him as though he is), Peele's attitude toward blacks is not immediately discernible. Nevertheless, he rejuvenated for the popular stage in England a metaphor which, without exaggeration, profoundly and adversely affected the way blacks were to be represented on the stage for years to come. By validating the revived metaphor with historical facts, Peele gave it renewed vitality. In its newest form, the metaphor informed the actual historical facts, making the historical event allegorical and the allegory real.

This fusion, of course, is what Peele's source does, but on the stage, he fused two dramatic styles, the older allegorical with the newer mimetic. The older allegorical morality play of *The Battle of Alcazar*, inseparable from the mimetic historical drama, instructs the audience on how to view history and the actions and the nature of men in the play. This older form performs the same role as the actual historian who tells his reader how to read history. Encoding the older dramatic form into the new mimetic drama does in effect what the play within the play in *Hamlet* does, and what Richard III, the Jew of Malta, and every other stage villain

---

13. *Ibid.*, sigs. Tiii r, Uiii r, and Xiv v.

does when he assumes the histrionic style of his ancestors. The audience is asked to view the new play not as the older dramatic form but as a new form that calls to mind the older one.

The writers of *Richard III* and *The Jew of Malta* did not want vices in their plays; they wanted villains. They did, however, want the audience to remember the vice as a way of understanding the villain. Witness Richard's comment: "Thus, like the formal Vice, Iniquity, I moralize two meanings in one word." The irony of these lines makes clear the fact that Shakespeare's character is not Iniquity, yet Shakespeare—as does Richard himself—wishes us to remember Iniquity as we judge Richard's actions as a man on the mimetic stage. The same process occurs, Howard Felperin suggests, as we judge Falstaff. Comparing Falstaff to Cowardice who masquerades as Courage, Felperin concludes: "Falstaff is like this Vice; yet he is also, as Shakespeare makes equally clear, unlike this Vice in so far as he expresses a range of emotion well beyond that of an allegorical abstraction."[14] Remembering Iniquity or Cowardice, the audience is able to recognize the metaphor of the vice as well as to distinguish the actions of the man from the personification.

Similarly, the audience, mindful of the older dramatic form while watching the new, is able to distinguish between the two, and the clear difference between them adds to the vitality of the mimetic representation and makes the act of interpretation more an exercise of judgment. The audience can recognize the difference between the historical character and the allegorical. That the former behaves so much like the latter reestablishes the validity of the older allegory as a method of viewing and interpreting the actions of real men. Thus when the audience sees Muly Mahamet behave in a manner in concert with its traditional views of blackness, the metaphor of blackness receives reconfirmation and renewed credibility in the real world.

The allegorical framework that Peele employs to accomplish this consists primarily of a Presenter and dumb shows that together introduce each of the five acts. Like the Vexillator in *The Castle of Perseverance*, the Presenter acts not only as the narrator

---

14. Shakespeare, *Richard III*, III, i, 82; Howard Felperin, *Shakespearean Representation: Mimesis and Modernity in Elizabethan Tragedy* (Princeton, 1977), 66.

of the historical drama but as a moral interpreter and commentator. Appearances in the dumb shows by such personages as Nemesis, Fame, Death, Furies, and even ghosts who cry "Vindicta" reinforce the moral interpretation of the actions and the characters.

The Presenter's first appearance and the first dumb show are the most important of the play, for the allegorical framework is laid and the lines of the historical and allegorical battles are drawn. That all of this is achieved simultaneously speaks to Peele's effectiveness as a playwright and the Presenter's effectiveness as a dramatic device. The Presenter, from his very first words, judges and interprets the characters and the action of the play:

> Honor the spurre that pricks the princely minde,
> To followe rule and climbe the stately chaire,
> With great desire inflames the Portingall,
> An honorable and couragious king,
> To undertake a dangerous dreadfull warre
> And aid with Christian armes the barbarous Moore,
> The Negro Muly Hamet [15] that with-holds
> The kingdome from his unkle Abdelmelec,
> Whom proud Abdallas wrongd,
> And in his throne instals his cruell sonne,
> That now usurps upon this prince.[16]

Continuing his exposition, the Presenter calls forth the villain of the play with these foreboding lines:

> Blacke in his looke, and bloudie in his deeds,
> And in his shirt staind with a cloud of gore,
> Presents himselfe with naked sword in hand,
> Accompanied as now you may behold,
> With devils coted in the shapes of men. (I, i, 14–18)

As damning as his description is Muly's appearance, for he has a black face, the livery of the devil. Nor does the Presenter cease after he has invoked Muly's presence. As if the sight of him alone

---

15. For the sake of meter, Peele frequently shortens "Muly Mahamet" to Muly Hamet, although this does lead to some confusion because Abdelmelec's successor is named Muly Hamet.
16. George Peele, *The Battle of Alcazar*, in *The Dramatic Works of George Peele*, Vol. II of Prouty, ed., *The Life and Works of George Peele*, I, i, 1–11.

were not evidence enough of his hellish nature, the Presenter specifies that "the Negro Muly Hamet" arrives accompanied by "devils coted in the shapes of men." If I am correct in assuming those attendants are black, not since the fall of Lucifer was last enacted had the English stage seen such a host of black devils.[17] Aided by these attendants, the Moor—as Muly is frequently called—performs in the first dumb show acts of treachery to add further ocular proof to the assertions of the Presenter. There before the eyes of the audience, Muly commits fratricide and parricide. Commenting on the acts of "this unbeleeving Moore," the Presenter warns that "Nemisis high mistress of revenge" will "inflict / Vengeance on this accursed Moore for sinne" (I, i, 32, 35, 39-40). The Presenter, before abandoning the stage to the action of the first act, commands the audience:

> Sit you and see this true and tragicke warre,
> A modern matter full of bloud and ruth,
> Where three bolde kings confounded in their height,
> Fall to the earth contending for a crowne,
> And call this warre the battell of Alcazar. (I, i, 49-54)

These departing words at the start of Act I make clear the rela-

17. Among those "devils" identified as Muly's companions is his son. The "Plott of the *Battle of Alcazar*" identifies a total of four others, two "moores attendant and two pages to attend the moore" (*Two Elizabethan Stage Abridgements: The Battle of Alcazar and Orlando Furioso*, ed. W. W. Greg [Oxford, 1922], 26). Although the text makes no mention of the color of the attendants, it seems reasonable to assume that at least the son is black. Information in the plott leads me to believe that the others also are black. According to the plott, the attendants in the dumb show are "mr. Sam, mr Hunt & w. Cartwright." In Act II, Scene iii, the attendants are "W. Cartwright and Mr. Hunt." In this scene Muly, in reference to his attendants, tells Calypolis: "Into the shades then faire Calypolis, / And make thy sonne and Negros here good chere" (566-67). Since the attendants are clearly identified as "Negros" in this scene, it seems reasonable that Cartwright and Hunt, at least, would be in blackface throughout the play since neither plays any part other than attendant. Sam does appear in the dumb show of Act III, but as a devil; blackface, we know, is not incompatible with that role. Also, Greg writes: "There is, namely, some ground to suppose that the allusion in the text (Q 23) to 'devils coted in the shapes of men' may not be merely rhetorical, but that at least one of the murderers in the dumb show was actually provided with certain diabolical attributes, which indeed seems implied by the words 'as now you may behold' " (*Two Elizabethan Abridgements*, 50). Blackness seems like the obvious diabolical attribute. See also Tokson, *Popular Image of the Black Man*, 55.

tionship of this play to the older drama. Specifically, the Presenter's speech calls to mind plays in which the devil was black, Nemesis did wreck vengeance, and the mighty did fall. The allegorical formulation employed reveals Peele's conscious desire that this "modern matter" be seen in terms of a psychomachia. By specifically mentioning the truth of the story and its modernity, the Presenter perhaps hints at Peele's own awareness that the play was fusing the older allegorical form and the new mimetic. The play demands that the modern be approached and interpreted through the older tradition, and by so doing, *The Battle of Alcazar* acquires the validity of history and of moral tradition.

The plot of the play proceeds in a predictable manner, with the characters and their actions conforming to the designs of the Presenter. Abdelmelec declares his cause "just and honorable" and acts always accordingly. Like Righteousness of old, this good Moor sends counsel to the deceived Sebastian to dissuade him from his wrongful course. Unfortunately, wise counsel is lost on the "carelesse christian prince," who like his allegorical antecedents, scorns Abdelmelec's "curtesie." Only when it is too late, after his countryman the Duke of Avero has fallen and the battle is lost, does Sebastian recognize that he has been deceived; then he repents his part in the battle.

As for the villain, the "ambitious Negro moore," he plays his role well. His followers boast of his stratagem to lure "the good and harmlesse king of Portugall" (II, iii, 515) to Alcazar with a false promise. Muly's son, reveling in his father's ability to play the villain, boasts that the usurper will

> Make shew of friendship, promise, vow and sweare,
> Till by the vertue of his faire pretence,
> Sebastian trusting his integritie
> He [Muly] makes himselfe possessor of such fruits,
> As grow upon such great advantages. (II, iii, 526–30)

The Moor himself dissembles boldly as he greets Sebastian:

> O brave Sebastian noble Portugall,
> Renowned and honoured euer maist thou bee,
> Triumph over those that menace thee.
> The hellish prince grim Pluto with his mace
> Ding downe my soule to hel, and with this soule

> This sonne of mine, the honor of my house,
> But I performe religiously to thee
> That I have holyly earst undertane,
> And that thy Lords and Captains may perceive
> My minde in this single and pure to be,
> As pure as is the water of the brooke,
> My dearest sonne to thee I doo ingage,
> Receiue him Lord in hostage of my vow. (III, iv, 923-35)

Later Muly reveals his true disregard for Sebastian when he proclaims to the audience:

> Now have I set these Portugals aworke,
> To hew a waie for me unto the crowne,
> Or with your weapons here to dig your graves,
> You bastards of the night and Erybus,
> Fiends, Fairies, hags that fight in beds of steele,
> Range through this armie with your yron whips,
> Drive forward to this deed this christian crew,
> And let me triumph in the tragedie. (IV, ii, 1133-1140)

Though there are echoes of Tamburlaine's masculine line in Muly's speech, his are the words of a villain, not a conqueror. True to his cowardly nature, he meets death "Seeking to save his life by shamefull flight" (V, i, l. 1430). It is the Moor's villainy that ultimately matters in Peele's representation, not his oratorical skills or his dubious relationship to Tamburlaine.[18] Indeed, unlike Tamburlaine, Muly Mahamet *acts* the villain. And his discernible villainous histrionics actually make his blackness redundant. Blackness is, however, part of his literal garb; he comes to Peele black via Polemon. When Peele dramatized his historical source, he continued to make a historical fact an allegorical signifier of Muly's spiritual state. No less than seven times is Muly called "blacke" or a "Negro moore." As an adjective, *Negro* seems to be synonymous with "cruell," "unbeleeving" or "accursed." And the value of *Negro* as an adjective cannot be underestimated because it is used to distinguish the villain from the Moors who fight a "quarrel just and honorable," who, as in Peele's source, are just

---

18. See Jones, *Othello's Countrymen*, 44-46, for a discussion of Muly's language and his relationship to Tamburlaine.

and white, literally and figuratively. The villain of *The Battle of Alcazar*, however, is the "ambitious Negro moore."

That color becomes a factor in identifying the good and the evil is not difficult to imagine; nor is it difficult to imagine how easily color slips from being an accidental physical characteristic to an intrinsic component of the character's spiritual being. After all, black is the color of evil. The continuing tradition that cites the story of Ham as the source of physical blackness of Africans—remember that Purchas did it in 1613—certainly facilitates the application of this interpretation of blackness to real black men.[19] The allegorical structure that Peele found in his source also offers further validation for such an interpretation. Thus when Peele dramatized his story he only translated onto the mimetic stage a reading of blackness that wanted no corroboration. His allegory simply employs traditional signifiers of good and evil. The assumption that real black men are as truly evil as fallen black angels, if ever in doubt, receives new validation and renewed dramatic vitality. Nor does Peele's allegory bother to prove that black men are evil; instead it reveals the machinations and methods of evil and the dangers of trusting and countenancing black men. More abstractly, the allegory of blackness presented later on the mimetic stage dramatizes the blackening of honor and soul that result from the indulgence and pursuit of evil.

A second Elizabethan treatment of the Battle at El Ksar et Kebir can be found in *The Famous History of the Life and Death of Captain Thomas Stukeley*.[20] The central focus of this episodic

19. See Jordan, *White over Black*, 35-36.

20. There were several other dramatizations of the Battle of Alcazar, most of which probably were more concerned with Sebastian and the legend that he survived the battle than with the war of succession fought between Muly Mahamet and his uncle Abdelmelec. Massinger's play *Believe as You List* (1631) adapts the Sebastian myth to ancient Greece. The only black character in that play is the king's devoted servant Zanthia, and she has only three lines. Another play on this subject, *Sebastian, King of Portugal*, was acted by the Admiral's Men in 1601; however, the text of this play is lost. A play entitled *Mahomet* was first acted in 1594, although its text too is lost. Dryden's *Don Sebastian* (1689) is discussed in Chapter Six. See Alfred Harbage and S. Schoenbaum, *Annals of English Drama, 975-1700* (2nd ed; Philadelphia, 1964), 78-79, and Earl Miner, "Commentary to *Don Sebastian*," in *The Works of John Dryden*, ed. H. T. Swedenberg, Jr., *et al.* (Berkeley, Calif., 1976), XV, 385.

romance is the swaggering demi-hero Thomas Stucley, and the play dramatizes the battle of Alcazar primarily to record Stucley's last adventure and death.[21] The Alcazar episode, which occurs in the last 500 lines of the play's 2755 lines, has the same principals as Peele's play; they include Muly Mahamet, Abdelmelec, and Calypolis. Because of the similarities between *Alcazar* and *Stukeley*, it seems useful to discuss *Stukeley* and its two villains in terms of its similarities and dissimilarities to *Alcazar*. Any discussion of similarities, of course, raises a question of influence, and this question must be addressed first.

How the present text of *Stukeley* came to be is a matter of much speculation, as is the date of the play, although it was certainly acted before it was published in 1605.[22] It is commonly agreed, though, that *Alcazar* is older than *Stukeley*. I also believe that the unknown author of Stukeley knew *Alcazar*; this opinion I base on several facts. The first is the popularity of Peele's play. Although *Alcazar* was not published until four years after it is believed to have been first acted, its publication and stage revival in 1598 indicate some continuing interest in the play. *Alcazar* was also parodied by Jonson in the *Poetaster* in 1601; his reference to the play indicates that it came to his notice at least as late as its revival. A second factor that leads me to believe the author of *Stukeley* knew *Alcazar* is the use of the name Calypolis.[23] The name is not in Peele's source, and its first known use on the English stage occurs in *Alcazar*.[24] That its next use as the name for a character occurs in *Stukeley* suggests more than coincidence.[25] Finally, while it is true that "not a single passage of Peele's *Alcazar* has been

---

21. It is worth noting here that the full title of Peele's play, as it appears on the title page of the 1594 quarto reads: *The Battell of Alcazar, Fought in Barbarie betweene Sebastian King of Portugall and Abdelmelec King of Marocco. With the Death of Captaine Stukeley.*

22. See Yoklavich, "Introduction to *Alcazar*," 247-73.

23. Greg calls "Calypolis" a "seemingly improbable name" and knew no source for it. See *Two Elizabethan Abridgements*, 83-84.

24. Of the female characters in *Alcazar*, Yoklavich writes: "The three women do not figure in the historical accounts of Alcazar" ("Introduction to *Alcazar*," 241).

25. See Thomas L. Berger and William C. Brandford, Jr., *An Index of Characters in English Printed Drama to the Restoration* (Englewood, Colo., 1975).

interpolated into the text of the Stukley play," there are at least two clear echoes of Peele's lines in *Stukeley*.[26] At line 992 of *Alcazar*, in a speech derived from information in Polemon's account, a member of Abdelmelec's train, Celybin, describes at length the size of Sebastian's entourage:

> The enemie dread lord, hath left the towne
> Of Arzil, with a thousand souldiers armed
> To gard his fleet of thirteene hundred saile,
> And mustering of his men before the wals,
> He found he had two thousand armed horse,
> And fourteene thousand men that serve on foot,
> Three thousand pioners, and a thousand cochmen,
> Besides a number almost numberlesse
> Of drudges, Negroes, slaves and Muliters,
> Horse-boies, landresses and curtizans,
> And fifteen hundred waggons full of stuffe
> For noble men, brought up in delicate. (*Alcazar*, IV, i, 992-1003)

In a similar scene in *Stukeley*, Muly Hamet, Abdelmelec's heir, and Antonio, later a claimant to the Portuguese throne, boast of the size of the armies. Speaking first, Muly Hamet says:

> Look on the power that Abdelmelek brings
> Of brave resolved Turks and valiant Moors
> Approved Alarkes, pussiant Argolets
> As numberless as be these Afric sands
> And turn thee then and leave thy petty power
> The succour failing you expect from Spain
> And bow thy knees for mercy Portugall.[27]

Retorts Antonio:

> Our very slaves, our negroes, muleteers
> Able to give you battle in the field
> Then think of those that you must cope withal
> The Portigall and his approved power
> Muly Mahamet and his valiant Moors
> The Irish Marquess Stukley and his troops
> Our war like Germans and Italians

---

26. Yoklavich, "Introduction to *Alcazar*," 260.
27. *The Famous History of the Life and Death of Captain Thomas Stukeley*, in *The School of Shakespeare*, ed. Richard Simpson (London, 1878), I, ll. 2469-75.

> Alvares, Caesar, Menesis and Avero[.]
> Proud Abdelmelek kneel and beg grace. (ll. 2476-84)

All the proper names used above by Antonio are found when Celybin in *Alcazar* continues his speech from line 1014 in Act IV. This is yet another coincidence that suggests knowledge of *Alcazar*. While the echoes do not make an unimpeachable case, it does seem likely that Peele's play was known by the author of *Stukeley*. Yoklavich is unwilling to dismiss the possibility, writing: "A good many scenes in both plays represent the same characters and the same events."[28]

Further support for this position can be found in the clear resemblance in the structure of the Alcazar episode in *Stukeley* to Peele's play. It has been suggested that this episode was added to an earlier version of *Stukeley* —maybe a version older than Peele's play—in order to ride the crest of interest in the battle.[29] This suggestion is supported by the difference between the earlier sections of the play and the Alcazar episode, which employs a chorus and a dumb show, devices not found in the earlier episodes. Although choruses and dumb shows occur frequently in Elizabethan drama, in the case of this play they seem less structurally appropriate than usual. Whether the chorus was added in imitation of Peele's play is uncertain, but its appearance at this juncture of the play suggests that it might have been.

The chorus first appears to move the scene from Portugal to Africa, and though there are three earlier scene changes, it is only this one time that a chorus is used to facilitate the change. Like the Presenter in *Alcazar*, the chorus performs an essentially narrative function, and in addition to setting the scene, it informs the audience of Muly Mahamet's duplicity in dealing with Sebastian and of the divine judgment against Stucley, Sebastian, the Moor, and his cause:

> But heaven, displeas'd with their rash enterprise,
> Sent such a fatal comet in the air
> Which they misconstruing shone successfully
> Do haste the faster, furrowing through the deep.

28. Yoklavich, "Introduction to *Alcazar*," 260.
29. See *Ibid.*, 258-60, and Richard Simpson, "*Biography of Sir Thomas Stucley*," in *The School of Shakespeare* (London, 1878), I, 140-44.

> And now suppose—but woe the wretched hour,
> And woe that damned Mahamet [by] whose guile
> This tender and unskilled but valiant king
> Was thus allured unto a timeless death. (ll. 2292-99)

Lacking the elaboration of Peele's Presenter, the chorus, as one would expect, establishes nonetheless the same moral outlines and invites the same judgments. Sebastian is "valiant" but "beguiled," the Moor "damned."

Even from the simplest outline, we can recognize the characters earlier met in Peele's play. Sebastian agrees to fight

> . . . but for honour's sake,
> For Portugals chief good, and to advance
> The Christian true religion through those parts. (ll. 1456-59)

Abdelmelek, too, acts like his analog in *Alcazar*. He tries but fails to persuade Sebastian to "leave that traitor that but trains thee on / Unto the jaws of thy destruction" (ll. 2420-21). And of course, the "damned Mahamet" is analogous to the "accursed Moor" in *Alcazar*. However, Muly is not the only villain in the play, a fact that necessarily affects his characterization. The other villain, Philip of Spain, first requires our attention.

Easily recognizable as a villain in this play, Philip deceives, dissembles, and boasts; in short, he acts the villain. In a scene that harkens back to the morality plays, Philip and two advisors, like vices of old, devise their policy toward Sebastian. Philip, intent on having Sebastian's crown by whatever means, agrees to deceive the Portuguese ambassador and consequently the Portuguese king with false pledges of military aid to Sebastian's African expedition. When the ambassador comes before Philip, the Spanish king proceeds as the dissembling villain that he is:

> My Lord Botellio we have weigh'd th'effect
> Of your imbassage; and in nature bound
> Beside the affection of near neighborhood
> To do our kinsman and your noble king
> All offices of kindness that we can. (ll. 1549-53)

After Botellio leaves, Philip wonders if the plot he has undertaken is not "too severe, ambitious / And more deceitful than becomes a king" (ll. 1569-1570). His words, however, ring more like a villain's vaunting since Philip never swerves from his resolve, and the Machiavellian response he receives from his advisers only serves to identify further Philip and his cronies as evil men.

Muly Mahamet, unlike Philip, does not act the villain. His villainy becomes known not by his actions but through the remarks of others. The chorus, as we have seen, plays a very important role in establishing this aspect of Muly's character. Philip too helps in characterizing Muly. In a reference to the civil war, Philip says: "The right is in Molucco [Abdelmelek]" (l. 1444). He continues:

> Besides, Mahamet is an infidel
> From whose associate fellowship in this
> And all things else we Christians must refrain. (ll. 1446-48)

Although there is irony in assigning these lines to Philip, the words themselves are not ironic. They describe accurately the way Muly is to be viewed.

As for Muly, he speaks in the same high-sounding rhetoric made famous by Tamburlaine and borrowed by so many other warriors, including Peele's Moor. However, the emptiness of Muly's rhetoric is only made clear when he proves himself a coward by attempting "to save himself by flight" (l. 2601) in the end. Muly displays neither villainous prowess nor self-conscious awareness of the discrepancy between what he truly is and what he says he is; he is deceitful because he is not what he says he is. There is, however, one brief moment when the Moor does speak like the villain that we know him to be. Seeing Sebastian rally his troops to the field, Muly boasts to the audience:

> Bravely resolved, my self will follow you.
> And so it happen that Mahamet speed
> I wreck not who, Turk or Christian, bleed. (ll. 2564-66)

We expect Muly to say this, not because we have witnessed him acting like a villain, but because we are told that he is one.

The distinction between the dramatic treatment of Philip's character and Muly's has greater significance in the absence of any mention of Muly's race in the text, an absence that must strike every reader since race is so important in Peele's play and Polemon's account. Two questions arise when we consider what seems to be an important omission. Why is there no mention of race? And, is Muly meant to be black? I think the answer to the latter question is yes. It seems hard to imagine that this essential biographical and dramatic feature could be so thoroughly overlooked, particularly if we assume some contemporary popularity for Peele's play. Surely the audience of *Stukeley* expected Muly to be black.[30] However, only the slightest bit of textual evidence can be found to support my opinion here. When the chorus calls Muly "that damned Mahamet" (l. 2297), it could be implying his blackness. As we know, a long tradition exists of representing the damned on stage and in paintings as black.[31]

If Muly is black, why then is there no mention of it? The text surely need not mention something that would be obvious to the audience. The sex of characters is not always mentioned, so why should the race, particularly when it is obvious and well-known? Also, if we agree that Muly was portrayed as black, we can better understand why he does not act more like a villain. With villainy stamped on Muly's face, the author of the play could proceed with economy to the conclusion. Since Muly's blackness is dramatically redundant in Peele's play, villainous histrionics are superfluous in *Stukeley* if Muly is black. This can be more clearly seen in light of the characterization of Philip. Because there is no outward sign of Philip's villainy, the playwright must employ dramatic conventions to convey the fact. Philip must act the villain; a black Muly need not do so because he looks the villain. Blackness as a signifier of sin is commonplace, and Peele and Shakespeare in *Titus Andronicus* had successfully transferred the allegory of blackness to the mimetic stage by the time these scenes in *Stukeley* were on the boards. *Stukeley's* author perhaps employed the allegorical possibilities of blackness silently.

A further observation on Peele's play can be made here. If we acknowledge the probability of Muly Mahamet being black in *Stukeley*, we can see the degree to which Peele employs the allegory of blackness for thematic purposes. Muly in *Alcazar* could be

30. Tokson includes this Muly Mahamet in his list of black characters (*Popular Image of the Black Man*, 139); in *Othello's Countrymen*, however, Jones makes no mention of this Muly's blackness, but then neither does he indicate that he believes Muly to be other than black.

31. See Chambers, *The Mediaeval Stage*, II, 142.

as quietly black; were he so, however, the play would be fundamentally different. The allegorical center of the play would be unspoken and therefore diminished. The recognition of Muly's blackness as a symbolic representation of his evil spirit would, of course, still exist, but the explicit endorsement of this allegorical system as one that is valid for representing, interpreting, and judging the characters and actions of "real" men would not.

Whether Muly in *Stukeley* is a black Moor like his analog in Peele's play will never be known with certainty. He is, however, indisputably different from the character in the earlier play. Appearing in a play with another villain diminishes his status as the singular source of evil. In *Stukeley*, Muly is one villain amongst other villains. Evil, we learn, may lurk in the hearts of Christian men, and goodness may even be found in the hearts of non-Christian white Moors. But whether the unique representation of evil in a play or one of several, black men remain the unredeemed heirs of the Prince of Darkness.

If the author of *Stukeley* does not exploit fully the allegorical possibilities of blackness, Shakespeare takes full advantage of them in *Titus Andronicus*. He draws Aaron, the Moor, directly from the same villainous type as Muly Mahamet. Black in color and evil in nature, Aaron enjoyed a long stage career and served as the model for at least two obviously related characters, Eleazar in Thomas Dekker's play *Lust's Dominion* (1600), and Mulymumen in William Rowley's play *All's Lost by Lust* (1619).[32] Together these three plays kept alive on the stage the villainous Moor and the allegory of blackness well into the eighteenth century. All three plays enjoyed revivals as well as adaptations, two of which, Aphra Behn's *Abdelazer; or, The Moor's Revenge* (1677), and Ravencroft's *Titus Andronicus, or the Rape of Lavinia* (1686), will be discussed later.

Aaron, Eleazar, and Mulymumen have more in common than their blackness and the evil it signifies; they also exhibit lecherousness, a vice commonly associated with blacks. Attributed to

---

32. Although the 1657 quarto of *Lust's Dominion* attributes the play to Marlowe, scholars generally agree that this is the same play recorded in Henslowe's diary as *The Spanish Moor's Tragedy*. See Cyrus Hoy, *Introductions, Notes and Commentaries to Texts in "The Dramatic Works of Thomas Dekker,"* Edited by Fredson Bowers (Cambridge, England, 1980), IV, 56-72.

Africans from a variety of sources, concupiscence has even been suggested as being Ham's sin. This supposed venery is common not only to the male characters to be discussed in this section but also to the female characters to be discussed in the next. Its pervasiveness in the plays indicates the significance with which playwrights endowed this reputed characteristic and therefore demands special consideration.

Of course, one could discuss this emphasis on black sexuality as the simple and unsophisticated rehearsal of facts garnered from various sources consulted by the playwrights and from popular opinion formed by those sources. However, that would be to deny the frankness with which Elizabethans wrote about sex in plays, poetry, and romances. It would also ignore a long religious tradition that focused constant attention on the sins of the flesh.[33] Even when carried on under a cloak of secrecy, sexual relationships were always of public interest because personal sexual relationships were thought to affect members of a community beyond the couple personally involved. As Spenser contends in *The Faerie Queene*, private lust leads to public lawlessness:

> The beautie, which was made to represent
> The great Creatours owne resemblance bright,
> Vnto abuse of lawlesse lust was lent,
> And made the baite of bestiall delight:
> Then faire grew foule, and foule grew faire insight,
> And that which want to vanquish God and man,
> Was made the vassall of the victors might;
> Then did her glorious flowre wax dead and wan
> Despised and troden downe of all that overran.[34]

It is the responsibility of the collective community to condemn such lust for the community's safety. In these plays, the black character's sexual relationships help to define his relationship to the community as a whole. Where the sexual relationship of a black character with a white character is sanctioned, the character is a lawfully accepted member of that society. Where the rela-

---

33. See Jordan, *White over Black*, 40–43, and Stephen Jay Greenblatt, *Renaissance Self-Fashioning: From More to Shakespeare* (Chicago, 1980), 246–51.

34. Edmund Spenser, *The Faerie Queene*, in *The Works of Edmund Spenser*, ed. Edwin Greenlaw *et al.* (Baltimore, 1935), IV, vii, 32.

tionship is unsanctioned, it serves but to reinforce the villain's unholy grip on the community.

Clearly Aaron's position of power in *Titus Andronicus* results from his sexual relationship with the Queen of the Goths, Tamora, the importance of which the reader is constantly reminded. From this base of power, Aaron expands his power over all the other characters and lets loose an avalanche of villainy on Rome and its inhabitants. Yet Aaron's position of power simultaneously acknowledges a position of dependency; his power is thematically and structurally contingent on Tamora's. The Queen of the Goths obtains political power as a result of her sexual power over Saturninus, the wicked emperor. But neither would possess power were it not for a miscalculation of the virtuous.

Aaron's age of villainy is unwittingly ushered in by the virtuous Titus Andronicus, who rejects his responsibility "to set a head on headless Rome" (I, i, 186), then ignores Saturninus' breach of the public peace, and finally proclaims the rebel as emperor. By so doing, Titus permits to begin a Saturnine age, an age of policy and stratagem. Once Saturninus' reign commences, so do Titus' woes, most resulting from the very dissembling and deceits of the new emperor and his newly elected empress. The concurrent rise of Aaron indexes the rise of chaos and the decline of virtue, justice, and order. When Titus laments in Act IV, scene iii, "Terras Astraea reliquit" ("Astraea has left the earth"), he recognizes indeed that the dark planet has replaced the light of justice, and Aaron is the black operative of that black planet.

Aaron himself recognizes Saturn as the presiding genius of his world and tells Tamora so: "Madam, though Venus govern your desires / Saturn is dominator over mine" (II, iii, 30-31). This proclamation links Aaron to Rome's malevolent emperor, Saturninus, and Aaron explicitly owns a superior unifying agent for the general malice of the play. Aaron's acknowledgment of hierarchy in no way lessens the quality or quantity of his evil; rather, his admission assures him of an even greater triumph. When his stratagem allows him to father an heir by the emperor's wife, he supplants the emperor and revokes his rights as husband, father, and emperor. Aaron's victories over Saturninus and Tamora are complete as the Moor betrays, beguiles, and overmasters his very masters. As he moves through the play, Aaron becomes the very symbol of the evil that is loosed upon Rome.

The Andronicus family quickly recognizes Aaron as the symbol of iniquity and his blackness as the outward manifestation of the evil within. When Bassianus rebukes Tamora for associating with Aaron, he equates Aaron's color with wickedness and warns Tamora lest she too be spotted:

> Believe me, queen, your swart Cimmerian
> Doth make your honor of his body's hue,
> Spotted, detested and abominable. (II, iii, 72–74)

Aaron's "abominable" color links him to the stage devils of old, an association not lost on Titus and his sons or on the audience. Four times in Act V, Aaron is called a "devil." Other allusions to Satan abound, including one in Act V in which Aaron is said to have a "fiend-like face" (V, ii, 66). Nor are Titus and his sons the only ones to so characterize Aaron and his kind; when the nurse brings in Aaron's heir, she calls it "A devil" and "A joyless, dismal, black, and sorrowful issue!" (IV, ii, 63, 66). The infant enters the world seemingly in possession of the powers and the mark of his father.

This baby provides an interesting crux in the play and offers us an opportunity to observe Aaron's attitude toward blackness and to compare his attitudes to others'. On the most literal level, what the nurse says of the baby is true because the baby witnesses the sin of its mother. Yet when the nurse speaks of the baby as the devil, she identifies the infant not only as the symbol of the empress' sin but also as the heir of his father's evil and the heir of both their theatrical forefathers. But neither the nurse nor Tamora's elder sons find sin itself loathsome; they detest the infant because he threatens them with discovery. And, moreover, it is really the baby's blackness that makes detection of Tamora's adultery certain. For this reason, Tamora's confederates hate not sin but rather only its signifier, blackness.

Aaron's response to his son reveals how important blackness has really become. He sees only his son, and his famous words in answer to demands that he kill the baby show that he understands the problem exactly. "Zounds," Aaron says, "ye whore! is black so base a hue? / Sweet blouse, you are a beauteous blossom, sure"

94

(IV, ii, 71–72). The Moor's immediate defense of his son addresses the loathing of his color, and Aaron rejects the demand that he slaughter his newborn heir because he is black. True, the baby's blackness betrays the guilt of Aaron and Tamora; Aaron himself acknowledges this in Act V. But the baby's *blackness* is what is seen as evil by Aaron's confederates in crime. And it is this attack on blackness that Aaron faces and rejects. When he continues his defense of his son, he does so with a defense of blackness.

That Aaron need defend blackness points to a real irony of this scene. Now that they fear betrayal by blackness, Chiron and Demetrius abjure it, though they still have not abjured sin. But their abjuration comes too late. By previously embracing blackness and sin, by indulging the black Moor and all that he signifies, Tamora's sons and the empress herself all become tainted by sin, revealed by blackness. Bassianus' earlier warning to the Queen of the Goths comes true; her honor and the honor of her wicked sons are spotted by their association with her "swart Cimmerian." Aaron hits home when he chides the elder sons: "Stay, murderous villains! will you kill your brother?" (IV, ii, 88). Their kinship to the black infant, to the black Moor, and to the black deeds done cannot be denied. And it is the baby's blackness that brings all of this to fruition, that makes these realities inescapable. Tamora, Saturninus, Aaron, Chiron, and Demetrius all parent a single heir, a black devil. And all are betrayed by the fruit of their sin: Aaron by the very cry of the baby and then its very blackness, all the others by Aaron. And although Titus achieves his revenge on Saturninus and his partisans without Aaron's aid, Titus' heir relies on Aaron to betray his associates so that the deeds of Titus may be justified to Rome. Ultimately it is the betrayal of sin by its own blackness that restores Astraea to earth.

But the signification of blackness is rendered more complex by Aaron's sense of self-determination. Before he defends blackness, Aaron denies the power of blackness to determine his nature; he insists that he chooses to be evil. Proud of his villainy, Aaron, after he has chopped off Titus' hand, gloats: "Let fools do good, and fair men call for grace, / Aaron will have his soul black like his face" (III, i, 204–205). By emphasizing his volition in the election of evil over good, Aaron rejects determination; for him, blackness *can* be a signifier of evil only when black men choose to be evil. Even after his capture he insists that he chose evil:

> Tut, I have done a thousand dreadful things
> As willingly as one would kill a fly,
> And nothing grieves me heartily indeed,
> But that I cannot do ten thousand more. (V, i, 141-44)

Aaron's emphasis on will here informs his defense of blackness in Act IV and makes more problematic the play's treatment of it. Operating in the end are two conflicting systems of blackness. One makes it an indisputable symbol of sin; the other holds that the signifier can signify falsely. Titus and his sons and their partisans undeniably see blackness as a symbol of evil; the symbolic role assigned Aaron's son bears out the determination of the Andronicus faction. But Aaron's rejection of the infallibility of the signifier sets things at odds. Aaron does not deny his role as an agent of evil; he does, however, insist unrelentingly that his was a free choice. If we allow Aaron this freedom of will, there is then no inconsistency with his behavior toward his son. It is only when we see Aaron as a unidimensional type locked steadfastly in the role of villainous Moor—a role determined by his blackness, without freedom for the slightest dramatic variation—that any touch of humanity seems uncharacteristic. A momentary comparison with Muly Mahamet makes this clear. In the end, Muly cares for no one but himself; like the earlier vice, he lacks, finally, humanity. Perhaps another relevant comparison can be made between Marlowe's Barabas and Aaron. Barabas, in the end, acts only characteristically, denying even his paternal bonds to Abigail. But by demonstrating some humanity, Aaron undermines the univocal symbolism of blackness, and the play says something about the nature of evil—in what others think of the baby and black men and white—and about blackness. This surely should surprise no reader of *Othello*.

How clearly this was perceived by an audience in the seventeenth century or even one in the twentieth, however, is a different problem. Placed in a historical context, Aaron is unquestionably the heir of Muly Mahamet. Nor is his relationship to the devil in any doubt; claiming not to believe in the devil only strengthens in the audience's mind his close kinship to the Prince of Darkness.

Aaron's talk of policy, stratagems, and villainy, his dissembling and deceptions, make him easily recognizable as a villain, and the last and lasting image of him in the play implants irrevocably in the mind of the audience an idea of Aaron's true villainous nature. Hurling his last curse, he asks no forgiveness but shouts instead:

> Ah, why should wrath be mute, and fury dumb?
> I am no baby, I, that with base prayers
> I should repent the evils I have done:
> Ten thousand worse than ever yet I did
> Would I perform, if I might have my will:
> If one good deed in all my life I did,
> I do repent it from my very soul. (V, iii, 184-90)

Reiterating as he does here that Aaron wills to be Aaron probably does little to undermine the vision of the black Aaron fulfilling his traditional role. In this case, the visual image probably overpowered the repeated stress on volition found in the text.

The very mention of volition and the acknowledgment of some self-consciousness, however, separates Aaron from his predecessor. As obviously as he is modeled after Muly, he as obviously diverges. Aaron's ability to recognize the role that his blackness plays in the minds of others and to deny its power over himself helps loosen somewhat the constrictions of type characterization. Though it does not effect a redemption, Aaron's uncompromising paternal devotion does soften the otherwise harsh and vile portrait of him. This chink in the allegory of blackness, however slight, separates Aaron from Muly Mahamet. Muly's awareness of himself in an allegory of evil is uncritical and uncomplicated. He acknowledges in no way his blackness, nor does he attempt to make it meaningless. Villains they both are; Aaron, however, seeks to identify himself as a character outside a preordained allegory. Aaron and *Titus* make us feel slightly uncomfortable about stigmatizing this black man.

No such discomfort exists in Ravenscroft's adaptation. If anything, we should feel only comfort at seeing "that dismall Fiend of darkness" racked and immolated at the end of the play, for in this adaptation Aron has not a jot of humanity.[35] Though there are

35. Edward Ravenscroft, *Titus Andronicus, or the Rape of Lavinia* (1687; facsim. London, 1969), V, i, p. 51. I distinguish between the characters in the two plays by

no great alterations of the plot, Aron is made more evil, more vicious, and if possible, more unrepentant. He is the source of *all* evil, and Ravenscroft establishes him as such immediately. Where in Shakespeare's play Demetrius encourages his mother to seek revenge for Alarbus' death (I, i, 132-41), in the adaptation, Aron appears to plant the seeds of revenge in Tamora's mind:

> To tremble said you? did you say to tremble?
> No Madam stand resolv'd but hope withall,
> That the same Gods that Arm'd the Queen of *Troy*
> May favor *Tamora* the Queen of *Goths*
> With like Successfull minutes, to requite
> These Bloody wrongs and *Roman* Injuries. (I, ii, p. 5)

In the next scene in which Aron appears, he instructs Saturninus to dissemble forgiveness to Titus, a role played by Tamora in the Shakespearean original:

> Hearken to this Counsel with attention,
> Dissemble all your griefs and discontents,
> You are but newly stept into your Throne,
> Lest then the People and Patricians too
> Upon a Just survey take *Titus* part,
> (You know he has a plausible pretence,
> He kill'd his Son, by him the Traytor fell)
> And so supplant you for ingratitude,
> Which Rome reputes to be a heinous Crime. (II, i, p. 13)

With but minor alterations, these were Tamora's words in the Elizabethan original (I, i, 442-48), and their reassignment in the Restoration revision clearly lessens her villainy and highlights Aron's.

Tamora, to be sure, is no innocent. She continues in this scene by encouraging Saturninus to implement Aron's plan:

> Yield at Intreaties, and let us alone,
> I'le watch a day that's fitted for Revenge,
> And race their Faction and their Family. (II, i, p. 14)

But these lines are part of a much longer speech by Tamora in the original that Ravenscroft reassigns to Aron. This speech indicts

---

using this spelling of Aron, which is found in the 1687 quarto of Ravenscroft's adaptation.

Tamora, but it is Aron who acts as the prime mover of these villainies. In fact, Tamora is clearly Aron's operative, saying so herself in Act III: "Now will I hence and seek my Lovely Moor, / to know what further mischiefs are in store" (III, i, p. 23). And like her analog's guilt, Tamora's extends beyond villainy to debauchery, and here again her illicit sexual liaison with Aron ushers him into the precincts of power. She actually recommends Aron to Saturninus, an act that gives Aron access to power and a guise of legitimacy to Tamora's dealings with him. Of course, that sexual alliance leads to her undoing when its fruit, their "black brat / This Babe of darkness" (V, i, p. 53) is discovered.

In Ravenscroft's adaptation, the disgust over the adultery, the miscegenation, and the actual blackness of Aron and the child exceeds greatly anything found in Shakespeare's *Titus Andronicus*. From its first mention, blackness is regarded unequivocally as a foul fault. Aron, himself disgusted by his blackness, says in his "Now climbeth Tamora" speech (II, i, 1-25 in Shakespeare): "Hence abject thoughts that I am black and foul, / And all the Taunts of Whites that call me Fiend" (II, i, p. 15). This is no insignificant alteration of Aaron's statement, "Away with slavish weeds and servile thoughts!" Shakespeare's Aaron only alludes to his color when he explicitly rejects his station; Ravenscroft's Aron, on the other hand, endorses the truth of others' judgments on his blackness and then attempts to displace one truth with another by saying: "I still am Lovely in an Empress Eyes" (II, i, p. 15). Aron's negative attitude toward his own blackness defines his behavior toward others and theirs toward him and those associated with him.

The play's overriding hostility toward blackness finds expression in Bassianus' horror at seeing Tamora with Aron; his disgust for the object of her affection is greater than is his revulsion against adultery:

> Hell—Kiss a Moor.
> Believe me Madam, your Swarthy Cymerion
> Has made your Honour of his bodies hue,
> Black, Loathsome, and Detested. (III, i, p. 20)

Nowhere is this attitude more clear than in the treatment of the child. Conceived and born before Tamora's marriage, the "black

Imp" is brought by a faithful Goth to Chiron and Demetrius for them to murder,

> . . . lest it shou'd
> Grow up to ruine you and the Empress,
> And all the *Goths* expose to *Roman* fury. (V, i, p. 39)

Never is the baby discussed without reference to its color. Even Aron's defense of it and blackness rings hollow by reason of his earlier comments on his own blackness and by the very conspicuous absence of his line, "is black so base a hue?" (IV, ii, p. 71). In the final scene, when Aron's and Tamora's villainies are exposed, the baby is but another example of their evil and is awarded epithets such as the "black brat," the "Babe of darkness," and the "Hellish infant." Yet with the emphasis so unwaveringly placed on the child's color, one senses that not just for Chiron and Demetrius but for the play itself that blackness is as horrible as the sin of the parents. As Demetrius puts it: "Would you to th'Empress shame preserve a thing / So foul and black?" (V, i, p. 39). Nor does anyone except Aron express any horror or sympathy when the baby's mother stabs it because it is the "off-spring of the Blabtongu'd Moor" (V, i, p. 55).

The play's unrelenting emphasis on Aron's blackness corresponds to the augmentation of Aron's wickedness; blackness and evil are essentially related. Aron, it must not be forgotten, holds his blackness as a token of his evil nature, and Ravenscroft purposely removes any possible ambiguities about blackness that appear in the Shakespearean text. Even Aaron's rejection of determinism is missing from the adaptation. Where Aaron "will have his soul black as his face" (III, i, 206), Aron takes leave gloating that "once the mind is to distruction bent, / How easy 'tis new Mischiefs to invent" (IV, i, p. 32). Expressed in the passive voice, Aron's boast here is at best a weak acknowledgment of some volition, and not at all like Aaron's emphatic claim. Moreover, Aron's line does *not* deny determinism.

In the end, Aron stands as the single worst creature in the play, surpassing Saturninus, Tamora, Chiron, and Demetrius for sheer cruelty, viciousness, perfidy, and wickedness. Saturninus moves toward repentance, if not redemption. Even Tamora compares favorably to Aron; she at least loved Chiron and Demetrius and calls

Titus an "Inhumane Villain!" when she learns that he tricked her into eating her two sons. Aron's paternal affection, on the other hand, is inconsequential. Though he earlier wishes to protect his son, Aron, afraid that Tamora has surpassed him in villainy by murdering their child, would prove himself more vile by eating the child's corpse:

> She has out-done me in my own Art—
> Out-done me in Murder—Kill'd her own Child.
> Give it me— I'le eat it. (V, i, p. 55).

Ignoring the obvious differences between Shakespeare's text and Ravenscroft's, a reader cannot ignore the emphatic association between evil and blackness in this play. Aron is the central focus of the play and the author of its evil. The questions we ask ourselves about Aaron, blackness, and the nature of evil while reading Shakespeare's play do not arise while reading Ravenscroft's, and this less complex play results from Ravenscroft's alterations, including important changes in Aron, Tamora, and Saturninus. Nor is it possible to minimize the relentless focus on blackness in the play. That evil is inseparable from blackness is seen by the relationship of the other villains to Aron's blackness. The more loathsome they find his blackness, the less villainous they are. Aron is ever the criterion.

Accounting for some of Ravenscroft's alterations is easy, particularly those that are avowedly political. In his preface to the reader, Ravenscroft writes:

> Compare the Old Play with this, you'l finde that none in all that Authors Works ever receiv'd greater Alterations or Additions, the Language not only refin'd, but many Scenes entirely New: Besides most of the principal Characters heighten'd, and the Plot much encreas'd. The Success answer'd the Labour, tho'it first appear'd upon the Stage, at the beginning of the pretended Popish Plot, when neither Wit nor Honesty had Encouragement: Nor cou'd this expect favour since it shew'd the Treachery of Villains, and the Mischiefs carry'd on by Perjury, and False Evidence; and how Rogues may frame a Plot that shall deceive and destroy both the Honest and the Wise; which were the reasons why I did forward it at so unlucky a conjuncture, being content rather to lose the Profit, then not expose to the World the Picture of such Knaves and Rascals as then Reign'd

in the opinion of the Foolish and Malicious part of the Nation (sig. A2 r-v).

Aron serves then as a model of evil and its power to subvert all who indulge it, however slightly. Titus (who loses his hand), Tamora, and the repentant Saturninus all learn the value of ever-constant vigilance; to be less is to lose. But the truly villainous cannot waver, nor can they express the remotest human feeling. This is perhaps one reason why Aron offers to do the unthinkable, to devour the corpse of his son, thereby losing what respect he may have had for showing some paternal affection. In the end, Aron can love only his villainy, perhaps as the tyrant loves only his tyranny. To make this point unmistakably clear the actions of the play and the cruelty of the villain are sketched more boldly than may seem necessary; such exaggeration, however, is common in plays with political themes. "Effective propaganda must be emphatic," John Loftis writes, "and Augustan drama written in the service of party or faction is emphatic indeed. The political motive led to intensification, whether of tragic seriousness or of comic satire; it led to the avoidance of ambiguity and even of subtlety."[36]

Other reasons, however, exist for the redoubling of Aron's villainy and the increased violence of the play. Technical advances in stage properties as well as architectural changes in the theaters themselves made possible the staging of spectacles. Whether it was because of these technical advances or the love of spectacle or some other reason, popular taste in the 1670s and 1680s favored plays that depicted brutal tortures and grotesque murders.[37] This accounts, in part, for Aron's being racked and immolated. Other changes that fed audience "predilection for gore and horror" also originated from Ravenscroft's desire to meet the demands of popular taste.[38]

Accounting for Ravenscroft's accentuation of blackness is not so easy; the renewed emphasis may have resulted from increased familiarity of the English with Africans in the 1670s, a familiarity brought about in several ways. By 1678, the earliest possible date

36. John Loftis, *The Politics of Drama in Augustan England* (Oxford, 1963), 161.
37. See Robert D. Hume, *The Development of English Drama in the Late Seventeenth Century* (Oxford, 1976), 290, and Montague Summers, *The Restoration Theatre*, (London, 1934), 201-12.
38. Hume, *English Drama in the Late Seventeenth Century*, 199.

for Ravenscroft's adaptation, Africans were common sights in the Lord Mayors' Pageants. Books by visitors to Africa and to plantations in the East and West Indies, as well as pictorial representations of Africans, were commonplace. These representations tend to make the African less threatening and more domestic, as they stress the two roles most common to him, slave or exotic extra. If Ravenscroft's play was not acted until 1686, when it was licensed, other images of blacks surely demanded the attention of the audience. Morgan Godwyn's and Thomas Tyron's pleas for the conversion of Africans had been published in 1680 and 1684 respectively, although calls for more humane treatment of African slaves began before then. Ravenscroft wished to use Aron's blackness thematically and to keep before the audience not the image of the impotent slave, mastered and humbled, but the morally repugnant overmastering villain whose blackness and physical repugnance signified his spiritual state. By emphasizing Aron's blackness, Ravenscroft emphasizes the significance of Aron's blackness and reminds the audience that the allegorical interpretation is still valid.

Before Ravenscroft adapted Aaron for the Restoration stage, his most direct descendant, Eleazar, had appeared in Thomas Dekker's play, *Lust's Dominion; or, The Lascivious Queen* in 1600. In a dramatic situation similar to Aaron's, Eleazar, beloved of the lascivious Queen Mother, deceives, plots, murders, and dissembles his way to power. His relationship to the community and to power, however, is more complex than Aaron's, even as Eleazar's characterization seems less ambiguous and less subtle. A villain, Eleazar is hindered by neither human compassion nor attachments; called "That damned Moor, that Devil, that Lucifer," he proves his epithets by his actions.[39] His blackness is seen as the symbol of his soul; as one character says of him, "Seeing your face, we thought of hell" (II, ii, 124). Eleazar himself encourages other Moors to make blackness the symbol of their souls, telling them: "Your cheeks are black, let not your souls look white" (II, ii, 80). And although he is regarded almost universally as evil, Eleazar still enjoys a sexual relationship that is sanctioned by the community

39. Thomas Dekker, *Lust's Dominion*, in *The Dramatic Works of Thomas Dekker*, ed. Fredson Bowers, (Cambridge, England, 1961), Vol. IV, II, i, 52. All future citations of this play are from this edition.

and that complicates both the community's view of him and the play's. Also, unlike Aaron, Eleazar lives amidst a community of Moors, and his relationship with them, and the relationship of the larger Spanish community with them, ultimately shift the play's focus from an isolated Moorish villain to a community of villains.

Like another famous though later Moor, Eleazar attains respectability in the community, presumably through military service, and for his valor—a virtue common to Moors on the stage in the seventeenth century—he is received with favor by King Philip. When Philip dies early in Act I, Eleazar becomes dependent on his wife and her family to keep him in the community. When he is threatened with expulsion, Alvero, his father-in-law, pleads: "Why should my sonne be banished?" (I, ii, 159). His wife, the virtuous Maria, buoys Eleazar's spirit in defeat and seeks redress from the king to "revenge my Lord's indignity" (I, ii, 192). The strength of Eleazar's legitimate claims to membership in the community even allows him to commit regicide with impunity, an act motivated by the Moor's characteristic villainy and jealousy, but which he argues to be an act of revenge against "that lecher King," who, he claims, "threw my wife in an untimely grave" (III, ii, 173-74).[40]

From this position of legitimacy, Eleazar displays his villainous nature, for he mocks the very law that guarantees his safety, as he mocks all decency. Neither love nor respect does he bear his wife, and he uses her instead only to further his claims on the community. To be rid of her, he plots her death as he plots the king's. His contempt for social and moral norms he displays by keeping as his mistress the lascivious queen of the play's title, and he uses this relationship as the power base from which to launch all his villainies.

Great and numerous are the crimes of Eleazar, too numerous to catalog here. His every act attacks the order of the state as it teeters on the brink of chaos. He imprisons, betrays, kills, or plots to kill Philip's two male heirs, Cardinal Mendoza, the Queen Mother, and the betrothed of Princess Isabella. He has the Queen Mother,

---

40. Leo himself reports of the inhabitants of Barbarie: "No nation in the world is so subiect vnto iealousie; for they will rather leese their lives, then put vp with any disgrace in the behalfe of their women" (*History and Description of Africa*, I, 183). The marginal gloss that appears just before these lines in Pory's translation reads: "*The Moores are a people of great fidelitie.*"

whom he abuses in every possible way, befoul her reputation and the Cardinal's by proclaiming Philip's youngest son the Cardinal's bastard. Eleazar even manages to obtain for himself the crown of Spain. But marvelously enough, he surrenders it. The crown is not his goal; Eleazar plots to position himself near Isabella. It is she he most desires, and when at last he has her alone, he confesses his lust and threatens her virtue:

> Coy? were you as hard as flint, Oh! you shou'd yield
> Like softned wax, were you as pure as fire,
> I'le touch you, yes, I'le taint you, see you this [his Rapier],
> I'le bring you to this lure. (V, i, 279–82)

Eleazar manipulates events in order to feed his insatiable lust, a lust like jealousy and evil that is believed to be constituent to all Moors. But his lust more than offends virtue; it threatens to destroy the state itself. Kings die, civil wars rage, villains reign, all consequences of the Moor's voracious sexual appetite. And to combat this stands Isabella, the virtuous yet helpless victim, indeed the very hope of Spain.

Isabella's vulnerability, however, does not result solely from Eleazar's schemes; he alone does not possess such power. Her woes in part arise from the moral failings of lustful Spaniards who, behaving like the Moor, help to create an environment conducive for him "to carry black destruction to the world" (II, i, 3). King Philip's heir Fernando succumbs to his own lustful desires and consequently dies at Eleazar's hand. Such criminal lust helps to put Isabella in danger. So too does her mother's sinful love for Eleazar. The Queen Mother, hoping to satisfy her sexual appetite, plots with Eleazar, but for this she loses honor and family. Cardinal Mendoza, to fulfill his longing for the Queen Mother, entraps himself and, like Fernando and the Queen Mother, learns too late what uncontrolled sexual desire reaps.

Opposition to Eleazar does exist, and the first person to act recognizes the Moor as a sexual threat to the community. Unwilling to gloss over even his mother's crimes, Prince Philip points boldly to the source of Spain's problems. He then denounces Eleazar's debauchery and reviles the Queen Mother for being the Moor's debauchee:

> . . . 'tis this villain
> Dishonours you and me, dishonours *Spain*
> Dishonours all these Lords, this Divell is he. (I, ii, 126-28)

Philip, a few lines earlier, lists those dishonors, a catalog of sexual sins, and rebukes his mother and those nobles who through complacency allow the adulterers to continue:

> My father whilst he liv'd tyr'd his strong armes
> In bearing christian armour, gainst the Turk,
> Whilst you at home suffered his [King Philip's] bed-chamber
> To be a Brothelry, whilst you at home
> Suffered his Queen to be a Concubine,
> And wanton red cheekt boy's to be her bawds
> Whilst shee reeking in that leachers armes ——(I, ii, 117-21)

Philip accuses not just his mother but all those who winked at her transgressions. The guilt and responsibility for these crimes extend to all in the community who were lax in their vigilance, to those who tolerated evil.

Isabella, however, does remain vigilant, and her vigilance sets into motion the forces that free her and Spain and that destroy Eleazar and his compatriots. When one of Eleazar's Moorish henchmen, Zarack, offers to rescue Isabella from Eleazar, she cleverly avoids placing herself in danger. Presuming lust to be Zarack's real motive, she proceeds to manipulate him while protecting herself. "Oh! *Zarack* pity me, I love thee well, / Love deserves pity, pity Isabel" (V, ii, 131-32), she tells the Moor's lieutenant. Zarack, like so many before him, surrenders to his lust and falls unwittingly into the power of Isabella's camp.

Isabella's presumption of guilt, and the contempt she, Philip, and Hortenzo have for Zarack, reveal the general attitude of the characters and the play toward Moors. Zarack says nothing explicitly about love to Isabella; in fact, his offer of assistance seems innocent and hints that revenge for his ill-treatment at Eleazar's hands motivates him:

> I'm weary of this office, and this life,
> It is too thirsty, and I would your blood,
> Might scape the spilling out: By heaven I swear,
> I scorn these blows, and his rebukes to bear. (V, ii, 127-30)

For reward he only asks that she "swear to advance me" (V, ii, 134). Is Zarack seeking revenge and possibly redemption? Or is he dissembling this compassion? From the nature of Isabella's response, we know that she at least does not believe any nobility of spirit exists in him. She plays the role that seems most expedient and that certainly proves productive. However, as soon as Zarack leaves to effect her plot, she says: "the plot is cast / Into the mold of Hell" (V, ii, 150-51). When Hortenzo inquires of Isabella how she won Zarack to her cause, she replies:

> I did profess; I, and protested too,
> I lov'd him well, what will not sorrow do?
> Then he profest; I, and protested too,
> To kill them both, what will not devils do? (V, ii, 154-57)

One can assume from Isabella's remarks that Zarack's actions betray more than his words. Perhaps there is a histrionic link between Zarack and Eleazar, one that the text cannot reveal. But then again, perhaps Zarack's blackness prompts suspicion enough or, at least to Isabella's mind, signifies guilt and precludes the possibility of goodness regardless of his actions. This point is brought home when Philip murders and damns Zarack, even after he has served Philip and Isabella well. Isabella is unmoved and admonishes Philip and Hortenzo for not assuming their new roles quickly enough:

> *Philippo* and *Hortenzo* stand you still?
> What; doat you both? cannot you see your play?
> Well fare a woman then, to lead the way.
> Once rob the dead, put the Moors habits on,
> And paint your face with the oil of hell. (V, ii, 167-72)

The virtuous Isabella's orders to Hortenzo and Philip equate what at first seem to be separate ideas: blackness and role-playing. In the dramatic world of *Lust's Dominion*, however, blackness and role-playing define the spiritually deficient state of the Moors. Isabella knows that Zarack is role-playing or dissembling when he protests charity. Because Zarack is black, he is evil. Actions that do not conform to this equation are simply counterfeit. The "oil of Hell" is the indisputable emblem of the wickedness of Eleazar and his henchmen. When Philip and Hortenzo balm themselves with it, they must assume a role; they must act opposite to what they are.

Role-playing, then, is not unique to Moors in this play. Isabella, Philip, and Hortenzo adopt certain roles; in fact, every important character in the play adopts a role at some point. How then is the role-playing of the Moors distinguishable from the role-playing of the other characters? The Spanish dissemble for expediency; each actor has a specific and limited end that he hopes to achieve by role-playing. Isabella feigns love to Zarack to win his aid; Mendoza plays the penitent adulterer to claim the Queen Mother. In contrast, the Moors must act to continue in the community; they must never uncover their true nature. Once they are recognized, their demise is assured. For the Moors, role-playing is a way of life, and life for them is but a succession of roles. And Eleazar is the master actor; he dissembles to everyone except his Moorish confederates, Baltazar and Zarack. They belong to a confraternity of villains, each knowing and acting his part. The parts they play change somewhat from scene to scene, but the players aim always at the same end: to obscure from the Spanish their evil natures as they pursue their wicked desires. Eleazar operates entirely under this ordinance. He beguiles the Spaniards who accept him, and he makes his every appearance but another demonstration of his thespian prowess. In the last act, he speaks of his intended triumph over the Spanish as though it were only theater:

> O! Saint revenge to thee
> I consecrate my murders, all my stabs,
> My bloody labours, tortures, stratagems:
> The volume of all wounds, that wound from me:
> Mine is the stage, thine is the Tragedy. (V, iii, 56–60)

Eleazar's boast betrays not only how he views the world but also instructs us on how to view him.

The tragedy that Eleazar would mount exploits the opposition between black and white and vice and virtue that is *Lust's Dominion*. But for him it will not be tragedy; he conceives his play as comedy for himself. Directing what he supposes to be a runthrough, Eleazar laughs at the thought of his intended victims in his clutches. Speaking to the disguised Hortenzo and Philip, whom the Moor believes to be Baltazar and Zarack, Eleazar gloats:

> Where thou stand'st now, there must *Hortenzo* hang,
> Like *Tantalus* in a man-eating pang:
> There *Baltazar* must Prince *Phillippo* stand,
> Like damn'd Prometheus; and to act his part,
> Shal have a dagger sticking at his heart.
> But in my room I'le set the Cardinall,
> And he shal preach Repentance to them all.
> Ha, ha, ha. (V, iii, 71-78)

But Eleazar's play is inverted by Hortenzo and Philip. Posing as their opposites Zarack and Baltazar, Hortenzo and Philip turn their play into a comedy and Eleazar's into the tragedy. When the Moor thinks he has a friendly audience of confreres, Philip and Hortenzo call forth a hostile audience to watch their play. With Eleazar manacled, the Spaniards are free to laugh, and to Eleazar's demands that he be unshackled, Philip mocks: "Then shall we mar our mirth and spoil the play" (V, iii, 108). Once Hortenzo and Philip are in control, order is restored. Life is comedy for the Spanish and tragedy for the Moors. This vision of order is made explicit in the last lines of the play. Restored to the throne, Philip proclaims:

> And now *Hortenzo* to close up your wound,
> I here contract my sister unto thee,
> With Comick joy to end a Tragedie.
> And for this Barbarous *Moor*, and his black train,
> Let all the *Moors* be banished from *Spain*. (V, iii, 179-83)

The play ends with everyone's return to his previous role. Philip declares his acting career over: "His [Eleazar's] acts are past, and our last act is done / Now do I challenge my Hereditary right" (V, iii, 168-69). Philip's real role is king. Eleazar's role, however, is actor, and Philip knows this and says so: "This is the *Moor*, the actor of these evills: / Thus thrust him down to act amongst the devils" (V, iii, 146-47). Eleazar, for his part, promises in death to "out act" the devils "in perfect villa[i]ny" (V, iii, 166).

To know Eleazar as actor makes him unacceptable to the community because the actor is a dissembler and is, therefore, untrustworthy. When Isabella understands Zarack is an actor, she is safe from him. Philip too understands this, and when he is an actor himself, he is made privy to the mind that conceives the role.

Ironically, in the scene in which Eleazar thinks he is directing Philip and Hortenzo as played by Zarack and Baltazar, Eleazar loses control of the play and his own role. From the safety of their disguise as Moors, Philip and Hortenzo discover Eleazar's true role in their community, recast him to suit their requirements, and finally unmask him.

The conclusion of the play, it should be remembered, goes beyond the expulsion of the Moors from Spain. It also removes Isabella from sexual danger; she is betrothed to Hortenzo. Her escape from tragedy is as much a part of the comedy as the return to order. The sexual threat to the community dies with Eleazar, who uses his last breaths to remind everyone exactly how he came to power and what he most desired:

> . . . ere my glasse is run,
> I'le curse you all, and cursing end my life.
> Maist thou *Lascivious Queen* whose damned charms,
> Bewitch'd me to the circle of thy arms,
> Unpitied dye, consumed with loathed lust,
> Which thy venereous mind hath basely nurst.
> And for you *Philip*, may your days be long,
> But clouded with perpetuall misery.
> May thou *Hortenzo* and thy *Isabell*,
> Be fetch'd alive by Furies into hell,
> There to be damn'd for ever. (V, iii, 153–63)

Eleazar wishes here for nothing more complicated than a return to power. He wants things as they were, not as they now are. But his return would mean a return to lust's dominion, and that cannot be. Philip sees to this.

In removing the sexual threat to the community, Philip also declares it safe for former transgressors. He forgives his mother and Mendoza for their "crimes" and thereby absolves them of any real responsibility. In the end, the kingdom is made safe by the exclusion of all Moors. To countenance their presence, no matter how legitimate their claims may appear, is to ignore the obvious and to allow the devil to act freely in one's midst. Moors must be known for what they are, not for what they pretend to be. They must not be allowed to obscure their black natures. Instead the Moors' blackness must elucidate and discover them, for they are black of soul as well of face.

A final question arises as we consider role-playing and blackness in *Lust's Dominion*: Are roles chosen or predetermined? For the Spaniards, roles are assigned. Philip acknowledges this when he seeks his "hereditary right." Problems result when people deviate from their assigned roles; this is most clearly true for the Queen Mother, Mendoza, and Fernando. However, those who faithfully execute their assigned roles are rewarded, even if only in death, as was Maria, Eleazar's wife. The belief in predestined roles seems to extend to the Moors as well. By the play's end, everyone recognizes the Moors' blackness as the sign of their predestined villainy. Eleazar, though, complicates this by tacitly acknowledging another possibility when he reminds Baltazar and Zarack: "Your cheeks are black, let not your souls look white" (II, ii, 81). He seems to be acknowledging that a choice is possible, but the choice is to deviate from their natural inclination, their natural condition. Later, as he lies about his involvement in imprisoning Hortenzo and Philip, Eleazar says:

> Because my face is in nights colour dy'd,
> Think you my conscience and my soul is so,
> Black faces may have hearts as white as snow,
> And 'tis a generall rule in morall rowls,
> The whitest faces have the blackest souls. (V, iii, 7–12)

The audience knows here that Eleazar lies. But what exactly is he lying about? Is he simply lying about his involvement in the imprisonment? Or is he lying about blacks? The irony of this situation falls heavily on the Moors because Eleazar most certainly lies about his own soul and conscience. His invocation of theatrical tradition only indicts him further, as it further complicates the matter because the dramatic tradition to which he refers uses blackness as a sign of evil. But Eleazar claims here to be real. He, in fact, is attempting to say that this is not a play and that therefore an allegorical reading of his blackness is inappropriate. Of course, his attempt only accentuates the obvious. *Lust's Dominion* is a play, and Eleazar has even less credibility in the dramatic world than he hopes to claim. Ironically, his role has been predetermined by the very tradition he invokes to liberate him from suspicion. For Eleazar and his kind, their moral roles have been determined, and that determination is witnessed by the blackness on their faces.

The play's internal references to theater point to an interesting paradox, a paradox that is obvious in the scene above. We may view Eleazar's lines above as entirely conventional; frequently, characters in plays like to remind us that they are not in plays. In this scene, we may also view Eleazar's blackness as a theatrical convention. On the stage black people generally are evil; offstage perhaps they are not. In this context, blackness reveals itself to be a conventional trope, and *Lust's Dominion* provides a counterbalance to the modern matter of *The Battle of Alcazar*. Yet the play as an imitation of life (and do not such internal references to plays within plays help to enhance the mimetic illusion), reconfirms suspicions of blackness because we know that the black man is lying and that Isabella must beware. How the individual viewer or reader reconciled this paradox is impossible to determine. Some probably recognized blackness to be just another theatrical convention; others, however, probably saw the play as a veracious comment on life outside of the theater.

Aphra Behn, in her Restoration adaptation of *Lust's Dominion*, made several notable changes. The first was in the title, which she changed to *Abdelazer; or, The Moor's Revenge*. As the new title implies, in this play the emphasis is shifted from lust to revenge. Though Eleazar unconvincingly hints that revenge motivates his villainy, Abdelazer makes much of this motive. In his very first monologue he links his villainy to his desire to avenge the wrongs he and his princely father suffered at Spanish hands:

> Now all that's brave and villain seize my Soul,
> Reform each Faculty that is not ill,
> And make it fit for Vengeance, noble Vengeance.
> Oh glorious Word! fit only for the Gods,
> For which they form'd their Thunder,
> Till man usurp'd their Power, and by Revenge
> Sway'd Destiny as well as they, and took their trade of killing.
> And thou almighty Love,
> Dance in a thousand forms about my Person,
> That this same Queen, this easy *Spanish* Dame,
> May be bewitch'd, and dote upon me still;
> Whilst I make use of the insatiate Flame
> To set all *Spain* on fire.——
> Mischief, erect thy Throne,

> And sit on high; here, here upon my Head.
> Let fools fear Fate, thus I my Stars defy:
> The influence of this [sword]—must raise my Glory high.[41]

Though he has reasons enough for revenge, reasons that include his father's loss of a kingdom and his own enslavement, Abdelazer does not attempt justice but instead an ignoble revenge, and his methods and aims denigrate his cause, as his speech so obviously reveals. For this reason, he gathers no sympathy for himself or his cause. Instead, he paints himself a villain and embraces mischief and villainy, and mischief and villainy soon come to be his greatest interests. And the plot, following very closely the plot of *Lust's Dominion*, provides Abdelazer with sufficient opportunities to commit several heinous crimes, including murder, betrayal, and attempted rape.

Like his predecessors in *Lust's Dominion* and *Titus Andronicus*, Abdelazer's unsanctioned sexual alliance with the Queen Mother allows him to prey upon the host community. He acknowledges this when he prays to Love to keep the lascivious queen infatuated and within his power. His legitimate status in the court, like Eleazar's, he acquires through marriage to a Spanish woman, Florella. This marriage, however, does not enjoy the approval of the entire community. The king, Ferdinand, laments the marriage not only because Florella is lost to him but also because marriage between a Moor and a Spaniard is foul. To Abdelazer's brother-in-law Alonzo, the king complains:

> How came thy Father so bewitch'd to Valour,
> (For Abdelazer has no other Virtue)
> To recompense it with so fair a Creature?
> Was this—a Treasure t'inrich the Devil with? (II, ii, p. 33)

Alonzo, after some slight defense of Abdelazer, agrees: "I did oppose it with what Violence / My Duty would permit" (II, iii, p. 34). Ferdinand and Alonzo, by objecting to Abdelazer's marriage, question Abdelazer's right to belong to their community. Furthermore, Ferdinand's suggestion that Florella's father was bewitched

---

41. Aphra Behn, *Abdelazer; or, The Moor's Revenge*, in *The Works of Aphra Behn*, ed. Montague Summers (1915; rpr. New York, 1967), Vol. II, I, i, pp. 14–15. All future citations of Behn's works are from this edition.

points to other dangers that may exist for the community that accepts the Moor.

The method by which the vengeful Abdelazer obtains legitimacy in Christian Spain points more directly to the nature of his threat to the community. Like his analog, he poses a sexual threat. Alonzo acknowledges this when he expresses surprise that anyone could love the Moor, particularly the Queen Mother. On this point Abdelazer taunts Alonzo: "How, Sir! that cou'd love me! what is there here, / or in my Soul, or Person, may not be lov'd" (V, ii, p. 84). The irony of Abdelazer's remark, of course, shows that no answer is really required because he and the audience know what makes him unlovable. Yet Alonzo responds because he wants to decipher for all Abdelazer's blackness and to expose the danger that exists:

> I spoke without Reflection on your Person,
> But of dishonest Love, which was too plain,
> From whence came all the Ills we have endur'd;
> And now being warm in Mischiefs,
> Thou dost pursue the Game, till all be thine. (V, ii, p. 84)

Alonzo focuses on the real and present sexual danger and demands that its broader meaning be recognized. His fears all too soon find corroboration, as the "Game" (and the obvious sexual pun is intended) the Moor pursues includes Leonora, King Ferdinand's sister.

Abdelazer himself constantly proves the truth of the growing fear of him. No single act of his better demonstrates this than his attempted rape of Leonora. As he moves against her, he employs figurative language that demonstrates unmistakably that he understands that his violation of the princess is also a violation of the community:

> Were you devout as Vestals, pure as their Fire,
> Yet I wou'd wanton in the rifled Spoils
> Of all that sacred Innocence and Beauty.
> —Oh, my Desire's grown high!
> Raging as midnight Flames let loose in Cities,
> And, like that too, will ruin where it lights. (V, ii, p. 89)

His metaphor of destruction focuses attention on the broader scope of his action. By expanding his act of sexual violence against

Leonora into an act of violence against Spain, Abdelazer aligns himself with the general fear and makes clear the fact that threats to the community proceed from the sexual.

When he is finally subdued, Abdelazer rehearses for his captors his sexual offenses; he knows well that these attacks and demonstrations of prowess are more disgusting to the Spanish than his other crimes. Philip rages as Abdelazer tells him of having "whor'd the Queen thy Mother." To enrage Philip more, Abdelazer tells him of the attempted violation of Leonora. The Moor takes further pleasure in taunting Philip with a promise that he will continue to lust after Leonora until his last breath:

> Yes and the last Sense that will remain about me,
> Will be my Passion for that Charming Maid
> Whom I'd enjoy'd e're now, but for thy Treachery. (V, iii, p. 96)

Responding furiously, Philip promises to kill Abdelazer presently: "Deflour'd my Sister! Heaven punish me eternally, / If thou out-liv'st the Minute thou'st declar'd it" (p. 96). Philip knows that safety can only be achieved by destroying the Moor.

The metaphor of sexual power finds its final enactment and resolution in Abdelazer's execution. The stage direction for this scene reads: Philip "Runs on him, all the rest do the like in the same Minute. Abd[elazer] aims at the Prince, and kills Osmin" (V, iii, p. 96).[42] Abdelazer's execution is a communal activity; all the men present on the stage participate. By stabbing him, the white men not only remove the sexual threat from the community, but they also reaffirm their own power over the Moor. Once he is removed, the community returns to normal. Philip assumes his throne and Alonzo claims Leonora's hand; order is restored, virtue preserved.

Abdelazer concludes as does *Lust's Dominion*, with Spain once again safe. However, there is a significant alteration that affects both the play's political attitude toward blacks and its representation of Abdelazer. In *Lust's Dominion*, Philip expels from Spain all the Moors; in *Abdelazer*, no such order is given. While this change indicates some recognition of Abdelazer as a distinct individual, it also points to a reality of life in the 1670s. Blacks were

---

42. Osmin is the rough equivalent of Zarack; however, Osmin behaves honorably and joins with the others to murder Abdelazer.

to be found everywhere, and English interests in the slave trade, as we saw in Chapter III, were long since established. Thus what may seem to be a decrease in overt racism is complicated by historical and economic factors.

The play also complicates our overall response to blackness by offering another black character against whom we may judge Abdelazer. Osmin, the only character Abdelazer kills in his last bit of mischief, earlier betrays Abdelazer and releases Philip and the others from prison. Obviously modeled after Zarack in *Lust's Dominion*, Osmin, however, is not motivated by lust; in fact, he seems to be an individual motivated by grace. After saving Leonora from Abdelazer's violence, Osmin promises: "I'll live to do you Service" (V, ii, p. 90). This redeemed Moor then reveals that he has already served her as the mysterious messenger who informed Mendoza and Philip of Abdelazer's plot against them. (In *Lust's Dominion*, the two friars, Cole and Crabb, are the messengers.) Nor does Osmin seek any reward for his deeds in Leonora and Philip's behalf. Osmin acts because Philip is king. And unlike their counterparts in *Lust's Dominion* who recognize Zarack as a dissembler, Philip and the others unhesitantly believe Osmin. Philip, after having been freed, thanks Osmin, proclaiming: "Thou art some Angel sure, in that dark Cloud" (V, iii, p. 93). And when Osmin partakes in the execution of Abdelazer, Osmin reveals his goodness and true allegiance and thereby demonstrates that some Moors can belong to the community. This fact saves the Moors from the wholesale expulsion that they suffer in *Lust's Dominion*.

The recognition by Philip and the play that righteous behavior is possible in a Moor relaxes somewhat the traditionally disparaging representation of Moors and the related moral judgments. But the difference between Osmin and Abdelazer and their stations requires some notice. A royal Prince of Barbary, Abdelazer seeks legitimacy and ultimately power in the community. Osmin, a faithful servant, recognizes the legitimate power of Philip, the grace of Leonora, and the tyranny of Abdelazer. As a nonthreatening faithful servant, this good Moor represents a type character as surely as does Abdelazer. They are just different types, both of which are common among black characters; they both represent extremes, one dangerous and the other benign. The latter accepts his role in the community and serves well; the former, always dangerous, seeks to pervert established order. The presence of Osmin in this play neither negates the type characterization of Abdelazer nor denies it. The emphasis placed on Abdelazer's blackness and diabolism constantly reminds us of his type and that long-held traditional view of blacks and blackness. Osmin simply proves that another type exists.

The predominant type, the villainous lecher, we find again in William Rowley's *All's Lost by Lust*, another play that is set in the Spanish court and that moralizes against sexual license. In *All's Lost*, the venereous King Rodorique of Spain loses his kingdom to the Moors, whose king is the viciously cruel and equally lascivious Mulymumen. A theatrical descendant of Aaron, the wicked Muly shows regard for neither life nor law and himself becomes the symbol of lawlessness and lust. With his usurpation of the Spanish throne, the play becomes a metaphor for the topsy-turvy world that results from sinful lust and rebellion against one's lawful king.

This theme is promoted by comparing the lustful but lawful King of Spain to the black King of the Moors. Although the play condemns Rodorique's crimes, which include the rape of his general's daughter, it nevertheless upholds his right to the throne under any condition. After Julianus, the injured father, avenges his daughter's honor, he realizes that by overthrowing his lawful king, he has unleashed tyranny on Spain. Rodorique's victim, Jacinta, laments to her father:

> Oh Iulianus, what hast thou done? th'ast 'scapt
> The raging Lion, to wrastle with a Dragon,
> He would have slaine with a majesticke gripe,
> But this with venome; better had bin thy fate
> By him to fall, then thus, by such a helhound.[43]

Yet as the symbolic representative of evil in the play, Muly must be seen as more wicked than the rapist-king, Rodorique, and this is economically achieved by simply employing the allegory of

---

43. William Rowley, *All's Lost by Lust*, in *William Rowley: His All's Lost by Lust and A Shoemaker, A Gentleman*, ed. Charles Wharton Stork (Philadelphia, 1910), V, v, 16-20.

blackness. Long before Muly appears on stage we know he is an evil, ugly, and black devil. Of his Moorish enemies Rodorique warns:

> They would deter us with their swarty lookes:
> Were they the same to their similitude,
> Sooty as the inhabitants of hell,
> Whom they neerest figure; cold feare should flye
> From us as distant as they are from beauty. (I, i, 31-35)

Recalling the traditional views of Moors as fiendish and ugly, Rodorique claims victory for "christian valour" against an enemy of "halfe-nak't Infidels" from a "sun-burnt Clymate" (I, i, 87, 84-85).

As with Aaron and Eleazar, Muly's danger extends beyond the battlefield because he hopes to secure and to compound his power through a sexual alliance. He wants to marry the ravished Jacinta. Such a marriage, he knows, would bind him more legitimately to the community, as well as secure for him sufficient cause to seek revenge against Rodorique and to justify his mischief. His request for Jacinta's hand clearly defines the political advantages he seeks:

> . . . to binde me faster to thee,
> Plight me thy ravisht daughter to my wife,
> And thou shalt see my indignation fly
> On wings of thunder. (IV, i, 180-83)

Jacinta rejects unequivocally and unhesitantly Muly's sexual offer: "O my second hell, / A Christians armes embrace an infidel" (IV, i, 184-85). The injured Jacinta equates marriage to Muly with her earlier ravishment, and though she bases her rejection on Muly's religion, she holds his infidelity to be innate and permanent. His infidelity, of course, is synecdochical for his blackness, which is really innate and permanent. And the earlier invocation of the allegory of blackness, of course, gives legitimacy to Jacinta's refusal: Muly is evil.

The Moor's anger and sexual frustration at rejection lead to the final calamities of the play. With Rodorique defeated and in flight from Spain and himself installed as king, Muly seeks vengeance against Julianus and the steadfast Jacinta, whom he threatens:

> . . . I shall be more frightfull,

> If thou repell a profferd arme of loue,
> There will rebound a hate blacker in Act
> Then in similitude. (V, v, 2-5)

But Jacinta, who finds the very sight of Muly "frightfull," vows suicide before she will submit. Angered, Muly devises a fiendish plan to secure his revenge. He blinds Julianus, who then unwittingly impales Jacinta upon his own sword. This deed crowns the Moor's treachery with villainy and guarantees his infamy. Over the bodies of the fallen Julianus and Jacinta, Muly ends the play with the command: "Let Chroniclers write, here we begin our raigne, / The first of Moors that ere was King of Spain" (V, i, 203-204). Echoing Philip's lines at the end of *Lust's Dominion*, Muly proclaims a new and horrific era, the beginning of the one that audiences heard Philip proclaim as closed. The conclusion of *All's Lost* offers a stern moral: lust and lawlessness beget lust and lawlessness. The reign that commences at the play's conclusion is literally and metaphorically a reign of darkness presided over by a "black monster."

Yet, even as Muly stands triumphant, his victory is declared subject to divine providence, his power achieved not through his own strength but through divine design. Muly serves as God's instrument of retribution, and so Julianus tells him:

> Thou laughest at misery.
> Tis well, thou giuest a grave unto my sorrowes,
> Yet wherefore shouldst thou glory in't? this worke
> Is none of thine, tis heavens mercifull iustice,
> For thou art but the executioner.
> . . . .
> I was a traytor to my lawfull King,
> And tho my wrongs encited on my rage.
> I had no warrant signde for my revenge,
> Tis the peoples sinnes that make tyrants Kings,
> And such was mine for thee, now I obey. (V, v, 132-36, 140-44)

Although Muly's viciousness is not compromised, his role in the allegory humbles him. Julianus' exegesis of the Moorish victory offers the comfort of continued divine order and divine judgment against the black foes of Christianity. As the unknown translator of *Destruccion de las Indias* warns: "By the wicked he [God] punisheth those that be wicked."[44] Muly triumphs precisely because he is wicked; the Moors, like the plague of locusts, are a visitation from God.

Wickedness is constituent to Mulymumen, Aaron, and Eleazar, and the belief that blackness signifies evil, a long-held popular notion, predetermines their type. For black men such as Osmin in *Abdelazer*, movement away from evil signifies movement away from the norm. Africans arrived on the stage, as they arrived in England, as players in an allegory, their color the most important signifier. Yet of all their crimes and cruelties, their greatest (at least in these five plays, and surely in *Othello*) seems to be their uncontrollable lust for white women. The reader must surely ask himself why this crime? Why does Aaron's fathering a son of Tamora entrap him and accelerate his fall? Why is Eleazar, one of many lechers and bawds in *Lust's Dominion*, beyond repentance and redemption? Why is murder at the hands of a white rapist preferable to marriage to a Moorish king? Why does sexuality define the black man's relationship to the community?

The answers to these questions can be found in both the dramatic tradition and popular opinions about sex, Africans, and Englishmen. Unrelenting, remorseless lust and virtue tried, common themes in English literature, were dramatized in the cycle plays and the moralities. Lust itself was personified in the moralities, as exemplified by Luxuria in *The Castle of Perseverance* and Voluptas and Sencualitas in *Susanna*. Later mimetic plays like *The Revenger's Tragedy* (1606) and *The Duchess of Malfi* (1613) also treat themes of concupiscence and luxury. The five plays discussed here reflect the continued interest in sexual matters. The black lechers of these plays are drawn from that tradition, their blackness a metaphor for the sins of the flesh that they embody. As moral exempla, they warn the audience of the blackness that results from sexual license and the sexual license that seems to accompany blackness.

Yet we know this characterization of black men has some historical basis. English and European travelers always reported on the supposed libidinousness of Africans. Recall that Leo reports

---

44. Bartolome Las Casas, *The Spanish Colonie*, trans. M.M.S. (London, 1583), sig. 4v.

"no nation vnder heauen more prone to venerie" than "Negros."[45] English playwrights then were only representing on the stage what was commonly reported and held to be true. But on the stage blacks represented more than licentiousness; they represented a threat. Unrestricted by the sexual mores imposed by Christianity, Africans were free, or at least perceived to be free, to indulge themselves. This itself is threatening to a people who had a repressive system that governed all sexual contact and interdicted most. The sexual freedom that Africans were believed to have, had to be condemned in order to justify the sexual codes of Christianity. Yet as Winthrop Jordan notes: "The life of 'savages' had attractions, even if civilized white men were not entirely aware what these attractions were."[46] In a very real way, the attraction itself was the danger, and the attraction and the danger extended to and endangered the very structure of English and European society. The satyric African, if admitted into the community, would undermine its basic organization, and the African's supposed libidinousness, if not condemned, could prove dangerously attractive.

An important yet intangible undercurrent remains unaccounted for here. What part did personal sexual insecurity and sexual anxieties play in determining the representation of Moors? Sexual tension between white men and black, and the accompanying myths (most of which persist to this day), can be traced back to those first encounters with Africans in the sixteenth century. Did the anxieties and myths inform the representation? We know that the "fact" of the African's venery did; surely it is not unreasonable to consider these other facts as influences. On the complex subject of white attitudes toward black men in the colonies Jordan writes:

> No matter how firmly based in fact, however, the image of the sexually aggressive Negro was rooted even more firmly in deep strata of irrationality. For it is apparent that white men projected their own desires onto Negroes: their own passion for Negro women was not fully acceptable to society or the self and hence not readily admissible. Sexual desires could be effectively denied and the accompanying anxiety and guilt in some measure assuaged, however, by imputing them to others. It is not we, but others, who are guilty. It is not we who lust, but they. Not only this, but white men anxious

45. Leo Africanus, *History and Description of Africa*, I, 180.
46. Jordan, *White over Black*, 40.

over their own sexual inadequacy were touched by a racking fear and jealousy. Perhaps the Negro better performed his nocturnal offices than the white man. Perhaps, indeed, the white man's woman really wanted the Negro more than she wanted him.[47]

These irrationalities articulated by Jordan help to explain why the greatest crimes and threats of the Moors were sexual. It is, of course, not possible for us to attribute these particular anxieties specifically to any of the authors, but these sexual dynamics clearly operate in these plays.

The more skeptical reader may seek to discredit this argument by citing *Abdelazer*, a play written by a woman. Behn's play, however, is not wholly of her imagination; it is an adaptation. Also several alterations in the play tend to support the idea that Dekker's Philip—if not Dekker himself—was susceptible to this anxiety. For Philip in *Lust's Dominion*, the question of power is a question of masculine prowess. In Act IV, Philip and Eleazar engage in a duel, Philip with a broken sword. Eleazar wishing to demonstrate his prowess offers Philip the longer sword:

> . . . I'le be sworn thy mother was a Queen;
> For her sake will I kill thee nobly:
> Fling me thy sword, there's mine, I scorn to strike
> A man disarm'd. (IV, ii, 102-05)

Philip, recognizing the obvious pun on *Queen* and the greater insult to his masculinity, replies: "For this dishonoring me / I'le give thee one stab more" (IV, ii, 105-06). He then suggests that he and Eleazar fight with weapons of equal length, that is if Eleazar is willing to surrender his advantage. Even the reader who is unwilling to accept the sexual symbolism of this scene must recognize the sexual nature of Eleazar's insult and challenge and of Philip's response. Philip must defend his honor and his masculinity against the man who has named his mother a queen.

Behn alters this scene significantly. Unlike Philip in *Lust's Dominion*, her Philip arrives "arm'd with more than compleat Steel" (IV, vi, p. 65). He claims justice too in his quarrel. Thus Philip declares himself not only equal to Abdelazer, but superior. In the ensuing struggle, the stage direction reads: "Philip *prevails*,

---

47. *Ibid.*, 152.

the Moors give ground" (IV, vi, p. 65). Philip seems not to have the anxiety that his analog in *Lust's Dominion* suffers, and he demonstrates this by his actions and words. But the sexual symbolism is obvious here, just as it is when Philip and the other men execute Abdelazer. Behn has only lessened the anxiety not eliminated it or the sexual conflicts.

The issue of masculine prowess raises the related issue of political power. To maintain power, the sexual freedom of Moors must be restricted. Failure by the community to limit Moors sexually leads to their exercise of power and terror. Had each been excluded from the community sexually, he would have had no power over it (remember Osmin). This is true even for Mulymumen. Had his demand for sexual power over Jacinta and sexual legitimacy been immediately rejected by Julianus, who seems oblivious to the danger, the resulting disaster would not occur. This connection between political power and sexual dominance, Jordan addresses in *White over Black*: "Any Negro insurrection, furthermore, threatened the white man's dominance, including his valuable sexual dominance, and hence the awful prospect of being overthrown was bound to assume a sexual cast."[48] In these plays, the connection is clear; the real political threat is necessarily linked to the sexual threat, making them the same issue.

This problem of sexual anxiety cannot totally account for the overwhelming emphasis placed on the sexual nature of the Moors. As I have tried to show, other factors, including hundreds of years of English dramatic tradition, play an important role. Nevertheless, we have seen that the Moorish villain operates from a place of sexual advantage, and the pervasiveness of this theme demanded some attempt at an answer. Now I shall move to the representation of Moorish women, who like their black brothers also belong to the most venereous nation under heaven.

Characterized in a manner similar to her male counterpart, the black Moorish woman stands as a symbol of everything evil and low. Legitimately she functions in the community solely as a waiting-woman, illegitimately as a bawd and whore. Unusually libidinous, the black woman uses her illegitimate sexual relation-

---

48. *Ibid.*, 153.

ships as a platform for treachery, treachery aimed specifically at her mistress and generally at virtue, order, and community. Nothing but the gratification of her lust concerns the Moor, and her blackness, of course, reveals her to be "hels perfect character."[49] Even in the few plays in which the Moorish woman is not a treacherous whore, she still finds herself in predicaments that impugn her virtue and veracity.

The popular notion that black women were whorish could be heard on the English stage as early as Shakespeare's *The Merchant of Venice* (1596?), in which the unseen black woman is abused by her lover, the clown Launcelot. When told "The Moor is with child by you," Launcelot retorts: "It is much that the Moor should be more than reason, but if she be less than an honest woman, she is indeed more than I took her for" (III, iv, 39-40, 42). An earlier exchange between Jessica, Lorenzo, and Launcelot reveals a general contempt for blacks and for interracial sex. When Jessica reminds her beloved Lorenzo that the Christian community will disapprove of his marriage to a Jew, he replies to this warning: "I shall answer that better to the commonwealth than you [Launcelot] can the getting up of the Negro's belly" (III, v, 38-39). This brief exchange encapsulates the attitude toward black women that received fuller development in other plays and that dominated the seventeenth-century English stage almost to the exclusion of all other views.

The first play to put the typical Moorish waiting-woman on the stage, and possibly the first to put a black woman on the stage, was John Marston's *Wonder of Women; or, the Tragedy of Sophonisba* (1606).[50] Named Zanthia, the woman is prototypical in many ways.

---

49. Francis Beaumont and John Fletcher, *The Knight of Malta*, in *The Works of Francis Beaumont and John Fletcher*, ed. A. R. Waller (Cambridge, England, 1909), Vol. VII, IV, i, p. 136. Unless otherwise noted future citations of Beaumont and Fletcher's plays are from this Cambridge English Classics edition.

50. It is impossible to determine if Calypolis was portrayed as black in *Alcazar* and *Stukeley*. Peele's source makes no mention of a wife, nor does the text of *Alcazar* indicate if she is black. Because she condemns Muly Mahamet's treachery (II, iii, 531-36), I am inclined to see her as white. To allow a black person to express any virtuous sentiment would be uneconomical thematically as well as racially uncharacteristic. Also, Muly calls Calypolis "fair" in II, ii, 566. While this is not unimpeachable evidence, I believe it to be of some significance when considered with the other evidence. However, since it cannot be determined from the text of

Vile, lascivious, and faithless, she serves the faithful, virtuous, matchless Sophonisba. From this position of trust, Zanthia betrays her mistress to the lust of Syphax. The reward the Moor anticipates for her treachery is sexual intimacy with the villain; she hopes to purchase pleasure, luxury, with her mistress' virtue. The scene that most demonstrates Zanthia's venery, however, also demonstrates Syphax's contempt for her. While courting Zanthia's assistance in his plot to rape Sophonisba, Syphax says to the Moor:

> Thou art not foul, go to; Some lords are oft
> So much in love with their known ladies' bodies,
> That they oft love their—[Maids]:[51] hold, hold, thou'st find
> To faithful care kings' bounty hath no shore.[52]

Syphax probably shouts "hold, hold" to an overexcited Zanthia who is unable to control her desire for him. That his overtures produce so prompt and violent a response in Zanthia presumably astonishes Syphax, who offers the Moor monetary rewards for her assistance. She, however, proclaims herself Syphax's "creature," an offer that he again rejects saying: "Be yet; tis no stain; / The god of service is however gain" (III, i, 66-67).

Zanthia's overzealousness and disregard for honor or virtue contrast with Sophonisba's uncompromising modesty and virtue. Sophonisba chooses death rather than lose her honor or tempt her husband. As they contrast in virtue, they contrast in color, and

---

Stukeley whether Muly himself is black, the case for Calypolis is even more uncertain. Here again, I believe her to be white. Unfortunately, there is little in the text to support my opinion. Muly again speaks of his "fair Calipolis" (2336), but this single phrase is not enough evidence to make a strong case. However, Calypolis plays such an insignificant role in this play—like the Moors in civic pageants she is not much more than an emblem of the exotic—that it hardly matters whether she is black or white. It should also be noted that in every play but *The Fair Maid of the West, Part II*, when a black character, either male or female, is involved sexually with another character, that character is white.

51. The text of the quarto of *Sophonisba* reads: "That they oft love their-Vails." The widely accepted emendation that I offer above, is suggested by Kenneth Deighton (*The Old Dramatists: Conjectural Readings* [Westminster, England, 1896], 13). A. H. Bullen allows the original reading to stand, which he says is an example of aposiopesis (John Marston, *Wonder of Women; or, The Tragedy of Sophonisba*, in *The Works of John Marston*, ed. A. H. Bullen [London, 1887], II, 274). See also Jones, *Othello's Countrymen*, 76.

52. Marston, *Sophonisba*, in *The Works of John Marston*, Vol. II, III, i, 61-64.

Zanthia's serves as an emblem of her evil. Interestingly enough, the text makes no mention of her color, the only implied reference to it is Syphax's "Thou art not foul."[53] Yet Marston employs a metaphor common to plays with black women. As the villain tempts virtue, he discovers that he can only have evil, and when he embraces the black woman, he represents metaphorically his moral state. In this metaphorical representation, Syphax embraces sin; never virtue, and Zanthia is almost abstracted to her essential blackness. This theme is again represented when Syphax discovers his black servant Vangue in his bed. Syphax thinks he finally has virtue in the person of Sophonisba in his bed, but he really has its opposite there. "Hah! can any woman turn to such a devil?" Syphax shouts at his discovery (III, i, 185). Perhaps the real meaning of these words is lost to Syphax, but surely not to the audience.

Zanthia is but the first black woman abstracted to a symbol of lust and sin. Yet she represents more than her sin and the villain's; she also represents a threat to innocence and virtue. As she seeks to satisfy her lewd desires, she endangers those who trust their safety to her. It is this breach of trust that exposes her venery for the hideous crime that it really is. Her double sin parallels the crimes of her black male counterpart and raises again the question of the safety of a community that openly admits Africans.

The community that readily admits Zanche, the Moorish waiting-woman in Webster's *The White Devil* (1611?), also admits into its midst the evil that Zanche's blackness represents. Presided over by the concupiscent Duke of Bracciano, this confederacy of bawds and lechers seeks to displace the virtuous community governed by Francisco de Medici, Duke of Florence. In this community of the wicked, Zanche fittingly serves as the waiting-woman to Bracciano's mistress, Vittoria, the white devil of the play's title, and also as bawd and lover to the pander Flamineo, her mistress' brother. Ironically, even in this community to which she seems naturally suited, Zanche betrays those who trust her; like Zanthia, she places lust before loyalty.

Much is made of blackness in *The White Devil*; the title itself reminds us that the devil is usually black. But in this play, white

53. Jones also believes "foul" to be a reference to Zanthia's blackness, as he does the very name "Zanthia" (*Othello's Countrymen*, 76). Tokson too believes Zanthia to be black (*Popular Image of the Black Man*, 84–85).

is tainted and corrupted, and each of the evil white characters in the play is figuratively colored black. Before Vittoria stands trial for the murder of her husband, she is condemned for "her black lust," which promises "[to] make her infamous / To all our neighboring kingdoms."[54] At the trial itself Vittoria's prosecutor reports that this "debauch'd" woman effected a "black concatenation / Of mischief" (III, ii, 28-30). Vittoria's lover, Bracciano, colors himself black as he confesses crimes that include uxoricide and adultery. Her brother Flamineo, while on his deathbed, also proclaims himself black because of the crimes he has committed:

> 'Tis well yet there's some goodness in my death,
> My life was a black charnel. I have caught
> An everlasting cold. (V, vi, 269-71)

The play's emphasis on blackness, of course, elevates the importance of its single black character, the "black Fury" Zanche. Although the degree to which she is truly wicked does not become known until Act V, Zanche acts in concert with the nefarious schemers Bracciano, Vittoria, and Flamineo. While telling Bracciano that he can trust Zanche to assist them in obtaining access to Vittoria, Flamineo reports the Moor to be "wondrous proud / To be the agent for so high a spirit" (I, ii, 14-15). Recognized universally as a devil on earth, she makes visible the blackness that is only figuratively present in Bracciano, Vittoria, and Flamineo. The willingness of these three to trust the "black Fury" declares them to be of the devil's party. When men finally come to end the reign of the lustful trio of Vittoria, Flamineo, and Zanche, one of the murderers shouts: "Kill the Moor first" (V, vi, 215). Perhaps the murderer believes that with Zanche's death, satanic rule will cease or that Vittoria, without her black servant, can no longer be so vile or dangerous.

Zanche's demise and that of Vittoria and Flamineo come more quickly because of the Moor's betrayal of her mistress and her lover. Ironically, it is Zanche's lust and the lure of blackness that prompts her to treachery and ensnares her. The virtuous Francisco blackens his face and disguises himself as a Moor in order to

---

54. John Webster, *The White Devil*, ed. J. R. Mulryne (Lincoln, Neb., 1969), III, i, 7-8.

uncover the crimes of the guilty and to bring them to justice. When Zanche sees Francisco so disguised, she confesses: "I ne'er lov'd my complexion till now" (V, i, 206). But to prove herself worthy of this black man, Zanche plans to steal Vittoria's jewels. As further proof, she voluntarily tells Francisco of the crimes of her masters and then confesses disingenuously: "I sadly do confess I had a hand / In the black deed" (V, iii, 246-47). But Zanche confesses not as a prelude to a new virtuous life; in fact, she confesses for quite another reason. She intends to start a new criminal life with a new accomplice. Her confessions and plottings acknowledge a camaraderie between her and Francisco, a camaraderie based on their blackness and the belief that as black compatriots they are both criminals. Francisco encourages her in this illusion by responding to her wooing as though he were a stereotypical lecherous Moor: "I . . . dreamt on thee too: for methought I saw thee naked" (V, iii, 225-27). By doing the expected, both Zanche and Francisco uphold the traditional view of blackness. He knows black men are lecherous and criminal, and Zanche's behavior reconfirms his opinions of black women.

By far the most malevolent of all the Moorish waiting-women in seventeenth-century drama is Zanthia in Beaumont and Fletcher's *The Knight of Malta*.[55] Not only does she willingly betray her mistress, she also wishes to murder her. Zanthia's perfidy and malice spring, as one might expect, from her uncontrolled, if not uncontrollable, lust. Zanthia serves as a symbol of sin and lust and, like her counterpart in *Sophonisba*, as an external representation of the spiritual state of the man who embraces her. But Beaumont and Fletcher employ more explicitly an allegorical structure implied by the allegory of blackness than do the two earlier plays. In fact, the play seems like an old psychomachia, with Mountferrat, the villain and Zanthia's lover, caught between virtue and vice. On one side stands Zanthia, "in . . . black shape,

---

55. The list of characters prefixed to the text of *The Knight of Malta* in the 1649 folio of Beaumont and Fletcher's plays identifies this character as "Zanthia alias Abdella." Zanthia, however, never goes by this alias in the play; apparently one collaborator failed to synchronize fully his portion of the play with the other's portion. See E. H. Oliphant, *The Plays of Beaumont and Fletcher: An Attempt to Determine Their Respective Shares and the Shares of Others* (New Haven, Conn., 1927), 398. See also pp. 392-98 for a discussion of authorship.

and bla[c]ker actions / Being hels perfect character" (IV, i, p. 136). Her opposite, Oriana, represents virtue that is ever constant even when besieged. She claims for herself "spotless White" as "the Emblem of my life, of all my actions" (II, v, p. 110). Although Mountferrat desires Oriana, he can only possess Zanthia. Oriana represents purity and the repression of sexual desire, Zanthia the opposite. Were Mountferrat to aspire virtuously to Oriana, he would achieve her spiritual perfection. Because he wishes to spoil her, he embraces only the spoiled Zanthia. But in this play, much is lost by uncontrolled sexual desire, for Malta depends on the chaste to protect it and to defend its cause. The safety of the state depends on the knight who "being young, vows chastity" (V, ii, p. 162). Oriana encourages chastity, order, and self-control; Zanthia venery, sabotage, and license.

To satisfy her lust, Zanthia encourages Mountferrat, the object of her desire, to forswear his vows to the knighthood that is sworn to protect Malta. By perjuring himself, Mountferrat also becomes treasonous, and in Malta perjury and treason are closely linked. The city, besieged by the Turks, relies on faithful Christians to protect it. When Mountferrat abjures his vow of chastity and couples with the devil Zanthia, he endangers everyone, and as she assists in his crimes, she promotes treason. The nature of their crimes is ironically commented on by Mountferrat himself when he falsely accuses Oriana of treason:

> How weakly do's this court then
> Send Vessels forth to Sea, to guard the Land
> Taking such special care to save one Bark,
> Or strive to add fam'd men into one cloak,
> When they lurk in our bosomes would subvert
> This state, and us, presuming on their blood,
> And partial indulgence to their sex? (I, iii, p. 91)

His words here far more accurately describe himself and Zanthia, for it is their blood that is lustful and they who wish only to indulge their lust.

Zanthia reveals the contempt she holds for the community when she mocks its greatest strengths: the church and Christianity. As the traditional godless Moor, she blasphemes against God and the church when she mocks Mountferrat as he shrinks from entering a church with criminal intent:

Mountferrat: Heaven bless me,
   I never enter'd with such unholy thoughts
   This place before.
[Zanthia]: Ye are a fearful fool,
   If men have appetites allow'd 'em,
   And warm desires, are there not ends too for 'em?
      (IV, ii, p. 142)

Her contempt for Christianity is most graphically displayed when she suggests to Mountferrat that they seal their marriage contract in blood:

> . . . come Mountferrat
> Here join thy foot to mine, and let our hearts
> Meet with our hands, the contract that is made
> And cemented with blood, as this of ours is,
> Is a more holy sanction, and much surer,
> Than all the superstitious ceremonies
> You Christians use. (IV, v, p. 149)

While the mockery she has already made of a Christian sexual union finds perfection in her grotesque and perverted rite, Zanthia's desired end is really the overthrow of Christianity. And the danger is very real because even now Malta is a city besieged by a non-Christian enemy. Nothing is safe from her, not state, church, or individual.

When the leaders of Malta recognize Zanthia's threat, they expel her and Mountferrat. But to further punish Mountferrat, the knights order him married to Zanthia, a marriage that foreshadows Mountferrat's eternal damnation and coassociation with devils. However, before the Grand Master of Malta pronounces the final doom of Mountferrat and Zanthia, she is cursed in the most abusive way. Her confession, though true, is qualified as "the only truth that ever issued out of hell, which her black jawes resemble," and the soldier who begins this abuse continues: "a plague o'your bacon-face, you must be giving drinks with a vengeance, ah thou branded bitch: do'ye stare goggles, I hope to make winterboots o'thy hide yet, she fears not damning: hell fire cannot parch her blacker than she is: d'ye grin, chimney-sweeper" (V, ii, p. 159-60). This abusive language, far worse than any offered to Mountferrat, points to the essential ethical disparity between the Moor and a sinful Christian and identifies Zanthia as the demonic agent of the play. As she is abused, chastity and purity, symbolized by the color white, are valorized. When these virtues are restored, when the state is safe from Zanthia's lust and power, when white has triumphed completely, then safety returns. Zanthia, then, is more than a debased whore; she is also a temptress. She appeals to men in such a way that they forsake the higher aims of community and Christianity, and they become like her, selfish and foul. She promotes sexual license, and Malta requires sexual repression to secure its safety.

The black temptress, the corruptress of morals and of community survived on the stage for centuries. The popularity of *The White Devil* and *The Knight of Malta* continued well into the eighteenth century, and through most of the seventeenth century, one of these two offered the only representation of a black woman found on the stage. Even the very few black women from that period who are neither whores nor villains nevertheless find themselves in situations wholly suitable for the evil meretrixes of these plays. Of course the emphasis placed on the fabled sexual license of black women resembles the similar emphasis employed repeatedly in characterizing black men, and like the myths that surround the sexuality of black men, those that influence the characterization of black women originate from the same sources.

Theatrically, black women are the heiresses of both Satan and the female temptresses and bawds of the moralities and mysteries. Black characters inherit their sinfulness directly from their black progenitor Satan, their wantonness from the harlot who, ever ready to tempt a man to sin, boasts of her amorous experiences and desires.[56] Women like Treasure in *The Triall of Treasure* (1567) and Willfull Wanton in *The Tide Tarrieth No Man* (1576) exemplify the type of meretrix found in post-Henrician drama. Possessing an insatiable sexual appetite, these women seek only their pleasure, though the price is ruin for everyone else. Possibly the ultimate expression of this dual heritage is the black succubus Lucifera in Beaumont and Fletcher's *The Prophetess* (1622). Her dramatic role is minimal (she dances once in Act III), but she unites the two traditions in a single hyperbolic exemplum.

56. Spivack, *Shakespeare and the Allegory of Evil*, 118.

Black women of flesh and blood were frequently thought of as no less demonic or licentious than Beaumont and Fletcher's succubus. Even when not directly describing black women as such, the travel literature that reports black men to be venereous implies that the women are too. Leo makes a direct statement about black women when he says the Negroes "have great swarms of Harlots among them." Another equally damaging assessment of black women can be found in John Lok's description of Libya[57] where he found a people "called Garmanes, whose women are common: for they contract no matrimonie, neither have respect to chastite."[58] These sentiments found their way into popular beliefs and onto the stage as well. But myths about black female sexuality, like those about black men, reveal more about the white men who invented and propagated the myths. Black women had no control over their representation—as indeed many had no control over their own bodies. Those white men who did control representation had to offer some justification and rationalization for the slippage of white men from their own moral codes. If white men weakened, it was because the temptress' power overwhelmed. "Not only did the Negro woman's warmth constitute a logical explanation for the white man's infidelity," writes Jordan, "but much more important, it helped shift responsibility from himself to her. If she was *that* lascivious—well, a man could scarcely be blamed for succumbing against overwhelming odds."[59]

Black women, then, really did pose a threat to the community. They did not do so actively but in a far more subtle and dangerous way. If white men, tempted to fornication, succumbed, they necessarily violated, if not abjured, community norms. A white man allied with a black woman visibly flaunted moral and social stan-

---

57. Libya as described by Lok is much larger than the present day country of that name. "Libya interior," he writes, "is very large and desolate, in the which are many horrible wildernesses, & mountaines, replenished with divers kinds of wilde and monstrous beastes and serpents." Of the people, he writes: "It is to be understood, that the people which now inhabite the regions of the coast of Guinea, and the middle parts of Africa, as Libya, the inner, and Nubia, with divers other great & large regions about the same, were in old times called AEthiopes and Nigritae, which we now call Moores, Moorens, or Negroes" (Hakluyt, *Principal Navigations Voyages, Traffiques and Discoveries*, IV, 58, 57).

58. *Ibid.*, IV, 58.

59. Winthrop Jordan, *White over Black*, 151.

dards and weakened the basic social structure of the community. No matter how common in practice, concubinage and miscegenation remained taboo. Nor did interracial marriage remove the stigma—remember, Mountferrat is married to Zanthia as punishment. The response of white men to black women could produce disastrous results for white society. Projected onto the black woman, the dangers were held to be of her making. This is one of the reasons that Zanthia receives the greater abuse and condemnation. As the temptress, she is held more responsible for the failing of Mountferrat than he is. She must be driven from the community in order to remove the temptation. Evil may not cease to exist with the expulsion of the black woman, but a viable and real danger is diminished.

Before leaving our discussion of black women, three more must be mentioned. These three differ from those discussed above in a most fundamental way: they lack evil intent. However distinguishable they may be in this most significant way, they still do not diverge totally from the type. The first of these, Celanta in Peele's *The Old Wives Tale* (1590), is the most divergent of the three. Black and ugly, Celanta possesses that inner beauty praised in the fifth chapter of the Song of Songs. "Though I am blacke, I am not the divell," she says.[60] Quite the opposite of Celanta is her sister Zantippa who, though "handsome," is "curst as a waspe" (ll. 221, 229). However, Celanta for all her goodness can find no husband until she meets a blind man who, unable to see that she is "so hard favoured, so foule and ill faced," marries her (ll. 233–34). Pleased with his match, the new husband declares his wife "the fairest alive" (l. 771). Of course, the allegorical intent of this fable renders Celanta more an emblem of those virtues a man should seek in a wife rather than a mimetic character. Nor would the most naïve reader believe that the play suggests that black women make perfect wives. The fable is not about real people, and Celanta is not a Moor. But for all its abstractions, the play employs a common and popular notion of blackness. Celanta is ugly because she is black, and regardless of the comment on her virtue, the play

60. George Peele, *The Old Wives Tale*, ed. Frank S. Hook, in *The Dramatic Works of George Peele* (New Haven, Conn., 1961), l. 621. Vol. III of Prouty, ed., *The Life and Works of George Peele*, 3 vols.

reinforces this primary signification of blackness. By emphasizing Celanta's goodness, the play acknowledges the traditional association of blackness with evil; Celanta's paradox is the paradox of the Song of Songs.

The faithful Moorish waiting-woman Kate in Beaumont and Fletcher's *Monsieur Thomas* (1615) finds herself the butt of a joke that relies heavily on traditional attitudes toward blacks and blackness for its humor. While asleep in her mistress Mary's bed, Kate is mistaken for Mary by Thomas, a would-be lover who thinks that he is revealing to Mary his passion for her. When he learns that Kate and not Mary sleeps in the bed, he abuses the Moor mightily: "Holy saints, defend me. / The devill, devill, devill, devill, O the devill."[61]

Kate, guilty of no crime greater than participating in her mistress' plan to humiliate Thomas, is rewarded for her abuse by a promise of a "new Petticoate" from her mistress. Mary's warm language shows Kate's faithfulness and a friendly relationship between the two. Yet in spite of Mary's kindness, the play exploits traditional notions of black women. It is, after all, Kate's blackness and strongly implied ugliness that move Thomas to horror and the audience, presumably, to laughter. Nor does the play treat this scene ironically. Kate's blackness suits her for the role of the devil in which Thomas unwittingly casts her. An audience in 1610 may have been as surprised by Kate's virtue as Thomas is by her face. Perhaps too Thomas' failure with Kate reveals him to be an even more laughable Lothario than the foolish figure he already presents, dressed as he is in his sister's clothes. (To humiliate Thomas further, he is told to disguise himself as a woman so that he may gain entrance to Mary's room more easily.) What is certain, however, is that Kate is as much a butt of the joke as is Thomas, and the petticoat offers small recompense for the loss of dignity she so calmly endures. Though neither treacherous nor venereous, Kate's portrayal retains enough of the stereotypical features of black women characters to make her recognizable as a gentler, nonthreatening Zanthia type.

61. Beaumont and Fletcher, *Monsieur Thomas*, in *The Dramatic Works of the Beaumont and Fletcher Canon*, ed. Fredson Bowers, (Cambridge, 1979), Vol. IV, V, v, 30–31.

The Moorish maid to Margaretta in *All's Lost by Lust* also belongs to the Zanthia type. Named Fydella, she proves her faithfulness through evil when she assists her mistress Margaretta in murdering a man Margaretta believes to be her husband. Though primarily an accomplice in the crime, Fydella never shrinks from encouraging Margaretta to revenge. Before the deed, Fydella counsels Margaretta to villainy by first reminding her distressed mistress of her husband's unfaithfulness, and then by urging her to dissemble:

> . . . know hees open,
> Plaine, and rusticall, and altered from his first condition,
> What ever your purpose is, let it not appeare to him. (III, ii, 17-20)

Immediately before Margaretta murders the man, Fydella again offers similar wicked counsel: "If I might counsell you, I would conceale it: / If you can fly, due not betray your self" (IV, ii, 45-46). Yet, in spite of all her ill-advice, Fydella does demonstrate remarkable and, for a black woman, uncharacteristic loyalty and fidelity to her mistress. When Margaretta asks, "Thou louest me Fydella," Fydella woundedly responds, "Do you make a question ont Lady?" (III, ii, 78-79). Fydella, however, quickly assures Margaretta of her devotion, saying, "To my second life Madam" (III, ii, 83).

Superficially, Fydella seems appropriately named as she proves herself loyal to her mistress. Yet the name is not wholly without irony, for in proving her fidelity to Margaretta, Fydella proves faithful to the stereotype of the malevolent Moor. In fact, one may ask to what is Fydella really faithful, her mistress or her type? The general state of faithlessness that pervades *All's Lost* augments the irony of Fydella's name. Infidelity exists on all levels of this society: Margaretta's husband commits bigamy, the Spanish king rape, Julianus treason, and Mulymumen all manner of crimes. Only Jacinta remains truly faithful to herself and to her king and religion. It seems as though fidelity itself, like its namesake in the play, is blackened, the maid serving as an emblem of the virtue's tainted condition. And Fydella's image is tainted by more than her ill counsel; she is also touched by the evil deeds of Mulymumen. His bloody crimes he proclaims to be but the first fruits of Moorish rule in Spain:

> . . . take hence their bodies[62]
> Give them to Christians, and let them bestow
> What ceremonious funerals they please.
> We must pursue the flying Rodorique.
> All must be ours, weele have no Kingdome sharer,
> Let Chroniclers write, here we begin our reigne,
> The first of Moores that ere was King of Spaine. (V, v, 198–204)

Whatever small acclaim she may win for her faithfulness, Fydella cannot resist the damaging effects that reverberate from Mulymumen's and her own words and deeds.

Black women, even when they are not posing a general threat to the community, seem never to be wholly free of the taint of the powerful and enduring stereotype of the black, malevolent meretrix. Celanta, Kate, and Fydella all retain some of the features that define black women on the sixteenth- and seventeenth-century stage. Tempered by some virtue, they nonetheless remain closer to the more notorious and more common type than distant from it, and while on the stage, these deviations from the stereotype serve as constant reminders of the absent Zanthias and raise in the audience expectations of greater though unrealized villainies. Nor did these three more ambiguously drawn women offer much competition to the real Zanthias for control of the stage. Of these plays, only *Monsieur Thomas* was somewhat successful, but never as successful as either *The White Devil* or *The Knight of Malta*. On the English stage, when black women are concerned, evil clearly triumphs.

Before concluding this chapter, a final variation of the type of the villainous Moor must be discussed. In five plays, *The White Devil*, *The Devil's Law-Case*, *The Parliament of Love*, *The Lost Lady*, and *The English Moor*, a white character blackens his or, more frequently, her face and pretends to be a black Moor.[63] Although none

---

62. The bodies on the stage at this point include those of Julianus, Jacinta, Margaretta, Lazarello, Antonio, and Dionysia. Mulymumen did not have a hand in all their deaths, but they all seem to be regarded as his victims in this scene.

63. The villainous Governor of Ternata in Beaumont and Fletcher's *The Island Princess* disguises himself "like a Moor-Priest" (*The Works of Francis Beaumont and John Fletcher*, Vol. VIII, IV, i, p. 141). Tokson includes the governor in his list of black characters and those disguised as blacks; however, no textual evidence exists to prove the governor a black Moor. I think that *Moor* is used here synony-

of these characters disguises herself with malicious intent, the plays rely on the traditional prejudices toward and apprehensions about black people for thematic and dramatic reasons. The earliest of these plays is *The White Devil*, in which Francisco, the duke of Florence, masks himself in order to unmask the true villains of the play. As stated above, Francisco's black face provides him with immediate access to the secrets of the villainous Bracciano faction. Flamineo, Bracciano, Vittoria, and Zanthia suppose Francisco's blackness to be a sign of his villainy and unhesitantly reveal to him their most horrible crimes. By dissembling blackness, Francisco has entrée into a confraternity of dissemblers. When he unmasks himself and reveals his true virtue, he unmasks the villains and exposes their spiritual darkness.

Interestingly, *The White Devil* is the only one of these plays in which a man disguises himself as a Moor. In the others, a woman duns herself, ironically, hoping to remain spotless and pure as she clears her sullied honor. This motif receives its most succinct treatment in Webster's *The Devil's Law-Case* (1617?). The heroine Jolenta, in order to help her brother, pretends to have had a child out of wedlock; the child's mother, however, is the perjured nun Angiolella. Jolenta, painting herself black to escape a trial, adopts the livery of evil that all assume she has earned. Before the court, her identity still obscured, she receives the customary abuse for being a "black one" (V, vi, 33). In response Jolenta challenges her judges and abusers:

> Like or dislike me, choose you whether:
> The down upon the raven's feather

---

mously with *Indian* and *Muslim*, and that the priest is dressed in feathers and beads and other conventional "Indian" garb. Several reasons lead me to this conclusion; the first is the play's setting, which is identified as a group of islands in "India." In Act V, the governor is vilified as a "damn'd Priest," a "cruel man," and a "false knave" (Vol. III, V, i, p. 166). He is personally associated with "Mahumet" and the perversion of religion. "Thou hast made the gods hard too, / Against their sweet and patient natures, cruel," the heroine tells him as she embraces Christianity (Vol. VIII, V, i, p. 161). Yet through all this condemnation, no one ever calls him black. This is highly unusual, and in the context of the play, it seems unlikely, if he were in fact black. Also the stage directions at his unmasking read: "[Pyniero] Pulls his [the governor's] Beard and hair off." Were he also in blackface, that too would probably have been mentioned. *The Island Princess* is more fully discussed in Chap. VI.

> Is as gentle and as sleek
> As the mole on Venus' cheek.
> Hence, vain show! I only care
> To preserve my soul most fair;
> Never mind the outward skin,
> But the jewel that's within;
> And though I want the crimson blood,
> Angels boast my sisterhood.
> Which of us now judge you whiter,[64]
> Her whose credit proves the lighter,
> Or this black and ebon hue,
> That, unstain'd, keeps fresh and true?
> For I proclaim't without control,
> There's no true beauty but i'th'soul.[65]

Recognizing Jolenta's wisdom is as indisputable as her honor, the judges proclaim her fair.

The same dramatic device is used by Philip Massinger in *The Parliament of Love* (1624). In this play, Beaupre, the spurned and abused wife of Clarindor, paints herself black in an effort to protect her honor.[66] Once in blackface, Beaupre enters the service of the virtuous Belliscant who, upon learning Beaupre's story, promises to restore the abused wife to her husband. Of course, while in blackface Beaupre receives the kind of treatment meted out to Moorish women. Her husband, desirous of Belliscant, proceeds along a path often traveled by lechers; he first attempts to win the maid as a way to the mistress. Obviously believing the myth that Moorish women are easily debauched, Clarindor flatters his disguised wife first with money, then with promises of sexual favors:

---

64. Jolenta, in blackface, compares herself to the white but deflowered Angiolella.

65. John Webster, *The Devil's Law-Case*, ed. Frances A. Shirley (Lincoln, Neb., 1972), V, vi, 34–49.

66. Not published until the twentieth century, *The Parliament of Love* exists in a single, incomplete, and severely damaged manuscript. It is possible to determine neither exactly how much of Act I is missing nor what occurred in those missing scenes. For these reasons, we do not know exactly what occurs between Beaupre and Clarindor. (See Philip Edwards and Colin Gibson, "Introduction to *The Parliament of Love*," in Edwards and Gibson (eds.), *The Plays and Poems of Philip Massinger* [Oxford, 1976], II, 98.)

> I am serious,
> The curtains drawne and envious light putt out
> The soft tuch hightens appetite, and takes more
> Then culler, Venus dressinge in the daie tyme,
> But never thought on in her midnight revells.
> Come, I must have thee myne. (II, iii, 11-16)

Clarindor's offer is far from complimentary, for he assures the blackfaced Beaupre that in the dark her apparent ugliness will be hidden. She resists these advances, however, and remains virtuous; she is, after all, really not a Moor.

By proving a loyal servant to Belliscant, Beaupre again behaves unlike a Moor. In fact, Beaupre, rather than betray her mistress, betrays her husband. She encourages Belliscant to be chaste and actively aids her in resisting Clarindor's advances. For her chastity and loyalty, Beaupre is finally able to unmask herself and to be restored to her husband who "receauve[s] her and aske[s] pardon / Of her" (V, i, 474-75). By proving herself not to be what she seems, Beaupre earns the respect that is her due.

This motif is found again, though in a somewhat more complex manner than in these two earlier plays, in William Berkeley's *The Lost Lady* (1638). Milesia, the play's heroine, puts on blackface to escape her uncle, who violently opposes her marriage to Lysicles. Presumed dead, Milesia pretends to be a famous necromancer. While in this disguise, she hears that Lysicles plans to marry her friend Hermione. Though no such betrothal exists, the jealous Milesia plots revenge against her supposedly unfaithful lover and friend. However, while disguised Milesia learns what happens to Moors. First, she learns that her blackness excludes her from the company of the virtuous. Regardless of her actions, she remains constantly suspect, her color denying her natural innocence and goodness. Hermione implies this when she comments on Milesia's virtue:

> Where cannot vertue dwell: what a stil shade
> Hath she [virtue] found out to live securely in
> From the attempts of men? [67]

---

67. William Berkeley, *The Lost Lady* (London, 1638), III, i, p. 28.

Hermione's comment, of course, reveals both contempt for Milesia and envy. Her virtue is thought secure, not because she is strong but rather because she is ugly and beyond desire.

Ironically, the blackness that Hermione and Milesia herself believe will protect her from sexual advances provokes only the opposite response. The lecherous prove their depravity by desiring the undesirable. One character, Phormio, hopes to gain a reputation for virility by satisfying the allegedly insatiable black woman. However, his persistent advances Milesia resists with equal persistence. Yet, his attempts on her virtue reveal both his contempt as well as his sexual desire for Milesia. He couches his initial interest in terms of contempt: "I have a strange Capriccio of love enter'd me: / I must Court that shade" (III, i, p. 32). When Milesia struggles to free herself from his grasp, he boldly chides her: "In the name of darknesse, d'ee thinke I am not / In earnest, that you coy it thus?" (III, i, p. 32). Phormio, when advised later by a friend to kiss the Moor to make her more responsive, responds not so surprisingly: "Not for five hundred Crownes" (III, i, p. 32). He would, however, lie with her to enhance his sexual reputation, so he tells his friend:

> . . . when this act is knowne, this resolute
> Incounter, rich widdowes of threescore will
> Not doubt my prowesse. (III, ii, p. 33)

This remarkable acknowledgment of sexual myths about Moors also reveals the degradation that Milesia must endure so long as she retains her disguise. As an object of desire and contempt, she is constantly in danger, a danger that also exists so long as she remains disguised.

Ultimately, Milesia imperils her very life by remaining obscured too long. This mortal peril she brings on herself when she advises Lysicles to go to his beloved's—that is, Milesia's—grave. There, Milesia pretends to be her own ghost, but unfortunately for her, she enjoys excessively her role as *eiron* and while dissembling, indicts herself by praising the forbidden powers of the Moor:

> All that I ever did shee's conscious of,
> And jealous of your love unto Hermione,
> Did place me here, to search into your thoughts,

> And now is prouder of this discovery
> Than if a Crowne were added to her. (IV, i, p. 36)

Hearing this, Lysicles rails against the Moor and necromancy, and vows vengeance, which he gets shortly thereafter by poisoning the Moor. And without the slightest remorse, Lysicles says of the dying woman:

> . . . nor should you pitty her.
> Those that doe trace forbidden paths of knowledge
> The gods reserve unto themselves, doe never doo't,
> But with intent to ruine the beleevers,
> And venders on their Art.
> . . . .
> I am confident she is fled her Country
> For the ills she has done there, and now
> The punishment has overta'ne her here:
> And for her shewes of Vertue, they are Masks
> To hide the rottennesse that lyes within,
> And gaine her credit with some dissembled acts
> Of piety, which levells her a passage
> To those important mischiefes, Hell
> Has imploy'd her here to execute. (V, i, p. 42)

Only when the black is removed from Milesia's face does Lysicles relent, and then only because he knows that what he has said is not possible. Milesia is neither necromancer nor black. In sorrow, a friend of the dying woman suggests to Lysicles:

> . . . the opinions which prejudice
> Her vertue, should thus be wash't away with
> Blacke clouds that hide her purer forme. (V, i, p. 43)

The opinions that prejudice her virtue are but the common responses to the black on her face. And the blackness continues to feed the prejudice and make possible Lysicles' spiritual and physical attacks and Phormio's sexual attack. Once unmasked, however, Milesia's whiteness redeems both her reputation and her life. The apothecary who provided the poison produces an antidote. She and Lysicles then exchange vows of undying love. Yet Milesia pays a dear price for her blackness. Only after Lysicles recognizes that he has misjudged—in fact, prejudged—her does she escape with her life. He was pleased to watch the Moor die. Of course, the playwright fails to recognize this final irony about *his* opinion of black women. The play serves as a warning to the virtuous woman to stay clear of danger, to never seem to be other than what she is—a discrepancy she might find perilous.

Richard Brome's *The English Moor* (1630?) exploits the same myths about black women and the same paradox of desire and revulsion. In this play, Millicent, angered by her new husband's lack of trust, determines to prove that her honor is hers to maintain. To demonstrate that neither husband nor gallant can tempt her virtue, she vows to remain a virgin for a month. Her husband, a usurer named Quicksand, agrees, with the condition that she disguise herself as a Moor during that time. He reasons:

> Now this [blackening] shall both
> Kill vain attempts in me, and guard you safe
> From all that seek subversion of your honour.
> Ile fear no powder'd spirits to haunt my house,
> Rose-footed fiends; or fumigated Goblins
> After this tincture's laid upon thy face,
> 'Twil cool their kindness and allay their hearts.[68]

Of course, while in black face the opposite happens; Millicent must, in fact, repulse the advances of Nathaniel, the gallant who deflowered her friend, Phyllis. And of course Nathaniel courts Millicent in the customary and abusive manner used with black women. Finding her both physically desirable and repulsive, he professes his interest to her, and then tells a fellow gallant: "This Devels bird, / This *Moor* runs more and more still in my mind" (IV, iv, p. 62). However great his disgust, his desire remains greater. Millicent, however, turns Nathaniel's libidinousness against him, and during an elaborate masque devised by her husband, she substitutes Phyllis for herself so that Phyllis can entrap Nathaniel and force him to marry her. With all but Phyllis unaware of the substitution, Millicent seizes the opportunity to escape unnoticed to find Theophilus, her beloved.

The masque that Quicksand produces is designed both to humiliate the gallants who earlier abused him and to proclaim his

---

68. Richard Brome, *The English Moor, or the Mock Marriage*, in *The Dramatic Works of Richard Brome* (London, 1873), Vol. II, III, i, p. 37.

triumphant possession of Millicent. Derived directly from Jonson's *The Masque of Blackness* and *Gypsies Metamorphosed*, Quicksand's "Masque of Moors" tells of the daughter of a black queen who comes to England to find a white husband. Once married to an Englishman, the damsel "should be white as he" (IV, v, p. 66). The inductor of the masque, after reading the palms of all the gallants, finds only Quicksand to be "the worthy man, whose wealth and wit, / To make a white one, must the black mark hit" (IV, v, p. 66). This domestic version of Jonson's masque only accomplishes half of its producer's goals. Indeed the perfumed gentlemen are humbled, but Quicksand cannot claim Millicent's hand. His masque stars not his spotless and chaste Millicent but the defiled Phyllis, who more fittingly becomes the role, her fame as spotted as her face. Indeed Phyllis lives the role she plays because only an "honest" marriage to an Englishman, specifically Nathaniel, can unblacken her reputation. Paradoxically, to gain a husband for herself and to regain her honor, Phyllis, while she remains blackened, must again commit that sin that darkens her name. For Millicent to lend herself to this spectacle, she must proclaim herself spotted too; something she cannot do since she knows, as do Niger's daughters, the meaning of blackness:

> This is the face
> On which the Hell of jealousie abus'd
> The hand of Heaven, to fright the world withall. (IV, iv, p. 64)[69]

Millicent must escape this public defilement as surely as she must escape Quicksand and Nathaniel.

When the unmasking finally occurs, it proves more extensive than Quicksand intends or wishes. Quicksand himself is unmasked as a fool, a usurer, a lecher, and, so he supposes, as a cuckold, the thing he so entirely dreads. Defeated, he pleads for a divorce, renouncing all claims to Millicent. Nathaniel is revealed to be a debaucher and is forced to marry Phyllis. Like the black women

---

69. One wonders whether Brome is commenting on his former mentor's masque here. Quicksand speaks in favor of the *Masque of Blackness*, saying: "even Queens themselves / Have, for the glory of a nights presentment / To grace the work, suffered as much as this" (III, i, p. 38). But then again Quicksand is a fool, and we believe nothing that he says. Perhaps Brome held an opinion closer to Dudley's than to Jonson's on this subject.

in the masque, Phyllis and Millicent, once honestly betrothed, remove their blackface and reveal themselves to be the white women they are. Once the blackness is removed, so is any stigma of unchastity or harlotry. This is particularly true for Phyllis who redeems her reputation through marriage.

Neither *The English Moor* nor any of these other plays, save *The White Devil*, was very popular; of the five, only *The White Devil* and *The Lost Lady* were revived in the Restoration. Their value in this study lies not so much in how they helped to propagate the image of blacks as lustful villains but rather as demonstrations of how that perception of blacks permeates all levels of dramatic representation. It is important to remember that the crisis in each of these plays takes shape around a threat to chastity and honor. Blackness is an ironic signifier that foreshadows what will occur if virtue is lost. Racial issues are at best secondary to the greater issue of female virtue. When a character blackens his or her face, that character and the play itself accepts unquestioningly certain widely shared assumptions about the nature and signification of blackness. As clearly as transvestism acknowledges various sexual roles and the power or weakness associated with those roles, so do other forms of disguising. When Portia in *The Merchant of Venice* dresses as a man, she acquires the social power that men were believed to possess; when Falstaff in *The Merry Wives of Windsor* dresses as a woman, the costume unmans him. Disguises serve symbolic functions as actively as they do dramatic. Because blackness itself is an overdetermined symbol, the character who disguises himself as black brings into the play all the various meanings that blackness itself conveys. Included among these various significations are those that are prominent in the nonmimetic and nondramatic genres we have examined earlier. Otherness, exclusion from the community, duplicity, servitude, danger, and physical and spiritual ugliness are all potentially present in the disguise. In the case of these plays, the disguised use these significations benignly and frequently pervert them to use them magnanimously. But always and unquestionably the blackened character acts antithetically to the generally received nature of blackness and in accord with his true—that is, white Christian—nature.

Of all the alleged truths about black men and women, the sexual myths and the allied threats receive general endorsement in these plays. In each, sexual crimes and the desire to escape or uncover them induce the characters to disguise themselves as black. In *The White Devil*, Francisco must uncover the crimes that are committed by the debauched. Ironically, as Francisco seeks to uncover the sin of fornication, he is tempted, but because he is not really a Moor, he can turn lust against itself, though first he must personally experience the fabled uncontrollable lust of a black woman and act the Moor's venereous part. Like the real Moors, Francisco links himself sexually to the confraternity of sinners; he then destroys it. This irony points out the real threat of real Moors.

There is a double irony involved with the women who disguise themselves as black, each of whom paints herself black with the hope that she will be so ugly that no man will make sexual advances. Motivated by a personal sexual crisis, each woman chooses to hide herself until she finds safety in a legal, community-sanctioned marriage. Thus, while wearing the color of sin, she masquerades as unchaste to protect herself from becoming what in disguise she seems to be. Yet she discovers that her blackness does not deter temptation but rather prompts it. The disguised maiden finds not relief but only greater problems, all sexual.

Of course, what is ironic in the dramatic situation of the women proves paradoxical from a larger perspective. Not one of these plays attempts to contradict the general opinion that black women are physically unattractive. Even when a gallant such as Nathaniel finds the Moor unusually attractive, he acknowledges both the universal ugliness of Moors and the specific ugliness of that particular one. No matter how strong his desire, the seducer's language always remains abusive and the Moor essentially repulsive. This paradox helps us to understand why the Zanthia type is viewed as threatening. How can someone be simultaneously repulsive and desirable? Although we approach the problem with greater sophistication, the answer to this question remains, in the end, as elusive for us as it was for the seventeenth-century audience and playwright. But the paradox finds resolution every time some white man succumbs to desire and reveals that the attractiveness of black women exceeds the accumulated disparagements promoted and cherished by the white culture. And in these plays, the man is most truly culpable because the women, unlike the Zanthias, repulse the sexual advances. Male weakness stands out in stark relief against a background of beleaguered virtue. When we recognize this, we see more clearly the danger that black women present to the community. Although white men may recast the virtues and attractions of black women, these same men do not always prove themselves successful at controlling their own libidinousness, affections, and desires.

This discussion of disguised Moors provides a useful transition point. Having observed the basic stereotypical characteristics of the Moor manipulated so that they might be used for good, we must now examine how these same features are employed and altered in the characterization of honest Moors.

V

Ethiops Washed White
Moors of the Nonvillainous Type

> I kiss the instrument of their pleasures.
> —William Shakespeare, *Othello*

During the seventeenth century, a few black characters appeared on the stage who, against their nature and kind, demonstrated that virtue stood not completely out of their reach. However, like their female counterparts, these virtuous few are clearly derived from the more commonly represented stereotype of the villainous Moor and are, more accurately, versions of that type rather than absolute departures from it. By demonstrating virtue, these few honest Moors offer further validation of the more common, harmful, and denigrating representations of black Moors because they prove that it is possible to resist the call of evil, though most unusual.

The earliest nonvillainous Moors to appear on the stage were Morocco in Shakespeare's *The Merchant of Venice* (1596) and Porus in Chapman's *The Blind Beggar of Alexandria* (1596).[1]

---

1. Another character, Alcade, the King of Africa, in *The Thracian Wonder* (1599), may be relevant here; however, I am uncertain that he is black. Tokson holds the opposite opinion; he writes that it "is quite clear that King Alcade is dark skinned" (93). He bases his judgment on Alcade's comment that in Europe "Men have livers there / Pale as their faces" (*The Thracian Wonder*, in *The Works of John Webster*, ed. Alexander Dyce [London, 1830], Vol. IV, III, iii, 209). This, however, could be a reference not to blackness but to sun exposure, much like

Morocco, by far the more interesting of the two, comes to Belmont to participate in the lottery for Portia's hand. In the two brief scenes in which he appears, he evokes from the play's heroine only ironic contempt. Her relief at the departure of the vanquished suitor reveals her disdain for him: "A gentle riddance / Let all of his complexion choose me so" (II, vii, 78-79).[2] Perhaps Portia means more than skin color by "complexion" here, yet because Morocco is identified as a "Tawny Moor," her choice of words intends to call some attention to his color. But more than Morocco's complexion casts an unfavorable light on him. His long speech before the caskets undermines any dignity he may have possessed, and his choice of the wrong casket proves him foolish.

Cleopatra's: "Think on me, / That am with Phoebus' amorous pinches black" (Shakespeare, *Antony and Cleopatra*, I, v, 27-28). Tokson also sees a reference to Alcade's daughter as a "white Moore" (V, ii, 249 and 250), as further corroborative evidence for his opinion. While we do know for certain that the daughter is white, I believe her whiteness raises questions about Alcade's supposed blackness rather than solutions. In a few medieval romances some black parents do miraculously have white offspring. (See Heliodorus, *An Aethiopian History*, Book IV.) Could Alcade be from this tradition? Although it is possible, I have been unable to locate an example in drama. A dramatization of *An Aethiopian History* entitled *The White Aethiopian* (1650?) exists in manuscript, but there is no record of performance. Alcade and his daughter seem to be more closely related to the King of Africa and his daughter, Angelica, in Greene's dramatization of *Orlando Furioso*, first published in 1594 and then again in 1599. Alcade also makes a rather curious statement that adds to my uncertainty. When he first appears in the play, he says to Sophos and Eusanius, the real heroes of the play: "In Africa, the Moors are only known, / And never yet search'd part of Christendom; / Nor do we levy arms against their religion, / But like a prince, a royal justicer, / To patron right and supplant tyranny" (III, iii, p. 204). Is Alcade claiming to be other than a Moor? If so, does he mean he is not a Muslim, or not black or neither? We have no way of knowing. Finally, many other white Africans exist in dramatic literature, most notably in plays about Rome and Carthage. It seems to me more likely that Alcade belongs to this tradition. My uncertainty about him, however, requires that he remain outside of this discussion.

2. It is difficult to say how dark Morocco really is. The stage direction at the start of Act II, scene i, reads: "Enter Morocco, a tawny Moor all in white." *Tawny* offers its own difficulties because Shakespeare uses it synonymously with *black* in *Titus Andronicus*. (In Act V, Aaron calls his son, who several times earlier is called black, a "tawny slave" [V, i, 27].) Morocco himself speaks of his complexion in figurative language that fails to provide accurate information. I am inclined to believe that Morocco is fully black, primarily because of the visual contrast his black skin would make with the white and presumably exotic clothes.

Morocco also presents an obvious and unwelcome sexual threat to Portia, and he makes known his desire for her before he chooses:

> "Who chooseth me shall gain what many men desire."
> Why that's the lady! All the world desires her;
> From the four corners of the earth they came
> To kiss this shrine, this mortal breathing saint. (II, vii, 37-40)

Only by leaving immediately and quietly does Morocco maintain any honor or dignity, as his earlier professions of valor are forgotten by the relieved mistress of Belmont.

Porus, the King of Ethiopia, fares better in love than does Morocco, but the circumstances surrounding his triumph with the Lady Elimine deny him a totally honorable victory. Present only in the last scene of *The Blind Beggar*, Porus comes to offer obeisance and tribute to his conqueror, Cleanthes. While there, the humbled Porus sees Elimine, who has come to plead for assistance from Cleanthes. She and her child have been deserted by Count Hermes, who, unknown to Elimine, is really Cleanthes disguised. Porus proclaims his love for Elimine as does the defeated King of Bebritia, Bebritius. Allowed by Cleanthes to choose a spouse from among the several defeated kings, Elimine chooses Porus. She chooses him, however, not out of love but to highlight her perverse fortunes:

> In my eye, now, the blackest is the fairest,
> For every woman chooseth the white and red.
> Come, martial Porus, thou shalt have my love.[3]

Elimine invokes here the paradoxical "Fair is foul, and foul is fair," and by choosing with this in mind, she expresses both her expectations and her hopes. She expects Porus to be foul; she only hopes that he proves to be fair. Bebritius, angered by his rejection, reminds Elimine of the traditional and, of course, seemingly more reasonable expectation: "Out on thee, foolish woman, thou hast chose a devil" (x, 164). By focusing on the risks involved in marrying a black man, both Elimine and Bebritius do much to disparage further the already humbled Porus, who cannot escape the

---

3. George Chapman, *The Blind Beggar of Alexandria* in *The Plays of George Chapman: The Comedies*, ed. Thomas Marc Parrott (New York, 1961), Vol. I, scene x, ll. 161-63.

traditional prejudice toward blackness and black men. However, because the play ends just fifteen lines after Elimine chooses, we have no way of knowing if she chooses wisely when she ignores the widely known risks.

Bebritius' comment, though, points out how every representation of a black person necessarily remains colored by his blackness. The conqueror Cleanthes may freely allow the vanquished Porus to marry a cast-off, former mistress; however, the conquered and again defeated Bebritius sees the danger. Portia too sees the danger, but she luckily escapes. It is important to note that in both these plays the danger is sexual and consequently social. Neither Morocco nor Porus commits any crime other than seeking to marry a white woman, but it is this ambition that brings down upon them racial abuse. No matter how innocent or noble, black men, once they attempt to involve themselves sexually with white women, become personae non gratae in the community. And we see in the similarity between these two minor characters how closely related vilification and villainy are to the fear raised by incursions into the community.

It is such an incursion by the valiant Moor Othello that first alarms Venice and later provides Iago with an exploitable situation on which to build his diabolic plot. It is this same sexual relationship that ultimately leads to Othello's and Desdemona's undoing. However, in *Othello* (1604), Shakespeare manipulates the stereotype of the Moor and, consequently, the expectations of the audience. In so doing, he animated for the stage possibly the most popular and important representation of a black man until the twentieth century. On the most obvious level, Shakespeare reassigns roles in what could be a rather conventional secular psychomachia. Rather than playing the villain, a role that should be Othello's by dramatic convention and popular tradition alike, the valiant Moor becomes the center of the psychomachiac struggle between good and evil. Shakespeare alters things further by redistributing in a somewhat startling manner various aspects of the stereotypical Moor among the principal characters, each in some way becoming what Othello alone ought to be. The audience, as it becomes more and more uncomfortable with the reassignment of roles and characteristics, finds itself finally forced to reevaluate the validity of interpreting real life through allegory.

No feature has proven more important in characterizing blacks than the traditional belief in their venery, and as we have seen, in all but the two Alcazar plays, villainy finds expression in sexual desires or intrigues. In *Othello*, frank and unencumbered sexual desire is not confined to the villains; rather, it is distributed among most of the major characters including Othello, Desdemona, Emilia, Cassio, and, of course, Iago and Rodrigo. But the sexual interplay between the three principals, Othello, Desdemona, and Iago, defuses the sexual center of the play away from its expected and traditional location, the Moor, and focuses instead on two rather distinct and antithetical views of sex.

That Iago rather than Othello is obsessed with sex is startling because sex is conventionally the black man's preoccupation. In some ways, Iago's obsession helps to explain why it is blacks who are represented as lascivious and sex-obsessed, for Iago never ceases to project onto others his own overriding sexual interests as he reveals his own sexual anxieties. But we know it is Iago who is so obsessed, not Othello. Iago seizes every opportunity to incite others to accept the traditional view of the Moor as lecherous, and as licentious any woman who could love such a man. But the obscenities Iago shouts under Brabantio's window reveal more about himself than anyone else. In his soliloquy at the end of Act I, Iago again lingers on sexual themes, exposing the prurience of his mind as well as his sexual anxiety. A similar soliloquy in Act II reveals Iago to be almost monomaniacal:

> That Cassio loves her [Desdemona], I do well believe it;
> That she loves him, 'tis apt and of great credit.
> . . . now I do love her too,
> Not out of absolute lust, (though peradventure
> I stand accountant for as great a sin)
> But partly led to diet my revenge,
> For that I do suspect the lustful Moor
> Hath leaped into my seat.[4]

Iago returns again and again to his own prurient musings, obses-

---

4. William Shakespeare, *Othello*, ed. M. R. Ridley (New York, 1958), II, i, 281-82, 286-91. Throughout my discussion of *Othello*, I quote from this Arden Shakespeare edition of the play because it, unlike many other editions, is based on the text of the first quarto of 1622.

sions, and anxieties to feed his plot, and finally he succeeds in engendering in Othello's mind a similar obsessiveness and anxiety.

On the opposing side in the battle for Othello's mind and soul stands Desdemona, the loving wife who offers her beleaguered husband redemption. But Desdemona is no innocent virtue; though chaste, she frankly acknowledges to the duke, her father, and the assembled lords of Venice her total devotion to her husband. "My heart's subdued / Even to the utmost pleasure of my lord" (I, iii, 250-51), she tells them.[5] When she later asks permission to accompany Othello to Cyprus, she again openly expresses her sexual desire for her husband:

> . . . if I be left behind,
> A moth of peace, and he go to the war,
> The rites for which I love him are bereft me,
> And I a heavy interim shall support,
> By his dear absence. (I, iii, 255-59)

In so unlikely a place as Desdemona's embrace Shakespeare places for Othello safety from sin, temptation, and, ultimately, damnation.

Uncomfortably set between these odd permutations of lust and chastity stands Othello. Perversely for him, lust demands abstinence while chastity and salvation require entering Desdemona's embrace. When Othello refuses Desdemona's final invitation to her bed, he rejects virtue and chooses evil. By opposing honest sexual desire to obsessive prurience and sexual manipulation, Shakespeare disperses and relocates these sexual and dramatic tensions away from one of their traditional sources, the Moor. In *Othello*, the Moor comes to be uniquely motivated, not by the usual desire for sexual gratification and power but by all-consuming sexual anxiety.

Othello most powerfully and explicitly articulates his anxiety when he assures the signory of Venice that he wishes Desdemona to join him for reasons other than sexual gratification. In his request for permission to take his wife to Cyprus, Othello employs a rhetoric of negation:

---

5. A variant reading found in the 1623 folio has Desdemona saying here: "My heart's subdued / Even to the very quality of my lord" (I, iii, 245-46).

> Your voices, Lords: beseech you, let her will
> Have a free way; I therefore beg it not
> To please the palate of my appetite,
> Not to comply with heat, the young affects
> In me defunct, and proper satisfaction,
> But to be free and bounteous to her mind;
> And heaven defend your good souls that you think
> I will your serious and great business scant,
> When she is with me; . . . no, when light-wing'd toys
> Of feather'd Cupid, foils with wanton dullness
> My speculative and active instruments,
> That my disports corrupt and taint my business,
> Let housewives make a skillet of my helm,
> And all indign and base adversities
> Make head against my reputation! (I, iii, 260-74)

Speaking here, just after Desdemona's rather frank avowal of her sexual desire, Othello attempts to diminish the impact of his wife's argument. However, Othello goes so far as to deny himself even the desire of "proper satisfaction," a phrase that jars against Desdemona's request for the "rites for why I love him."[6] Whereas Othello will later incorrectly choose abstinence and, paradoxically, damnation to defend his honor, here he chooses abstinence to prove his manhood.

Of course, Othello's sexual anxiety is an intrinsic component of his larger fear of being a stereotypical stage Moor, and his attempt to deny his interest in "proper satisfaction" is an attempt to deny his kinship to his immediate predecessors Aaron and Eleazar. Characterized by their lechery and villainy, Aaron and Eleazar achieve power and overmaster their masters through a display of real sexual power. Aaron cuckolds the emperor; Eleazar whores the king's mother and "boys" the king. Othello seeks no such power

---

6. Although this line is frequently construed to refer to the "rites of war," I read it as meaning the "rites of love." (See *Romeo and Juliet*, III, ii, 8, and Ridley's note to this line.) In the line immediately following this, Desdemona says that during Othello's absence "I a heavy interim shall support." Shakespeare, as well as other Renaissance playwrights, frequently uses the figure of women bearing weight as a metaphor for coitus. It seems reasonable to assume that Desdemona speaks frankly and as a sexually mature adult.

over his masters, and though he retains real military power, he does not translate that power into a metaphor for sexual prowess. In fact, Othello humbly denies himself parity with the signory in terms that imply sexual and social submission. When he is accused of having "corrupted" Desdemona by "spells and medicines," Othello begins his defense by saying, "Most potent, grave and reverend signiors, / My very noble and approv'd good masters." He continues with his self-deprecation, saying, "Rude am I in my speech, / And little blest with the set phrase of peace" (I, iii, 76–77 and 81–82). Even in the most immediate circumstances of the play, Othello's humility seems excessive, but in contrast to his precursors, his behavior is remarkable. To imagine a typical stage Moor saying these words is but to witness him dissemble. However, Othello, unlike his predecessors, *sincerely* means what he says, as he demonstrates by his attempts to diminish whatever threat he may pose to the state. But his marriage itself compromises the state's security; he was called before the signory to begin defending Venice, not himself. And although Othello intensely wishes not to be a typical stage Moor, he finds himself in exactly that position. He is the black man who provokes a crisis by his sexual relationship with a white woman. He must, therefore, immediately and uncompromisingly identify his state of subservience and remain there; by so doing, he at least can assuage one fear and dismiss one threat. With that done, he is then free to move against the Turk, who is after all not a totally different sort of threat.

Yet in spite of his best efforts to the contrary, Othello cannot escape the role fated to Moors on the stage, and as he moves to free himself of the confines of the role, he moves inexorably closer to it. The irony of his fate finds no clearer emblem than Othello as dupe to the play's villain, the most atypical role in which Othello finds himself. And Iago's intentions as villain directly counter Othello's, for Iago wishes to ensnare Othello in the confines of the stereotype that Othello struggles so desperately to escape. As the playwright of Othello's demise, Iago directs Othello toward the traditional role of villainous Moor, toward making Othello fit the maxim that Iago himself will not fit: "Men should be that they seem, / Or those that be not, would they might seem none!" (III, iii, 130–31). By provoking Othello to jealousy, an attribute believed not uncommon to Moors and earlier witnessed in Eleazar, Iago achieves his goal.[7]

Othello, as Iago points out and as the audience would immediately recognize, has ample reason to be jealous of Cassio, for unlike himself, "Cassio's a proper man" (I, iii, 390). "A fourth eminent cause of jealousy may be this," Burton determines in *The Anatomy of Melancholy*: "when he that is deformed . . . will marry some fair nice piece . . . [he] begins to misdoubt (as well he may) she doth not affect him. . . . He that marries a wife that is snout-fair alone, let him look, saith Barbarus, for no better success than Vulcan had with Venus, or Claudius with Messalina."[8] Othello's blackness is deformity enough for Brabantio and Iago, and they both press this fact on Othello's mind as they remind him to be wary of his wife.

Once planted in Othello's mind, the seeds of jealousy take root quickly and swiftly bear fruit. Preoccupied with the alleged wantonness of his wife, the gullible and jealous man sees signs of guilty love everywhere:

> What sense had I of her stol'n hours of lust?
> I saw't not, thought it not, it harm'd not me,
> I slept the next night well, was free and merry;
> I found not Cassio's kisses on her lips. (III, iii, 344-47)

Othello's jealousy and the fear that it promotes, as well as his response to Iago's lies, precisely match Burton's description of the impotent man: "More particular causes [of jealousy] be these

---

7. Lois Whitney suggests in her article "Did Shakespeare Know 'Leo Africanus'?" that Shakespeare while writing *Othello* relied heavily on Pory's 1600 translation of Leo Africanus. On the subject of Othello's jealousy she writes: "In the matter of love, jealousy, and wrath Leo's characterization has a bearing also." (*PMLA*, XXXVII, 1922, p. 482.) See also Tokson, *Popular Image of the Black Man*, 17.

8. Burton also cites Leo as his source for "Incredible things almost of the lust and jealousy of his countrymen of Africa, and especially such as live about Carthage." Burton then points out that "every geographer of them [Moors] in Asia, Turkey, Spaniards, Italians," reports of the lust and jealousy of Moors. It should be noted that *The Anatomy of Melancholy* was not published until 1621, and hence could not have been known by Shakespeare. However, as a copious amalgamation of fact and lore, the book codifies opinions that were in currency long before its publication. Robert Burton, *The Anatomy of Melancholy*, ed. Holbrook Jackson (London, 1977), Part 3, pp. 264, 270-71.

which follow. Impotency first, when a man is not able of himself to perform those dues which he ought unto his wife: for though he be an honest liver, hurt no man . . . and therefore when he takes notice of his wants, and perceives her to be more craving, clamorous, insatiable and prone to lust than is fit, he begins presently to suspect, that wherein he is defective, she will satisfy herself, she will be pleased by some other means."[9]

The relationship between impotency and jealousy seems clear to Iago, who seizes upon the irony of Othello's steadfast denials of sexual interest and perverts them. Fixated and full of his own prurient musings, Othello now moves closer toward being the stereotypical Moor. But he is not consumed by lust and desire for gratification; instead, he fears that someone else performs his office. Nor does Iago let slip an opportunity to press this point home, until finally Othello is convinced that Cassio plays the role of lecher, the role Othello so steadfastly rejects. Once Othello, under Iago's direction, has cast Cassio in the role which by tradition should be his own, the tragic irony for Othello follows because he loses his sense of who he really is and begins to reclaim the role that he has rejected. Now maddened by jealousy, Othello, like his predecessors, becomes obsessed with sexual desire, but this time with Cassio's and Desdemona's rather than his own. From here Iago can easily persuade Othello to dissemble, yet another mark of all Moorish villains.

Othello himself records his fall to that previously rejected role in his comments on his own blackness. Although the allegory of blackness and its characteristic language surround him throughout the play (Iago uses it, as do Brabantio and the duke), when Othello succumbs, saying, "Haply, for I am black, / And have not those soft parts of conversation / That chamberers have," he identifies himself with the outsider his enemies have cast him as (III, iii, 267–68). He quickly completes his metamorphosis when he calls forth "black vengeance, from thy hollow cell" (III, iii, 454). (Here the folio reads "the hollow hell.") Calling down on himself the spiritual blackness of his theatrical forebears, Othello identifies himself finally with the devil.

9. Ibid., 266–67.

Ethiops Washed White

The success of Othello's transformation finds quick confirmation when those who knew and loved the former Othello fail to recognize him as the jealous, raging Moor. Emilia, Lodovico, and Desdemona all comment on the change in Othello and use a similar trope to express their confusion. Desdemona says of Othello: "My lord is not my lord, nor should I know him, / Were he in favour as in humour alter'd" (III, iv, 121-22). Lodovico, equally puzzled by Othello's behavior, asks: "Is this the noble Moor, whom our full Senate / Call all in all sufficient?" (IV, i, 260-61). Othello no longer seems to be Othello.

But the discrepancy between what Othello thinks he has become and what he has become tragically becomes clear to him only when it is too late. The role he attempts when he comes in to murder Desdemona is Justice, but Iago is much too good a stage director, for we recognize the Moor, finally, for what he is. Othello becomes the villain, reclaiming at that crucial moment over Desdemona's bed the role he has so long sought to avoid. And although there is a discrepancy between his perception of himself and the audience's perception of him, that distance collapses as Othello, welling with sexual desire, comments on Desdemona's beauty:

> It is the cause, it is the cause, my soul,
> Let me not name it to you, you chaste stars:
> It is the cause, yet I'll not shed her blood,
> Nor scar that whiter skin of hers than snow,
> And smooth, as monumental alabaster. (V, ii, 1-5)

Othello tries our sympathies for him even further when he bends over Desdemona's bed to kiss his doomed wife before he exacts his price:

> ... when I have plucked the rose,
> I cannot give it vital growth again,
> It must needs wither. I'll smell it on the tree,
> A balmy breath, that dost almost persuade
> Justice herself to break her sword: once more:
> Be thus, when thou art dead, and I will kill thee,
> And love thee after: once more, and this the last,
> So sweet was ne'er so fatal: I must weep,
> But they are cruel tears; this sorrow's heavenly,
> It strikes when it does love. (V, ii, 13-22)

Surely these are chilling moments for any audience as it watches the determined murderer linger over kisses stolen from the sleeping Desdemona. Each additional kiss calls to mind those other black Moors who sought to abuse other innocent women, for who can forget Othello's purpose for approaching Desdemona's bed? His final hint at necrophilia, and in this context Othello surely means physical love, captures the prurience of this scene. Othello's protestations of sorrow and love may be real, but his kisses are not kisses of tenderness or forgiveness. Were they, he would not, could not, reject Desdemona's offer of connubial love and, ironically, redemption.

When Othello finally discovers the disjunction between what he supposes he has done and what he actually has done, he learns his tragedy. And what exactly he learns is something that the audience has witnessed; he learns that the noble Moor, the adversary of a stereotype, has collapsed into that now victorious stereotype. When he sees this, the noble Moor calls down justice on the villainous:

> Whip me, you devils,
> From the possession of this heavenly sight,
> Blow me about in winds, roast me in sulfur,
> Wash me in steep-down gulfs of liquid fire! (V, ii, 278–81)

The Moor now condemns himself with the language commonly used to damn black fiends, as though he has assumed not only the role of the tormented but also of the tormentor, the damned and the damning.

In his final assault upon himself, Othello continues to apply to Othello the murderer the language and character of the typical Moor:

> . . . I pray you in your letters,
> When you shall these unlucky deeds relate,
> Speak of them as they are; nothing extenuate,
> Nor set down aught in malice; then must you speak
> Of one that lov'd not wisely, but too well:
> Of one not easily jealous, but being wrought,
> Perplex'd in the extreme; of one whose hand,
> Like the base Indian,[10] threw a pearl away,

---

10. The folio reads "Judean" here.

Ethiops Washed White

> Richer than all his tribe.
> . . . .
> And say besides, that in Aleppo once,
> Where a malignant and turban'd Turk
> Beat a Venetian and traduc'd the state,
> I took by the throat the circumcised dog
> And smote him thus. (V, ii, 341-49, 353-57)

Now fully cognizant of the discrepancy between what he thought himself to be and what he is, Othello speaks calmly of the man duped by the villain, of his honor and sense of being wronged. However, none of this extenuates his guilt. The "base Indian," the "circumcised dog," committed a crime, and Othello, who once served Venice well, executes justice for the state and finally merges his two roles. He is both villainous Moor and, at last, Justice. His ability to destroy one role by using the other helps win for him our sympathy.

Several other important factors contribute to eliciting a sympathetic response from us. Cast as the villain, and even having effected his and Iago's policy, Othello, however, is never fully and resolutely a villain; he lacks the love of evil that underlies the villain's every act. Othello is the misguided victim, as much sinned against as sinning, and this fact alone moves us to pity. This fact also points to the irony of Othello's tragedy; he falls victim to his own struggle. He struggles to destroy evil as he struggles to escape the identity of a Moor. But he escapes neither and becomes both. Othello, in fact, fulfills the worst suspicions that his worst enemies hold of him. Gratiano reminds us of this when he comments sadly:

> Poor Desdemona, I am glad thy father's dead;
> Thy match was mortal to him, and pure grief
> Shore his old thread atwain: did he live now,
> This sight would make him do a desperate turn,
> Yea, curse his better angel from his side,
> And fall to reprobation. (V, ii, 205-210)

Brabantio's nightmare has come true, and were he alive, this would provoke him to disclaim all faith. But the real horror here is that Brabantio's nightmare is also Othello's, and Othello becomes what he was most loath to be. We sympathize because he fell not for pride's sake but for honor's and because he remains vulnerable to that which he is and is made to be, no matter how that differs from what he wishes to be. In the end we, like Othello, wish he had not fallen victim to himself, victim to his fate.

Our sympathy for Othello, however, is sympathy for his struggle to escape his fate, not sympathy for what he is fated to be. For that there is no sympathy. Thus Brabantio can sympathize with Othello until he sees only the typical stage Moor, the man who bewitched his daughter. Those who sympathize see Othello as a brave warrior in control of his own destiny. Is not this the moral of his tale to Desdemona, who he says "lov'd me for the dangers I had pass'd" (I, iii, 167)? Brabantio himself was once beguiled by Othello's ability to overpower fate:

> Her father lov'd me, oft invited me,
> Still question'd me the story of my life,
> From year to year; the battles, sieges, fortunes,
> That I have pass'd. (I, iii, 128-31)

Othello's repetition of "pass'd" is deliberate and gives explicit expression to both the trials he conquered and the dangers he escaped. Brabantio loses respect immediately and irrevocably when he no longer sees Othello as the Moor who defies fate but instead as the Moor who threatens family and state. Brabantio, after all, is incredulous that Othello could at this time be called by "special mandate for the state affairs," and Brabantio's vulgar and bitter suggestion about Desdemona exemplifies again his changed perception: "Look to her, Moor, have a quick eye to see: / She has deceiv'd her father, may do thee" (I, iii, 72, 292-93). Angered by Desdemona's change in loyalty from father to husband, Brabantio holds her to be entirely faithless.

Those who, like Brabantio, in the end see only the Moor, surrender judgment to prejudice. Surely the most articulate spokesman for this point of view is Thomas Rymer, who finds much of *Othello*, including the status of the hero, ludicrous: "With us a Black-amoor might rise to be a Trumpeter; but *Shakespear* would not have him less than a Lieutenant—General. With us a *Moor* might marry some little drab, or Small-coal Wench; *Shake-spear* would provide him the Daughter and Heir of some great Lord, or

Privy-Councellor; and all the town should reckon it a very suitable match."[11]

Rymer's comments point to a problem that is not unique to *Othello* but is still of great significance. In the end, we can only be sympathetic to Othello's plight if we are first open to Othello himself. If we are immovable in our contempt or incredulity, the play is then all that Rymer says it is. The problem of sympathy for Othello is doubly important when we recall that of all the plays in English dramatic history, no other play until the twentieth century offered a black hero of Othello's stature. And always there to undermine the most positive aspects of Shakespeare's representation of a noble black is Othello's lapse into the stereotype. Justice smites a Moor. Fate seems to control not only Othello but his representation. However successful Shakespeare's manipulation of the stereotype may be, Othello remains identifiable as a version of that type. We may see Shakespeare's hand more subtly, if we see Othello's and Desdemona's tragedy as a personal tragedy. After all, chaos does not come again; order always exists in Venice and even its outposts. Shakespeare's black Moor never possesses the power or desire to subvert civic and natural order.

Shakespeare comments with similar subtlety on Othello through the internal playwright Iago. In the hands of this malicious playwright, characters must be what they seem; black men must be villains. The irony here, of course, is that villains must seem to be what they are not and vice versa. How differently from Iago Shakespeare represents Othello is witnessed in part by the sympathy Shakespeare evokes from us for Iago's victim. But this points to the basic duality of Othello's character, a duality that is constantly at work in the play. In the end, however, the separate parts become one in Othello, and the good becomes inseparable from the evil, Justice from the Moor, the playwright from the dissembler.

The importance of Othello as the dominant representation of an African on the stage cannot be overestimated. Unlike any of the other plays discussed in this or the previous chapter, *Othello* seems to have been always in revival. Not until *Oroonoko* was staged in 1695 was there a close rival to *Othello* for putting a

---

11. Thomas Rymer, *A Short View of Tragedy*, in *The Critical Works of Thomas Rymer*, ed. C. R. Zimansky (New Haven, Conn., 1956), 134.

dramatic representation of a black character before English audiences. Between 1604 and 1687, *Othello* was in production not less than fourteen times. No generation of seventeenth-century playgoers could not have seen the play in several revivals. The publication history of *Othello* also indicates significant popularity. Although the first publication did not occur until 1622, almost twenty years after its first performance, *Othello* was published in quarto seven times in the seventeenth century and was included in the four seventeenth-century folios. In spite of the remarkable endurance of *Othello*, its ability to influence positively the portrayal of Africans on the stage is, not surprisingly, almost negligible; the stereotype remains vigorous even into the Restoration, as the adaptations of *Titus Andronicus* and *Lust's Dominion* suggest. While a single play could not be expected to reverse centuries of tradition, one senses that *Othello* had virtually no effect on the representation of Moors in the seventeenth century. How much of this is due to Othello's own tragic relapse to the stereotypical Moor cannot be determined, but surely that must be a factor. Indeed, audiences may have learned other lessons from this play as they remembered the sight of the black Moor murdering the innocent and white Desdemona. Perhaps too, Emilia's stinging charge, "O gull! O dolt! / As ignorant as dirt!" (V, ii, 164–65), lingered in their ears. Or perhaps when Emilia cries, "O, the more angel she, / And you the blacker devil!" (V, ii, 131–32), the age-old conflict between black and white, between good and evil, received an all-too-believable and terrifying reconfirmation. For some, like Rymer, the belief that Othello was even high enough to fall was merely fabulous anyway. Perhaps *Othello*, like its hero, simply could not replace everywhere the long-held perceptions of black men.

Thomas Heywood's *The Fair Maid of the West*, Part I, probably dates from some time in the last years of Elizabeth's reign and therefore may have been acted before *Othello*.[12] The principal Moorish character of *Fair Maid*, Mullisheg, King of Fez, undergoes significant alteration between Parts I and II (Part II was written around 1631), alterations that in fact suggest that villainous Moors

12. Robert K. Turner, Jr., "Introduction to *The Fair Maid of the West, Parts I and II*," in *The Fair Maid of the West, Parts I and II* by Thomas Heywood (Lincoln, Neb., 1967), xiii.

were dramatically more desirable than virtuous ones. Found in both parts are all the major themes that surround black characters, most notably the problems of sexual power and the related sexual and political dangers posed by black men. Mullisheg's initial appearance in Part I raises immediately these issues; in that scene, he demands concubines to glorify his newly established reign:

> Find us concubines.
> The fairest Christian damsels you can hire
> Or buy for gold, the loveliest of the Moors
> We can command, and Negroes everywhere.
> Italians, French, and Dutch, choice Turkish girls
> Must fill our Alkedavy. (IV, iii, 27-33)

The king's ominous yet predictable first choice in women forebodes no good for the play's heroine, Bess Bridges, who in the previous scene departs England aboard her ship the *Negro* in search of her beloved Spencer.

The threat to Bess becomes real when she arrives in Fez, and Mullisheg desires her above all else. However, before he demonstrates his power, he allows Bess to rule his heart and to command him as freely as she had earlier commanded her tapsters. But once Mullisheg sees that Bess is enamored of another, he swiftly turns from the generous and doting lover into a cruel and jealous tyrant. He inquires of Bess, "What's he of that brave presence?" (V, ii, 87). She identifies her Spencer only as "A gentleman of England and my friend. / Do him some grace for my sake" (V, ii, 88-89). However, Mullisheg reacts viciously, and though he pardons all for whom Bess has earlier interceded, this time he responds to the fair maid:

> For thy sake what would not I perform?
> He shall have grace and honor.—Joffer, go
> And see him [Spencer] gelded to attend on us.
> He shall be our chief eunuch. (V, ii, 90-94)

Mullisheg's order to unman Spencer squarely identifies the paramount issue; the struggle to possess Bess becomes a struggle for manhood and power. Bess, however, will not permit such an atrocity to occur and steps in to save English manhood:

Not for ten worlds! Behold great King, I stand
Betwixt him and all danger.

Seize what I have, take both my ship and goods
Leave naught that's mine unrifled; spare me him. (V, ii, 94-97)

From her Christian name, Elizabeth, the fair maid partially derives the power to interpose herself between Mullisheg and Spencer. Earlier when the Moor learns her name, he recognizes the virtue of the English queen and her sway in Bess:

> There's virtue in that name.
> The virgin queen, so famous through the world,
> The mighty empress of the maiden isle,
> Whose predecessors have o'errun great France,
> Whose powerful hand doeth still support the Dutch,
> And keeps the potent King of Spain in awe,
> Is not she titled so? (V, i, 88-94)

The power of Christian-female virtue and English Elizabeth overcome Mullisheg, as it is steadfast female virtue that, by resisting temptation, offers support to English manhood. By being uncompromisingly virtuous, by resisting the luxury of the Moor, Bess (like Isabella in *Lust's Dominion*), saves her beloved from disgrace; had she chosen to act like Tamora, weak in spirit and flesh, Spencer's manhood literally would have been lost to the Moor.

Yet not everyone escapes unscarred; the clown, Clem, falls victim to Mullisheg through no fault other than his own foolishness. Clem has neither judgment nor a sense of irony. He believes Mullisheg intends Spencer an "honor" and offers himself to be gelded in Spencer's place. After he is emasculated, Clem runs back shouting: "No more of your honor, if you love me! Is this your Moorish preferment, to rob a man of his best jewels?" (V, ii, 126-27). The point to be learned by Clem's loss is that it is indeed the result of "Moorish preferment," and although the scene attempts comedy through the character of the clown and through staging, the situation it dramatizes is not comic. Clem's wound is real, as is Mullisheg's power and cruelty. To mistake this is to suffer Clem's fate, just as to approach Moors unwarily is to court danger. Like the Trojans who failed to recognize the danger of Epeus' horse, Clem mistakenly believes honor can be offered by the Moor. Vigilance, like the vigilance of Bess and Spencer, must never slacken when one traffics with Moors.

Bess's vigilance and her power over Mullisheg are symbolized in her handling of her ship, the *Negro*. As the ship is wholly owned and dominated by her and her men, so too must Mullisheg be dominated and controlled. The *Negro*, outfitted in black, stands as a testament of Bess's love for Spencer and her indomitable spirit in adversity. Although she is warned that a black ship "Twill be ominous / And bode disaster fortune" (IV, ii, 80-81), she embarks nonetheless in command of it, her fate, and her fortune. By extension, Bess learns that she must command the Negro Mullisheg, and that she does, guaranteeing her safety and her power over her own destiny.

At the end of Part I, the Moor too attempts to control his own destiny by forswearing lust and revenge and by adopting virtue:

> You have waken'd in me an heroic spirit;
> Lust shall not conquer virtue.—Till this hour
> We grac'd thee for thy beauty, English woman,
> But now we wonder at thy constancy. (V, ii, 118-21)

Mullisheg speaks as though he were involved in a psychomachia and plays both the role of mankind caught in a struggle between Lust and Virtue and, more suited to his blackness, the role of Lust to Bess's and Spencer's Virtue. Both his roles are suited to his type. By deposing lust and surrendering to virtue, however, Mullisheg moves away from the typical Moor and wins for himself redemption. He closes the play in the spirit of this conversion, promising to reward Bess and her companions.

In Part II, which begins just after the marriage of Spencer and Bess has taken place, the Englishmen find themselves in a predicament similar to Clem's in Part I. Virtue's victory over lust is not long lived in Mullisheg, and the English, having trusted in Mullisheg's promises of honor, now find themselves in danger. His desire for Bess rekindled, Mullisheg laments his earlier magnanimity and wants nothing more than to ravish Bess and to cuckold Spencer. The Moor sees his former goodness and generosity as self-treason, as though through some false action of his own, the wrong side won in the psychomachia between lust and virtue, between the typical Moor and the atypical. "I was a traitor to my own desires / To part with her so slightly," he states (I, i, 201-202).

Later he complains:

> I should commit high treason 'gainst myself
> Not to do that might give my soul content
> And satisfy my appetite with fulness. (I, i, 237-39)

From this moment, Mullisheg intrigues against Bess and Spencer and acts loyally to the type of the villainous Moor. Were it in his power, he would ravish Bess, but only the astute machinations of the English save her. And when the lecher king thinks that he has finally maneuvered Bess into his bed, the bed actually contains his wife Tota, although his partner is not discovered to him until the next day. For his part, he believes himself to have "had the sweetest night's content / That ever king enjoy'd" (III, i, 21-22). When he learns later that Bess has escaped a virgin still, he vows:

> ... all our injuries
> Upon the English prisoner we'll revenge.
> As we in state and fortune hope to rise,
> A never-heard-of death that traitor dies. (III, ii, 97-100)

The competition between Mullisheg and Spencer that appeared to have ended in Part I begins again, but unknown to Mullisheg, the field of competition has expanded to include his own wife Tota. She is as enamored of Spencer as Mullisheg is of Bess, and Tota plots to sleep with Spencer, both to satisfy her lust and to avenge herself on her negligent husband. Like her spouse, she does not know that the Englishman escapes safely from her lust and that she lies with her own husband, the Moor.

As judge, Tota happily proclaims the Englishman, or at least so she thinks, the champion in the fields of eroticism and gentility:

> The English stranger
> Is stol'n from forth mine arms. I am at full revenged.
> Were I again to match, I'd marry one
> Of this brave nation, if a gentleman,
> Before the greatest monarch of the world,
> They are such sweet and loving bedfellows. (III, i, 3-8)

Tota reduces herself to her type, and her lines could come from any of the Zanthias. Like them, she proves lascivious and untrustworthy, interested more in sexual gratification with a white man than in preserving her honor. The irony of her lines about Spencer, as with Mullisheg's about Bess, is that they are not about an Englishman but about a Moor. Yet Tota and Mullisheg discredit the compliments they unwittingly offer Moors by their own untrustworthy actions. Heywood cleverly has the English proclaimed the more virile and the more desired while he allows them to remain virtuously above the cesspool of the sexual intrigues of the Moors. The surrogates satisfy each other's wanton desires as they acknowledge their own general inferiority when compared to the English.

In the competition between the Moors and the English, the most important battle is waged to crown the more valorous, virtuous, and honorable; here too, of course, the Moors prove to be the losers. Mullisheg's and Tota's perfidy and dissembling remove them from the competition quickly, though they in fact have no interest in the prize. Bess and Spencer, however, tirelessly demonstrate their superior moral virtue. She remains a virgin throughout her stay in Fez, she and Spencer presumably not having had the time to consummate their marriage. Spencer demonstrates his superior valor by overpowering forty guards, and "with his good sword" killing six of them (III, ii, 80). He is captured by no less than the captain of the guard, Joffer, who, awed by Spencer's military virtue, trusts his moral virtue and allows him to visit Bess with the condition that he promise to return. Spencer rises to the challenge, promising that if he does not return, "May I be held a scorn to Christendom / And recreant to my country" (III, i, 112-13).

Believing all men as untrustworthy as himself, Mullisheg condemns Joffer for trusting the Englishman:

> Why canst thou think a stranger so remote
> Both in country and religion, being embark'd
> At sea and under sail, free from our hands,
> In the arms of his fair bride,
> His captain and his sailors all aboard,
> Sea room and wind at will, and will return
> To expose all these to voluntary dangers
> For a bare verbal promise? (III, iii, 25-32)

Joffer, unlike Mullisheg, believes in virtue and honor and is proud that even if purchased with his own death, "A Moor a Christian thus far did exceed" (III, iii, 34). But the Christians greatly exceed the Moors in what becomes a virtuoso display of honor and altruism. First Spencer comes to make his "honor shine," and he is subsequently followed by Bess and her train, all of whom offer their lives in exchange for Spencer's. Joffer, awed by the selflessness of the English, laments that they did not allow him to ransom them with his head. Even Mullisheg finally responds to this show of virtue:

> Shall lust in me have chief predominance?
> And virtuous deeds, for which in Fez
> I have been long renown'd, be quite exil'd?
> Shall Christians have the honor
> To be sole heirs of goodness, and we Moors
> Barbarous and bloody? (III, iii, 139–44)

Once more inspired by the virtue of the English, Mullisheg promises again to follow their example:

> These English are in all things honorable,
> Nor can we tax their ways in anything
> Unless we blame their virtues. (III, iii, 151–53)

Mullisheg also follows Spencer's lead in recognizing and rewarding the virtue and renown of Joffer. Finally the penitent King of Fez rewards Bess and Spencer, who, laden with gifts, depart the kingdom with a promise to report Mullisheg's "bounties" and "royalties," although it is their virtue that most deserves reporting.

Although the African episode of *Fair Maid* ends with Mullisheg and Tota reclaimed by righteousness, only one African, Joffer, never really wavers, and when he encounters the English again, they remember him for his constancy. In battle and as the captive of a Florentine general, Joffer's virtue continues to outshine that of all the other Africans. In recognition of Joffer's unflagging virtue, Spencer offers to ransom the captive Moor, even at the price of his own liberty. This offer overwhelms Joffer and prompts him to declare Christians to be the exemplars of all good:

> Such honor is not found in Barbary.
> The virtue in these Christians hath converted me,
> Which to the world I can no longer smother.
> Accept me, then, a Christian and a brother. (V, iv, 184–87)

The Moor's conversion signals the final and greatest victory of

Spencer and the Englishmen. But Joffer's conversion also records his personal triumph over his birth, as he implicitly renounces family, faith, and country.

Joffer deserves special notice here because he is unique in English drama and because he offers a valuable gauge by which to measure other Africans. That he is special should not be doubted, and the ways in which he distinguishes himself from other black characters point out those characteristics in blacks that were considered particularly good and particularly evil. First we should not forget that Joffer is loyal in service. Although he may be of rank, he knows his station. After Joffer captures Spencer, he tells his prisoner:

> Sir, though we wonder at your noble deeds,
> Yet I must do the office of a subject
> And take you prisoner. (II, vi, 1–3)

These same offices lead to Joffer's capture in Italy. He does not fail in his duty while in Italy: "Duke, I am prisoner, put me to ransom or to death. But to death rather, for methinks a soldier should not outlive bondage" (V, iv, 152–54). Unlike other "ambitious" Moors, Joffer never forgets his station. When Spencer seeks to embrace his old friend, the humbled Joffer replies: "I know you not; and I could wish you did not know me now I am a prisoner, a wretch, a captive and such a one as I would not have my friends to know" (V, iv, 158–60). Although there is something of nobility in Joffer's shame at being captured, his relationship with the English is always one of deference.

Most of all, Joffer distinguishes himself from other blacks by desiring virtue above all else; no other black Moor in *Fair Maid* or any other play so fervently pursues this goal. And an essential component of Joffer's quest is his total lack of sexual involvement throughout the play (a fact that may not have gone unnoticed by Aphra Behn when she created Osmin some forty-five years later). Joffer neither tempts nor threatens Bess's chastity; in fact, he seems to be celibate since there is absolutely no mention of a wife or other sexual liaison. Uncharacteristically for a black Moor, Joffer shows absolutely no sexual desire, and its absence allows him to pursue virtue singlemindedly, a quest that necessarily leads to Christianity. At the end of the play, Joffer uncomfortably calls to mind another convert to Christianity, the valorous and then unmarried (possibly celibate?) Othello. Joffer's celibacy, in fact, could be the single greatest influence Othello had on the dramatization of other Africans. To create a truly noble African, playwrights merely had to keep him away from women. In other words, playwrights had to create a new type, one that desired virtue exclusively and never women. Perhaps black men who desire virtue must be like the prototypical black Christian, the Ethiopian eunuch converted by the apostle Philip (Acts 8:27–39).

If Joffer reminds us of the valiant, bachelor Othello, Mullisheg in Part II resembles the married Moor, the Moor who is unable to control permanently his baser spirit and fleshly desires, and who relapses into his natural state. Mullisheg's relapse must not be seen only as a simple elaboration of the characteristics he briefly displays in Part I. His actions suggest that for a Moor, temptation is always too great to withstand, that his resolve is always weak. By embracing evil again, Mullisheg betrays a trust; he perjures himself. When Bess and Spencer leave Fez, surely the audience must be relieved that they are gone; one should not tempt the devil twice. On the other hand, Joffer's atypical behavior throughout, and particularly his conversion, remind the audience of the untrustworthiness of Mullisheg and of Moors in general. In the end, Joffer no longer wishes to be a Moor; he converts to Christianity because he believes it leads men to virtue. He renounces his religion and his kind, perhaps hoping to be more like that eunuch of whom Jerome writes: "By reading the prophet the eunuch of Candace the queen of Ethiopia is made ready for the baptism of Christ. Though it is against nature the Ethiopian *does* change his skin and the leopard his spots."[13] Yet had Heywood written a third part of *Fair Maid*, do we actually believe that Joffer could have retained this nobility of spirit? Surely we can guess what the nature of his temptation would have been.

The almost thirty years between the appearance of Parts I and II of *Fair Maid* point to the continued persistence and vitality of the type of the villainous Moor. And although we have seen far worse Moors than Mullisheg, he diverges from the type by *again* renouncing his prior preference for evil; surely not much trust can

---

13. Jerome, Letter LXIX, *Letters and Works*, 146.

be placed in his constancy. Joffer only shows that virtuous Moors are possible, at least in drama, but they are extraordinary Moors; no one, not even Joffer himself, believes there are many more like him. Nonetheless, Joffer and Mullisheg are not Aaron and Eleazar; they do display inclinations that are genuinely noble and virtuous. Unfortunately, the two parts of *Fair Maid* do not appear to have been very successful on the stage, and thus their slightly more positive representation of Moors seems to have had little influence.

In the plays discussed in this chapter and the previous one, the black characters have been found either in North African countries or in Europe, most frequently as servants. When in Europe, these characters are clearly meant to be Moorish in color as well as in culture. The first play to introduce black characters in a New World setting is William D'Avenant's *The History of Sir Francis Drake* (1658).[14] Although *Drake* is more a musical entertainment than a mimetic drama, it brought to the popular stage the kind of black characters that were becoming common in the streets of London during the Lord Mayors' Pageants. This change acknowledges what seems to be a growing change in the perception of Africans. Black Moors in dramatic works written after 1650 are treated less as threats to Christianity and European culture and more as property, exotic puffery, or slaves. This view of Africans reached its zenith on the stage in Southerne's *Oroonoko*; before moving to that play, however, some discussion of *Drake* is required.

The Moors in *Drake* are runaway slaves who have established a kingdom in Peru. Brought to America by the Spanish, these noble Africans, called Symerons (Cimmerians), rebel to escape the excessive cruelty and brutality of their Spanish captors. The theme of Spanish cruelty is not incidental to the characterization of these Moors; as we have seen in Chapter III, when tensions arose between the English and Spanish, a corresponding rise in anti-Spanish propaganda occurred. D'Avenant ennobles these Africans, in part, to emphasize how brutal and uncivilized the Spanish were.[15] The

---

14. *Drake* was first performed as a one-act opera and was later incorporated into *The Playhouse To Be Let* (1663), in which *Drake* was the third of five acts.

15. The Catholic Spanish continued to assist Charles II and the royalist cause until 1659 when Spain signed a truce with the Puritan government. D'Avenant's *The Cruelty of the Spaniards*, performed earlier in 1658 than *Drake* and then later

Symerons, at their best, are faithful to their English conquerors for whom the Africans serve as reliable guides and loyal soldiers. Chief among them in virtue is Pedro, who is nothing more than a devoted servant. The Symerons also have a sufficiently humble king who, like the King of the Moors in *Wolston Dixi*, offers praise to the English and then assistance.

The Symerons, however, are neither wholly civilized nor wholly trustworthy, and they demonstrate their barbaric nature in a thoroughly conventional manner. When unguarded and unsupervised, several members of the tribe seize a young Spanish bride and attempt to rape and torture her. The stage directions for the scene read: "The Scene is suddenly changed into the former prospect of the rising of the morning, and Venta Cruz; but about the middle it is varied with the discovery of a beautiful lady tied to a tree, adorn'd with the ornaments of a Bride, with her hair dishevel'd, and complaining, with her hand towards Heaven; About her are likewise discern'd the Symerons who took her prisoner."[16]

The English move promptly to rescue distressed virtue from the power of darkness; however, action by them proves unnecessary because Pedro manages to free the bride and the other white captives. In keeping with D'Avenant's propagandistic intentions, Pedro then justifies the behavior of his fellow Africans as a misguided demonstration of their fervor to serve their English masters and as an overreaction to the crimes of their former Spanish masters:

> They thought their duties was to take their foes.
> Be merciful, and censure the offence
> To be but their mistaken diligence.
> . . . .
> And, noble Chief, the cruelties which they
> Have often felt beneath the Spaniards' sway,
> Who midst the triumphs of our nuptial feasts
> Have forc'd our brides, and slaughter'd all our guests,

---

as Act IV of *The Playhouse To Be Let*, was "very welcome as propaganda at a time when the Spanish war was becoming unpopular" (Godfrey Davies, *The Early Stuarts*, [2nd ed; Oxford, 1959], 230-36, 398-99. Vol. IX of *The Oxford History of England*, ed. Sir George Clark, 15 vols.).

16. William D'Avenant, *The Playhouse To Be Let*, in *The Dramatic Works of Sir William D'Avenant* (London, 1873), Vol. IV, Act III, 68.

> May some excuse even from your reason draw:
> Revenge does all the fetters break of law. (III, p. 70)

The obvious point of the comparison is to make the Spanish appear even more barbaric than these black savages. Yet another very important point cannot be lost: black men, no matter how noble they may otherwise be, pose a real danger to the community, a danger that always seems to be effected sexually. This is the real point of D'Avenant's graphic scene, and this proves particularly true when we recognize that only the woman is presented on stage bound and threatened. The captive men appear only after they have been released from danger.

D'Avenant's *Drake* was the first new play in more than twenty years to put black characters on the English stage, and though the setting of the play is no longer Italy or Spain, the Moors in Peru still threaten as they do in Europe. When D'Avenant later incorporated *Drake* into *The Playhouse to Be Let*, he became the first contemporary playwright to bring this theme to the Restoration stage. This is not to say that London audiences had to wait long to see the lecherous black man threaten virtuous white women. Elizabethan plays depicting this theme were to be found soon enough. Oddly enough, however, it was mostly through the older plays or adaptations of them that this vision of black men was represented on the stage in the second half of the seventeenth century. *The Playhouse To Be Let* was not very popular and probably was not performed after 1663. Excluding Behn's and Ravenscroft's adaptations, only a few Restoration playwrights used black characters in their plays. Crowne's *Calisto*, although performed at court in 1675, was never on the public stage. Settle had black dancers in *The Empress of Morocco* (1673); Wycherly's *The Gentleman Dancing Master* (1672) has a black servant, and a nameless slave appears in the anonymous play *The Unnatural Mother* (1697).[17] If anything about these characters is noteworthy, it is that none is of the

---

17. The only scene in *The Unnatural Mother* in which the slave appears is worth mentioning here. To entrap a white woman and to prove her unchaste, this black slave is drugged and placed in her bed. She, of course, is innocent, but the black man's presence in her bed seems to be proof enough of her wantonness. He is stabbed while in his drug-induced stupor, but she is later exonerated.

villainous type that so commonly had appeared on the stage. However, none plays a role of any real significance. The only Restoration playwright to create a black character of any real dramatic significance was Thomas Southerne, and we must now turn to his *Oroonoko*.

When Southerne's adaptation of Aphra Behn's novella *Oroonoko* appeared on the stage in 1695, it introduced to the English popular stage a new kind of black character. Although the audience was not totally unprepared for this kind of black man (it had already seen similar characters in the Lord Mayors' Pageants and in D'Avenant's *Drake*), Oroonoko was nonetheless unique. A man from Africa, enslaved in the New World, he was yet a man noble in mind and soul, whose plight, whose disgrace, whose treacherous enslavement the audience was expected to bemoan. Oroonoko, in fact, served as the prototype for the "noble slave" who in the eighteenth century became a familiar figure on the stage and in literature.[18] Yet even as Oroonoko harbingers a new type character, he maintains many of the characteristics found in other earlier seventeenth-century black Moors.[19] In fact, not to see a resemblance between Oroonoko and Othello would be impossible. Although their origins and conditions are different, Oroonoko, like Othello and his precursors, remains trapped within the unbreachable confines of the stereotypical Moor.

Like the other "good" Moors, Oroonoko's position is one of subservience, in his case, utter subservience. Even in this state of bondage, Oroonoko speaks eloquently in defense of his own enslavement. When asked by his own slave Aboan to participate in a revolt, Oroonoko rejects the plan outright, refusing to "murder the innocent," those being his owner and the other slave owners. He tells Aboan:

> If we are slaves, they did not make us slaves,
> But bought us in an honest way of trade

[18]. In *Guinea's Captive Kings: British Anti-Slavery Literature of the XVIIIth Century* (New York, 1969), 108, Wylie Sypher writes: "Aphra Behn can be called the originator of the Oroonoko legend, or perhaps even the originator of the noble Negro."

[19]. It is interesting to note that the word *Moor* does not appear in Southerne's play. Behn, however, describes Oroonoko as a "gallant Moor" (*Oroonoko: The Royal Slave*, in *The Works of Aphra Behn*, V, 134).

> As we have done before'em, bought and sold
> Many a wretch and never thought it wrong.
> They paid our price for us and we are now
> Their property, a part of their estate,
> To manage as they please.[20]

Oroonoko finally agrees to revolt only when he learns that his beloved Imoinda could be seized from him by the young "Luxurious, passionate, and amorous" governor (III, ii, 198). The princely African responds as he must, with outrage and defiance:

> Ha! Thou hast roused
> The lion in his den; he stalks abroad
> And the wide forest trembles at his roar.
> I find the danger now; my spirits start
> At the alarm and from all quarters come
> To man my heart, the citadel of love.
> Is there a pow'r on earth to force you [Imoinda] from me?
> And shall I not resist it? Not strike first
> To keep, to save you? To prevent that curse?
> This is your cause, and shall it not prevail?
> O! You were born all ways to conquer me.
> . . . .
> I'll undertake
> All thou wouldst have me now for liberty,
> For the great cause of love and liberty. (III, ii, 205-15, 218-20)

Significantly, Oroonoko's response conforms to the conventional demands of heroic drama which require that the hero always be in love, and this love motivates him to action as often as it raises conflicts for him. Southerne's hero acts much like the heroes in Dryden's great heroic plays: he moves to action in defense of his love. Like Almanzor, the prototype of all heroes in Restoration heroic drama, Oroonoko defies fate and seeks to determine his own destiny. As he exhorts his fellow slaves to revolt, he places his faith in his own prowess and will:

> Impossible! Nothing's impossible.
> We know our strength only by being tried.
> If you object the mountains, rivers, woods

---

20. Thomas Southerne, *Oroonoko*, ed. Maximillian E. Novak and David Stuart Rodes (Lincoln, Neb., 1976), III, ii, 106-13.

Unpassable that lie before our march:
Woods we can set on fire, we swim by nature.
What can oppose us then, but we may tame?
All things submit to virtuous industry:
That we can carry with us, that is ours. (III, iv, 1-8)

Yet the conventional demands of heroic drama are not the only conventions satisfied in *Oroonoko*, for indeed the hero finds himself in a situation remarkably similar to that of Othello and all the other black characters, both vicious and virtuous. The danger that Oroonoko faces is sexual. He must defend his wife Imoinda or lose her and his manhood. Once again the battle takes shape around issues of sexual power and relationships between black men and white women. And the fact that Southerne changed Imoinda's race from black, as she is in Behn's novella, to white underscores just how conventional the dramatic situation really is. On the stage, black men seem never to be in love with black women, and Southerne surely must have known that the interracial marriage would heighten dramatic tension. He could have observed this just a few months before the first production of *Oroonoko*, had he seen the revival in March, 1695, of Behn's *Abdelazer*. Oroonoko will fight the governor not for the love of an African princess but for the love of a white woman. The realities of chattel slavery transmute this traditional theme, however, for now it is the black man who suffers the disadvantage, sexual myths notwithstanding. Oroonoko is clearly vulnerable, and in the reversed situation, it is he who must demonstrate prowess and virility. Perhaps this is Southerne's greatest achievement as a playwright, because he makes real for Oroonoko what was only feared by Othello. By so doing, Southerne may actually diminish the volatility of the interracial marriage. Oroonoko threatened can be made a worthier object of pity and sympathy than an irrationally enraged Othello.

Oroonoko's vulnerability, however, is really political, and therefore he translates his defense of honor and sexual power directly into an act of political defiance. When he exhorts his fellow slaves to rebellion, he combines the two explicitly, as he hopes to arouse them to protect their honor *and* their wives, as well as to forge a new state:

Ethiops Washed White

> We wonnot wrong
> The virtue of our women to believe
> There is a wife among'em would refuse
> To share her husband's fortune. What is hard
> We must make easy to'em in our love. While we live
> And have our limbs, we can take care of them;
> Therefore I still propose to lead our march
> Down to the sea and plant a colony
> Where, in our native innocence, we shall live
> Free and able to defend ourselves. (III, iv, 17-26)

Oroonoko's defense against cuckoldry is political; he will found a utopian state that is characterized by prelapsarian innocence. Of course, Southerne here invokes the topos of the noble savage, the man who knows only honor and innocence. This savage wishes most to escape a politically corrupt system in which the "innocent" are unable to defend themselves. But here as in other plays, that which is unflattering to English society is meant to prompt improvement in English society. "The foreigner," writes G. K. Hunter, "could only 'mean' something important, and so be effective as a literary figure, when the qualities observed in him were seen to involve a simple and significant relationship to real life at home. Without this relationship, mere observation, however exact, could hardly make an impact on men caught up in their own problems and their own destiny."[21] Comparing the nobility of the African to the decadence of the governor, therefore, is intended to criticize corrupt Christians, not to laud Africans.[22] As Wylie Sypher comments: "Southerne, of course, had *his* homily—that of Mrs. Behn—the depravity of the white man."[23] Southerne himself means for the audience to draw a similar conclusion, as the closing lines of the play so clearly demand:

> I hope there is a place of happiness
> In the next world for such exalted virtue.
> Pagan or unbeliever, yet he lived
> To all he knew; and if he went astray

---

21. G. K. Hunter, "Elizabethans and Foreigners," in *Dramatic Identities*, 13.
22. See Novak and Rodes, "Introduction to *Oroonoko*," in *Oroonoko*, for their discussion of the comic subplot of the play.
23. Sypher, *Guinea's Captive Kings*, 116.

> There's mercy still above to set him right.
> But Christians guided by the heavenly ray
> Have no excuse if we mistake our way. (V, v, 305-11)

That Southerne chooses to comment on English vice by contrasting the governor with an African, of course, testifies to the continued vitality of the traditional views of Africans; nor is Oroonoko's general superiority to his fellow Africans incompatible with this point. What better way is there to point out the moral failing of a superior people than to have that group surpassed by a uniquely virtuous member of a supposedly inferior race? This surely is the moral of the closing lines of the play.

Nor is the general inferiority of all the other Africans ever in doubt. Southerne's Oroonoko, like Behn's, distinguishes himself and is distinguished from his debased countrymen.[24] When he arrives in Surinam, the royal African declares himself "above the rank of common slaves" (I, ii, 233). When the rebellion fails and he is abandoned by his less hearty followers (who were persuaded to surrender by their wives), Oroonoko showers them with bitter contempt:

> I own the folly of my enterprise,
> The rashness of this action, and must blush
> Quite through this veil of night, a whitely shame,
> To think I could design to make these free
> Who were by nature slaves—wretches designed
> To be their master's dogs and lick their feet.
> Whip, whip 'em to the knowledge of your gods.
> . . . .
> I would not live on the same earth with creatures
> That only have the faces of their kind.
> Why should they look like men who are not so?
> When they put off their noble natures for
> The grovelling qualities of down cast beasts,
> I wish they had their tails. (IV, ii, 57-63, 67-72)

Oroonoko's condemnation of his fellow Africans reveals more than contempt for those who live by other than his heroic ideals. By their cowardice, Oroonoko claims that the others show them-

---

24. See Behn's *Oroonoko*, in *The Works of Aphra Behn*, V, 134-37, for her description of the hero.

selves to be less than men, that they are only men in form. Yet the articulation of this heroic sentiment seems to accommodate some racist theories, and Oroonoko's words outside of their heroic context may easily be construed as further endorsement of chattel slavery.

The noble African's opinions on ordinary blacks never want other spokesmen in the play. Oroonoko is universally recognized as superior to all other Africans, and all agree that the inferior breed deserves its debased and subhuman station. Almost as startling as Oroonoko's expression of this sentiment is the one found in Act I, in which two women are discouraged from sympathizing with the plight of the newly arrived African captives:

> Lucy: Are all these wretches slaves?
> Stanmore: All sold, they and their posterity all slaves.
> Lucy: O miserable fortune!
> Blanford: Most of 'em know no better; they were born so and
> only change their masters. But a prince,
> [Oroonoko] born only to command, betrayed and sold!
> My heart drops blood for him. (I, ii, 188-93)

The same caste system that Oroonoko later endorses is adopted by slave owners to justify the enslavement of the wretches. In effect, the play says to us that most blacks *deserve* their lot; only the unique, the princely Oroonoko proves worthy of sympathy.

The end of the play reinforces this system of human valuation because our sympathies are limited to the long-suffering royal Moor. There is some passing sadness at the death of Aboan, the faithful slave, but as we know, a slave if called upon is supposed to die in service to his master. Like Osmin, Aboan wins praise not for being heroic but for being loyal. The other Africans by the end of the play have all met their ignominious and deserved fate. But Oroonoko remains clearly visible as the central object of sympathy, and as such he may prove more worthy of this role than Othello. Although the circumstances at the end of the two plays are similar, the details are different. Imoinda lies dead, but a suicide; Oroonoko claims responsibility for her death, but he has none. He nonetheless adopts the role of Justicer and moves against himself and the truly guilty governor:

> The deed was mine.
> Bloody I know it is and I expect
> Your laws should tell me so. Thus self-condemned,
> I do resign myself into your hands,
> The hands of justice—but I hold the sword
> For you—and for myself. (V, v, 295-300)

Although he assumes guilt for a crime he does not commit, his words more appropriately suit the crime he does commit: the murder of the governor. No one doubts that the guilty governor receives deserved punishment, yet Oroonoko recognizes the supremacy of law, even though it has constantly upheld his inferior status and now demands his death. But by upholding the law, Oroonoko minimizes his threat to the community and makes possible our continued sympathy for him. Even as the play reminds us that he "went astray," it never demands more of him than the justice he himself exacts. (This starkly differs from the end of the novella, in which Oroonoko first suffers emasculation, then dismemberment, and finally, while still alive, incineration at the stake. These atrocities inflicted on Oroonoko, of course, were perpetrated against all too many black men, both enslaved and freed.) But here again Oroonoko must be viewed as unique because he demonstrates that he can live within a Christian community in full accord with both its more demanding heroic code and its essential and basic legal code. Were there such another Moor as Oroonoko, perhaps the other was more fortunate and escaped the miserable fortune that the rest of black humanity deserved and that the unfortunate Oroonoko endured.

Oroonoko and the other plays discussed in this chapter all acknowledge the possibility that a black man could be a hero, and in acknowledging that possibility, the plays lead us to believe that some slight chink has been made in the monolith of the black stereotype. And slight it was, for never gone from the stage was the black villain; Behn's adaptation of *Lust's Dominion* was revived just months before *Oroonoko* was first performed. Yet as we survey these honest Moors, we cannot fail to recognize that the threat that they pose to the community is ever present. Each in his own way reminds the audience of those dangers, sexual and hence political. Nor does the audience lose sight of this even in the plays in which black men are the victims of cruelty. Othello, Oroonoko, and the Symerons may earn our sympathy, but they never lull us into false security. Perhaps this lesson was more vitally important at the end of the seventeenth century, when the realities of African slavery demanded that contemporary playwrights offer a more accurate representation of the nature of the relationship between black men and white. The stage history of *Oroonoko* and of its various adaptations clearly demonstrates this point, for as each generation of audiences required a stronger abolitionist statement, the play was altered to meet that need. Of course, literature was written to provide the opposite view as well.[25] But representing the real relationship between black men and white makes other demands. Probably the most important was the realization that as victim, the black man was at least as dangerous, if not more so, than he was as villain. This recognition finally demanded a mediation, a tempering of the audience's sympathies, which was achieved by linking the black victim to his villainous past, a firm reminder to the audience that it must yet be wary. Simultaneously, the uniqueness of those blacks with whom we do sympathize was stressed, so that it was never forgotten that all Africans did not deserve sympathy, only the few. The many earned but their lot.

25. See Sypher, *Guinea's Captive Kings*, 116–21.

VI

White Men Burdened
White Moors on the English Stage

> They are false and desperate people, when they find
> The least occasion open to encouragement,
> Cruel, and crafty souls, believe me Gentlemen.
> —Francis Beaumont and John Fletcher, *The Island Princess*

One final topic remains to be discussed in this study of Moors on the English stage: the role played by white Moors in the larger question of Moorish representation. By understanding this role, we can learn the extent to which blackness ultimately establishes type and then can either reconfirm or revise our earlier observations about blackness and black Moors. Because our interest in these white Moors rests primarily in their relationship to black Moors, our discussion will reflect this in both scope and method.

White Moors share with black two essential features: both are non-European and primarily non-Christian. Although these two important distinctions help to determine the characterization of white Moors as well as black, we shall see that the resulting portrayals are often strikingly different. First, however, we must identify exactly who is a white Moor. In the plays examined in the three previous chapters, all the black Africans, with the notable exception of Oroonoko, are identified as Moors in the texts of the plays or pageants. While Pory would have us believe that "Africani bianchi" are "white or tawny Moors," playwrights tend to distinguish between three varieties of white Africans. The white Africans in Greene's *Orlando Furioso* (1591) and *The Thracian*

Wonder (1599) are not identified as Moors, and this proves significant because neither are they identified as Muslims. Africans supply the exotic element needed for these heroical romances, and these characters are the latter-day Carthaginians and Egyptians, the non-Islamic non-Europeans. The white Africans in Daborne's *A Christian Turned Turk* (1610) and Massinger's *The Renegado* (1624) are identified as Turks, and this too is a very meaningful distinction. Both plays are set in Tunis, one of the many holdings in Africa of the Great Turk. By acknowledging at least the political reality of Tunis, the playwrights also seem to recognize the ethnic difference of the conquerors of Tunis. The word *Turk* itself carries many of the same connotations that *Moor* does, but *Turk* almost always means Muslim and hence an enemy of Christianity. The single greatest difference between *Turk* and *Moor* seems to be the recognition of the ethnic difference and the Eurasian origin of the former group. We see this distinction clearly at work in *Othello* when the Moor leaves Venice to fight the Turk. The Turk may be an enemy of Christianity, but he is neither African nor black. Of course some slight qualification of this is required because these terms in the end adequately express the essential and perceived otherness of these non-Christian, non-European groups, so to that extent *Turk*, *Moor*, or *Indian* is never precise.

Relying on the playwrights' distinctions, we find very few white Moors on the stage in the sixteenth and seventeenth centuries. In fact, not until the heroic drama of the Restoration are they present in any real numbers. The adversaries of Muly Mahamet in *Alcazar* and *Stukeley* were perhaps the only white African Moors on the stage until Dryden's *The Conquest of Granada* in 1670. In *Alcazar*, the whiteness of the white Moors is as thematically significant as the blackness of the play's black villain. The righteous Abdelmelec stands as a beacon of moral virtue and rightful kingship, and his most notable trait is the affection he bears for the "careless Christian prince" (III, ii, 842). In the scheme of *Alcazar*, Abdelmelec's whiteness is more significant than his religion, and his absolute moral righteousness mediates his failure to profess Christianity.

More like the wicked Muly Mahamet is the villainous Governor of Ternata in Beaumont and Fletcher's *The Island Princess*, and the symbol of his villainy is his disguise as a "Moor-Priest." Neither an African (Ternata is in the Moluccas) nor black, the governor is most certainly an enemy of Christianity and of the European Christians in the Spice Islands. Presumably Asian, his ethnicity qualifies him as a "tawny Moor," though he is never explicitly called such in the text. His religion is a nonspecific admixture of idolatry and nature worship, though his gods are labeled "Mahumet gods."[1] It seems to be this religion that earns for him the title "Moor-Priest"; however, we shall discover that race is not entirely insignificant in this play.

The primary action of *The Island Princess* (1621) is the triumph of Christianity over the governor's "Mahumet gods." As in many other plays in which Christians come into contact with members of a non-Christian religion, the victory in *The Island Princess* is achieved by the conversion of a female non-Christian who recognizes the virtue of her Christian suitor. The triumphant Christian in this play is a Portuguese adventurer, Armusia, who proves his valor by rescuing the King of Sidore from the evil governor. This task he undertakes because the king's sister, the island princess, promises her hand to her brother's "redeemer." Armusia, however, is but one of the princess' suitors; several others, including the governor and another Portuguese, desire her hand.

It is in his quest for the princess' hand that the governor dons his priestly garb, and while posing as a priest, he deceives the innocent king and his sister, entrapping them by manipulating their sincere religious faith. Expressing only contempt for religion and honest believers, the deceitful governor blasphemes as he reveals his scheme and intentions:

> . . . my main end is to advise
> The destruction of you all, a general ruine,
> And when I am reveng'd, let the gods whistle. (IV, i, p. 143)

As a priest, the governor stands for duplicity, impiety, and impurity; significantly, his impiety is never separated from the play's notion of Islam. This failure to distinguish between the governor's villainy and his fraudulent religious fervor makes general the indictment of all believers in those "Mahumet gods." When the Christian Armusia is pressed by his captors to convert, his attack

1. Beaumont and Fletcher, *The Island Princess*, in *The Works of Francis Beaumont and John Fletcher*, Vol. VIII, IV, i, p. 156.

on the non-Christians stops not even with the woman he loves. He condemns them all:

> . . . I hate and curse ye,
> Contemn your Deities, spurn at their powers
> And where I meet your *Mahumet* gods, I'll swing'em
> Thus o'r my head, and kick'em into puddles
> Nay, I will out of vengeance search your Temples.
> And with those hearts that serve my God, demolish
> Your shambles of wild worships. (IV, i, p. 156)

Armusia's steadfastness in the face of adversity, his unshakable faith in his God, and his virtue win the admiration of the princess, who chooses to endure with Armusia his harsh fate:

> Your Faith, and your Religion must be like ye,
> They that can shew you these must be pure mirrors,
> When the streams flow clear and fair, what are the fountains?
> I do embrace your faith, Sir, and your fortune. (V, i, p. 163)

It does not matter that the governor is shortly revealed to be not a priest but instead the wicked usurper; he is inseparable from his fraudulent religion and its horrors. Like the princess, anyone who is swayed by virtue cannot deny the moral superiority of Christianity.

The "wild worships" of the islanders is, of course, but one manifestation of their complete inferiority to the European Christians; a second and equally important manifestation is their racial inferiority. So closely combined are the two that a distinction between moral and ethnic character becomes indiscernible. The very first description of the islanders warns the Portuguese against them:

> . . . let the guards be careful of their business,
> Their vigilant eyes fixt on these Islanders,
> They are false and desperate people, when they find
> The least occasion open to encouragement,
> Cruel, and crafty souls, believe me Gentlemen. (I, i, p. 92)

The only islander distinguished from this general horde is the princess, who unlike the others does not wear the sun's "tawny Livery":

> ... by my life I hold her a compleat one,
> The very Sun, I think affects her sweetness,
> And dares not, as he does to all else, dye it
> Into his tawny Livery. (I, i, p. 93)

The untainted princess proves the most easily moved by virtue, as she is the only islander won over to Christianity; the tawny color of the rest comes to symbolize their separation from the light of Christianity.

It is, however, important to remember that this group is not entirely beyond redemption; at least one islander converts. Yet as significant as the color of the saved is the gender. The island princess is won by Armusia's virtue and *virtus*. The European Christians, therefore, represent the force of enlightenment and strength to these "fusty villains" (V, i, p. 158). Christian valor and manhood overthrow the tyranny of the governor and restore the weak and helpless King of Sidore. The king himself recognizes the superiority of his "redeemer" Armusia and describes him as "this all Man, this all valor / This pious Man" (II, i, p. 122). Such unqualified praise from the island king comments on more than Armusia; it in fact speaks directly of the fundamental inferiority of the islanders, who must look to the Christians to define and exemplify manhood, valor, and piety.

The superiority of European Christians and the corresponding inferiority of Moors are important themes in Dryden's *The Conquest of Granada* and *Don Sebastian*. Although the Moors in both of these plays are white, Dryden makes ethnic differences as significant as ethical and religious differences in distinguishing the Moors from the Europeans. At the end of these plays the truly noble and virtuous Moors are discovered really to be the progeny of noble European Christians, and those other real Moors who desire spiritual correction and enlightenment forsake the religion of their misbelieving ancestors and embrace Christianity. The path to these discoveries and conversions proves long and arduous, but Dryden intends it to be because his goals in these plays are avowedly didactic. In the dedication to *The Conquest*, Dryden writes: "And Poets, while they imitate, instruct. The feign'd Heroe inflames the true: and the dead vertue animates the living. Since, therefore, the world is govern'd by precept and Example, and both these can only have influence from those persons who are above us, that kind of Poesy which excites to vertue the greatest men, is of greatest use to human kind."[2] Through the moral growth of his heroes and heroines who face and conquer adversity, Dryden makes vivid and dramatic his ethical and political concerns, as well as his belief in the racial superiority of Europeans. No better example of this can be found than in Almanzor, the hero of *The Conquest of Granada*.

In pursuit of fame and glory, Almanzor comes to Granada to assist the besieged Moorish King, Mahomet Boabdelin, in his battle against the advancing and victorious Spanish. Almanzor, however, finds himself caught in the midst of "intestine strife" between two warring Moorish tribes. The factionalism weakens the kingdom in addition to exposing the duplicity of the Moors and the weakness of their king. But it is Moorish duplicity against which we must measure Almanzor. Although he pretends to be above the law and unconcerned by questions of ethics, Almanzor adheres steadfastly to his own high moral standards and distinguishes himself from the other Moors by behaving in a manner antithetical to Moorish norms. The other Moors, conforming to the dramatic stereotype, reveal themselves to be deceitful and unscrupulous. Conversely, Almanzor always acts forthrightly, never duplicitously; he acts openly and honestly, never furtively. Almanzor never dissembles.

The acts of treachery performed by the Moors in *The Conquest* are as numerous as those performed by any of their black Moorish counterparts. Abdalla, brother of the king, betrays his brother for love of the ambitious Lynderaxa. She, however, will only be satisfied with a king, and she cares not who is king. Therefore, she plays her two lovers, Abdelmelech and Abdalla, against each other. Lynderaxa's brother Zulema encourages her in this treachery and articulates the Moorish standard when he prompts Abdalla to treason:

> If, when a Crown and Mistress are in place,
> Vertue intrudes with her lean holy face;
> Vertues then mine, and not I vertues foe;

---

2. John Dryden, "The Epistle Dedicatory," in *The Conquest of Granada, Part I*, in *The Works of John Dryden*, ed. H. T. Swedenberg, Jr., et al. (Berkeley, Calif., 1978), XI, 3. All future citations of Dryden's plays are from this edition.

> Why does she come where she has nought to do?
> Let her with Anchorit's not with Lovers lye;
> States-men and they keep better Company. (Part I, II, i, 208-13)

Almanzor never claims virtue as his foe; in fact, he respects virtue and the virtuous. Yet this hero claims as his guide not codified morality, which he considers sometimes to be faulty, but instead natural law:

> But know, that I alone am King of me.
> I am as free as Nature first made man
> 'Ere the base Laws of Servitude began
> When wild in woods the noble Savage ran. (Part I, I, i, 206-209)

Almanzor's adherence to natural law, however, does make some of his acts questionable by traditional moral standards. For instance, when he enters a fight, he claims to be unconcerned for the right and instead fights for the weak and for his friends: "I cannot stay to ask which cause is best; / But this [cause] is to me because opprest" (Part I, I, i, 128-29). Almanzor's words here seem to be an eccentric paraphrase of Paul's injunction to the Romans: "We then that are strong ought to bear the infirmities of the weak, and not to please ourselves" (Romans 15:1).

Perhaps Almanzor's most questionable moral act and ethical violation occurs when he promises to assist Abdalla in his treason simply because they are friends:

> When for my self I fight, I weigh the cause;
> But friendship will admit of no such Laws:
> That weighs by the lump, and, when the Cause is light,
> Puts kindness in to set the Ballance right.
> True, I would wish my friend the juster side;
> But in th'unjust my kindness more is try'd. (Part I, III, i, 23-28)

Here again, Almanzor's defense of himself recalls yet another biblical precedent: "Greater love hath no man than this, that a man lay down his life for his friend" (John 15:13). Almanzor's ethics demand faith in friendship and the use of strength to protect the "opprest." This moral code Dryden calls "excentrique vertue," and in the dedication to *The Conquest* he writes of his hero:

> But a character of an excentrique vertue is the more exact Image of humane life, because he is not wholy exempted from its frailties.

> Such a person is *Almanzor* . . . . I design'd in him a roughness of Character, impatient of injuries and a confidence of himself, almost approaching to an arrogance. But these errors are incident only to a great spirits; they are moles and dimples which hinder not a face from being beautifull; though that beauty be not regular; they are the number of those amiable imperfections which we see in Mistrisses: and which we pass over, without a strict examination, when they are accompanied with greater graces. And such, in *Almanzor*, are a frank and noble openness of Nature: an easiness to forgive his conquer'd enemies; and to protect them in distress; and above all, an inviolable faith in his affection. (p. 6)

Almanzor's virtue is quite literally eccentric. Only when he learns of his Christian heritage and accepts it does he move to the center; then his virtue, physical and moral, finds proper divine, political, and familial guidance.

Of his deviance, Almanzor first learns from the ghost of his mother, whom we later learn to be the sister of the conquering Ferdinand of Aragon. Predestined by God to divert her son from error and toward Christianity, nation, and family, the Ghost warns Almanzor:

> From antient Blood thy Fathers Linage springs,
> Thy Mothers thou deriv'st from stemms of Kings.
> A Christian born, and born again, that day,
> When sacred Water wash'd thy sins away.
> Yet bred in errors thou dost mis-imploy
> That strength Heav'n gave thee, and its stock destroy.
> (Part II, IV, iii, 123-28)

The wayward son does not, however, immediately desert the path of error; not until his father recognizes him through the device of "A ruby Cross in Diamond bracelets" does Almanzor cease defending Islam and battling Christianity and his destiny. With their arms raised against each other, the noble Duke of Arcos recognizes the identifying cross and birthmark and falls back from his son. Almanzor moves in for the kill, but heaven intercedes again as the ghost of his mother demands that he spare his adversary. He does and is then received once more into the Christian family by a paternal embrace. Almanzor concludes the play by embarking on a Christian mission to rid Spain of the Moors and to establish a Christian dynasty:

> The toyles of war shall help to wear each day;
> And dreams of love shall drive my nights away.
> Our Banners to th' *Alhambra's* turrets bear;
> Then, wave our Conqu'ring Crosses in the Aire;
> And Cry, with shouts of Triumph; Live and raign,
> Great *Ferdinand* and *Isabel* of Spain. (Part II, V, iii, 343-48)

As for Almanzor's former comrades, those who deplore the duplicity and cruelty of their fellow Moors abandon Islam and adopt Christianity. The most notable of these converts is Almahide, the last Moorish Queen of Spain. Falsely accused of adultery by her husband the king, Almahide must depend on Almanzor to defend her honor and virtue. But Almahide sees in her husband's lack of faith and in the mockery of her fellow Moors an example of a more significant wanting. As she goes to her trial, she laments:

> See how the gazing people crowd the place:
> All gaping to be fill'd with my disgrace.
> That shout, like the hoarse peel of Vultures rings,
> When over fighting fields, they beat their wings.
> Let never woman trust in Innocence;
> Or think her chastity its own defence;
> Mine has betray'd me to this publick shame:
> And vertue, which I serv'd, is but a name. (Part II, V, ii, 1-8)

Offered solace by her Christian maid, appropriately named Esperanza, Almahide then prays:

> Thou Pow'r unknown, if I have err'd forgive:
> My infancy was taught what I believe.
> But if thy Christians truely worship thee,
> Let me thy godhead in thy succour see:
> So shall thy Justice in my safety shine,
> And all my dayes, which thou shalt add, be thine. (Part II, V, ii, 15-20)

After her champion succeeds, the king desires Almahide to return to him. But his lack of faith she cannot overlook, so she forsakes him. Later she professes Christianity, and from Queen Isabel herself Almahide receives her new Christian name of Isabella. Renamed and reborn, Almahide will be a proper wife for her beloved Almanzor.[3]

---

3. The conclusion of the romance between Almahide and Almanzor resembles the conclusion of Corneille's *Le Cid*. In Corneille's play, Chimene is allowed a year

In the last act, two other Moors "beg to learn" the Christian faith: the lovers, Ozmyn and Benzayda. Members of two warring tribes, the two initially find comfort only at the Christian court of Isabel and Ferdinand. The Spanish queen, recognizing a parallel between her marriage to Ferdinand and the plight of these two young Moorish lovers, offers them sanctuary because

> Loves a Heroique Passion which can find
> No room in any base degenerate mind:
> It kindles all the Soul with Honours Fire,
> To make the Lover worthy his desire. (Part II, I, i, 145-48)

That the Moorish parents fail to recognize this only points to yet another failing of Islam and Moorish culture. Only after Ozmyn and Benzayda prove selfless and heroic by saving their fathers' lives are they received by the previously bitter and cruel men. But these two lovers recognize the superior example of the Christians and sue to be accepted into that faith.

Significantly, a common bond exists between the three converts, Almahide, Ozmyn, and Benzayda: each knows how to love selflessly. Each possesses that heroic passion of which Isabel spoke, and each is willing to sacrifice himself for the beloved. Perhaps it is this ability to love that opens their minds to Christianity; Isabel's heroic passion is, after all, a version of John's maxim on the power of love in his first epistle: "God is love; and he that dwelleth in love dwelleth in God, and God in him" (1 John 4:16). The unregenerate Moors, by contrast, love selfishly and lustfully. Perhaps no statement captures this difference better than Zulema's remarks to Almanzor about Almahide. Each warrior claims the queen's hand as his reward for assisting the renegade Abdalla. When Abdalla cannot honor his promises to both, he requests that one of the men surrender his claim. Almanzor suggests that both "set her free." Zulema retorts:

> If you will free your part of her you may;
> But, Sir, I love not your Romantique way.

---

of mourning for her father, after which she will marry Don Rodrigue, her father's murderer. Almahide asks a year's mourning for her deceased husband, after which she will yield to Isabel's command and marry Almanzor.

Dream on; enjoy her Soul; and set that free;
I'm pleas'd her person should be left for me. (Part I, III, i, 487-90)

Zulema's love is far from the heroic passion that is the standard for Christians and the truly virtuous; his lust and greed, however, are common to the Moors. This lust, according to Christian misconception, is totally compatible with the teaching of the Koran and "Mohammedan superstition."[4] Treachery and deceit, needless to say, are but other manifestations of the same meanness of spirit and ethical lack that characterizes Dryden's Moors.

Although Dryden does not exclude Moors from the company of the saved, there exists a higher category of redemption in this play. Almanzor is saved from both the error of Islam and the race of its adherents. The ghost of his mother is charged with more than saving his soul; she gives him a family history. She tells her son that "From antient Blood thy Fathers Linage springs" (Part II, IV, iii, 123). For Almanzor, the discovery of his parentage elevates him into the highest circles of power and virtue. Moreover, Almanzor, once properly situated, recognizes an external and hereditary source for his own virtue:

> This honor to my veins new blood will bring:
> Streams cannot fail, fed by so high a Spring:
> But all Court-Customs I so little know
> That I may fail in those respects I owe.
> I bring a heart which homage never knew;
> Yet it finds something of itself in you [Ferdinand].
> Something so kingly, that my haughty mind
> Is drawn to yours; because 'tis of a kind. (Part II, V, iii, 278-85)

The valiant Almanzor no longer finds himself at odds with the rest of mankind because he has found the center. His prowess and

---

4. In *The Crescent and the Rose*, Samuel Chew gives a brief history of Christian European attitudes toward the Koran and the unfounded myths about the book from the twelfth century through the seventeenth. On the subject of Islam and sexual license, Chew cites Edward Aston's *The Manners, Lawes and Customes of All Nations* (1611): "The 'incredible allurement' that has drawn countless men to Mahomet has been 'his giving people free liberty and power to pursue their lustes and all other pleasures, for by these meanes this pestilent religion hath crept into innumerable nations" (New York, 1937), 442. In Elegy XIX, "Going to Bed," Donne summarizes popular misconceptions when he writes that a sexual experience is similar to being in "A heaven like Mahomets Paradice" (l. 21).

haughtiness derive from Christian European kings; his race is the race destined by God to triumph over the misbelievers.

When Dryden again writes about Moors in *Don Sebastian* (1689), he expresses a racial and cultural ideology similar to that found in *The Conquest of Granada*. Inspired by a legend that Don Sebastian survived the battle of Alcazar, Dryden moves the moral struggle from the battlefield to the court of Muley-Moluch. (This is the name Dryden uses for the character named "Abdelmelec" in the other Alcazar plays.) There the young, vanquished king endures the humiliation of captivity with heroic fortitude and nobility of spirit. Predictably, his captors prove themselves to be brutally cruel, immoral tyrants. Only one Moor, Almeyda, does not participate in the general treachery and plotting that occurs in Alcazar, and she, we learn later, is the illegitimate sister of Sebastian, her father being the late King of Portugal.

As in *The Conquest of Granada*, the racial difference between the Europeans and the Moors proves significant because it seems to account for the Moors' brutality and meanness of spirit. Dryden makes the Emperor Muley-Moluch, a cruel and brutal tyrant, unrecognizable as the actual historical figure so kindly treated by Peele and Polemon. Although this is an obvious departure from history, Dryden claims that his design required this alteration. In the preface to the play, he writes:

> I must likewise own, that I have somewhat deviated from the known History, in the death of Muley-Moluch, who, by all relations dyed of a fever in the Battel, before his Army had wholly won the Field; but if I have allow'd him another day of Life, it was because I stood in need of so shining a Character of brutality, as I have given him, which is indeed the same, with the present Emperor Muley Ishmael, as some of our English Officers, who have been in his Court have credibly inform'd me.[5]

Dryden makes the cruelty of Muley-Moluch more vital and significant by linking it to a contemporary Moorish tyrant, Muley Ishmael. Moreover, to emphasize the cruelty of Muley Ishmael, Dryden in effect has the progenitor, the historic Muley-Moluch, inherit the flaws of his heir, Muley Ishmael. This makes Moorish

---

5. Dryden, "Preface to *Don Sebastian*," in *The Works of John Dryden*, XV, 70.

cruelty continuous and inherent, not that this had to be reaffirmed for an English audience in 1690. Dryden, therefore, is able to characterize all African people as monsters, beings who do not share the humanity of Europeans. Sebastian twice extends the metaphor to the Moors, the first time quite explicitly claiming for himself and denying to the Africans the qualities of man: "*Affrica* is stor'd with Monsters; Man's a Prodigy, / Thy Subjects have not seen" (I, i, 372-73).

In addition to this broad description of brutishness and brutality, individual Moors are portrayed in the traditional stereotypical manner. They are duplicitous, untrustworthy, greedy, and licentious. The emperor is described by a fellow Moor as "luxurious, close and cruel, / Generous by fits, but permanent in mischief" (I, i, 25-26). Muley-Moluch himself praises a priest for his hypocrisy: "How happy is the Prince who has a Churchman / So learn'd and pliant to expand his Laws!" (III, i, 105-106). Of course, having the Moors themselves acknowledge and praise those vices generally attributed to them emphasizes the thematic importance of those vices and provides additional credibility to the stereotype.

The racial inferiority of the Moors finds further expression in Dryden's treatment of Almeyda. Until the revelation of her parentage, she seems to be the only Moor fully at odds with the immoral pragmatism, greed, and lust that characterize Moorish Alcazar, its rulers, and its inhabitants. When we learn that Almeyda is really the daughter of a Christian, European king, we learn that her nobility of spirit is really inherited and therefore racially determined. On the subject of heredity and his heroine, the playwright contends that "the greatness of their Souls [Almeyda's and Sebastian's] was intended for a preparation of the final discovery, and that the likeness of their nature, was a fair hint to the proximity of blood."[6] Long before she discovers her true heritage, Almeyda demonstrates her greatness of soul and her quest for virtue by repudiating her kinship to Muley-Moluch and the Moors, all of whom she despises for their treachery and general immorality. She bitterly lambastes the emperor when he claims theirs to be "kindred Soul[s]":

6. *Ibid.*, 71.

> . . . if I thought my Soul
> Of kin to thine, soon wou'd I rend my heart-strings,
> And tear out that Alliance: but thou, Viper,
> Hast cancell'd kindred, made a rent in Nature,
> And through her holy bowels gnaw'd thy way,
> Through thy own Bloud to Empire. (II, i, 376-81)

When Muley-Moluch later professes his love, she rejects him for the captive Christian king. Muley-Moluch mocks her for having "chosen well, / Betwixt a Captive and a Conqueror" (III, i, 172-73). Defending her choice, she retorts:

> Betwixt a Monster and the best of Men.
> He was the envy of his neighb'ring Kings;
> For him their sighing Queens despised their bands,
> And Virgin Daughters blush'd when he was nam'd.
> To share his noble Chains is more to me,
> Then all the salvage greatness of thy throne. (II, i, 174-79)

For Almeyda, the difference between Sebastian's condition and Muley-Moluch's only highlights the moral superiority of the Christian king. And it comes as no surprise when she expresses her desire to share Sebastian's religion as well as his chains. When Almeyda publicly proclaims herself a Christian, she more closely aligns herself with her true race as she further separates herself from the Moors.

Christianity proves to be an essential component of European superiority. The Moors find ways to accommodate their religion to their own weakness and desires; their emperor praises hypocrisy in churchmen. By contrast, Christians, as Dryden portrays them, adhere uncompromisingly to a stringent and absolute moral code. At the play's end, the Christians meet the demands of their faith regardless of the consequences to their lives. Sebastian willingly surrenders a kingdom rather than violate—even accidentally and unwittingly—the tenets of his faith and conscience. When he and Almeyda learn that they are siblings, they know also that they are guilty of incest. Although they unknowingly commit this sin, they accept their guilt and their fate. Each acknowledges the higher demand of Christianity and the need for repentance. Sebastian refuses to return to his throne for fear "that were to show / Triumphant Incest, and pollute the Throne" (V, i, 537-38).

As the play ends with its reaffirmation of the superiority of Christianity, it also ends with yet another, this time explicit, avowal of the central role of heredity in human life:

> And let *Sebastian* and *Almeyda's* Fate,
> This dreadfull Sentence to the World relate,
> That Unrepented Crimes of Parents dead,
> Are justly punish'd on their Children's head. (V, 1, 724-27)

As Almeyda inherited her "greatness" of soul from the "proximity of Blood," she also inherited the sin of her parents. Hard is their fate, but Sebastian and Almeyda prove the moral superiority of European Christians by accepting that fate and desiring virtue above even life itself.

One final observation must be made about parentage, and consequently about interracial marriage, in the Dryden plays. Almeyda's father is European, not her mother. The real importance of the race of her mother is political. The extent to which this is true becomes clear when we consider that Sebastian would have married Almeyda, even while she was yet thought to be a *pure* Moor. Her conversion to Christianity, though essential in making her a suitable wife, does not entirely remove the question of race. However, there is nothing extraordinary in Sebastian's conquest of Almeyda; in marrying her, he would have only made legal an alliance similar to his father's with Almeyda's mother. For Sebastian's father, however, the question of marriage seemed insignificant, at least to some degree. He had an extramarital affair with a Moor and cuckolded a Moorish prince. In spite of all the reports of love between her parents, the central fact of Almeyda's birth cannot be dismissed, and as we recall the circumstances of her birth, Almeyda's bastardy becomes a more powerful symbol of Portuguese dominance and power than the strength of will that she derives from Portuguese blood. The discovery of a situation in the reverse, of a Portuguese queen bearing the child of a Moorish king, would produce on the stage the loudest cries of "whore" imaginable. Although not an entirely perfect example of this, Philip's response to his mother's affair with Eleazer in *Lust's Dominion* does offer some parallels.[7] As a vanquished king, Sebastian has

---

7. *Titus* also offers some interesting parallels. The virtuous Andronicus faction publicly and vociferously disapproves of Tamora's relationship with Aaron. Tamora's

much at stake in the battle for Almeyda's hand; his success serves as another example of his superiority, just as the triumph of Sebastian's father records his superiority. Similarly, in *The Conquest of Granada* Almanzor's success in isolating Almahide from her race is but the first step of his total triumph over her. That she can be persuaded by Isabel to marry Almanzor after a year of mourning demonstrates that Almahide is powerless to resist the total triumph of the Christian Spanish. Her conversion to Christianity is but the first step in her regeneration into a suitable wife for the newly recovered Christian prince. She is also renamed "Isabella," which totally consumes and masks Almahide's Moorish identity and reidentifies her as a Christian. Almahide is fortunate, however, because her fate coincides with her desire.

The common feature in all these situations is male dominance. As in *The Island Princess*, Almahide, Almeyda, and Almeyda's mother all recognize the superior virtue of Christianity and Christian men. These women submit to both, but more than spiritual dominance results. Political superiority too becomes inseparable from the power to father in interracial sexual relationships. Fathering children through the women of the enemy represents the ultimate symbol of political and cultural conquest. Like Aaron in *Titus Andronicus*, this is the moment of complete conquest because it denies the vanquished race future generations. By usurping the right to generation, the conqueror kills the enemy and his children's children, and establishes firmly his continued power over the enemy.[8] Thus the conquest of the Moors could be achieved in ways other than military victories.

---

wicked sons, however, are more concerned with the discovery of the affair by the emperor.

8. Miscegenation between white male slave owners and black slaves in America raised constant problems for the church and state, yet the fact that copulation between white women and black men received general condemnation points to the political significance white men placed on interracial sex. Winthrop Jordan writes: "It is scarcely necessary to resort to speculation about the influence of tropical climates in order to explain this situation for life in the islands was in large degree shaped by the enormous disproportion of Negroes to white settlers and characterized by the concomitant brutal nakedness of planter domination over the slaves. In the West Indian islands and to less extent South Carolina, racial slavery consisted of unsheathed dominion by relatively small numbers of white men over enormous numbers of Negroes, and it was in these colonies that Negro men were most

Black Face, Maligned Race

A brief mention of one of Dryden's rivals, the successful playwright Elkanah Settle, is warranted here before closing this chapter. In two of his plays, *The Empress of Morocco* and *The Heir of Morocco* (1682), Settle also writes about white Moors. These plays are quite different from any plays I have discussed thus far; they are the only plays I have found in which there are no white Christian Europeans to serve as exemplars of moral and spiritual perfection. What we find instead is a society much like the Italian society in *The White Devil*. In Settle's Morocco plays there are virtuous and evil Moors, forthright and duplicitous Moors. Settle's plays present the range of humans we generally expect to find in drama. Although we observe this to a degree in Dryden's plays, particularly in *The Conquest of Granada*, we still cannot ignore the distinction between Moor and Spaniard, and Muslim and Christian. Dryden's Moorish characters either lack grace or are incipient Christians. Although clearly non-Christian, the virtuous Moors in Settle's plays pray as faithfully as their Christian counterparts, and they demonstrate their goodness as fully. By being spared the unfavorable comparisons to European Christians, the Moorish heroes of the play are also spared the necessity and humiliation of disowning family, nation, and faith. Their identity as Moors—heroic Moors, honest Moors, virtuous Moors—remains intact.[9]

---

stringently barred from sexual relations with white women. Sexually as well as in every other way, Negroes were utterly subordinated. White men extended their dominion over their Negroes to the bed, where the sex act itself served as ritualistic re-enactment of the daily pattern of social dominance. In New England, at the other extreme, white men had no need for aggressive assertion of their dominance in order to sustain slavery on a major scale and hence in New England Negro men were accorded some measure of sexual freedom" (*White over Black*, 140-44).

9. Although not pertinent to this specific discussion, it is important to note that *The Empress of Morocco* makes important distinctions between black Moors and white Moors, if we are to rely on the plates found in the quarto of the play. In a musical scene, the singers and dancers are clearly black, though none of the major characters of the play are black. Tokson suggests that the Empress of the play is, but I disagree with him on this point. A specific comment of hers about punishing her daughter makes it seem impossible that the empress could be black. She orders her daughter's face "with some deep poys'nous Paint, / Discolour'd to a horrid black be stain'd. / Then say 'twas as a mark of Vengeance given, / That she was blasted by the hand of Heaven" (*The Empress of Morocco*, [London, 1673], IV, ii, p. 52). It is hard to imagine that the empress is black and that her daughter is white.

In considering these plays, we ought to recall Hamlet's words about *The Mousetrap*, for these plays too are tropical. The real concerns in Dryden's plays and the briefly mentioned plays of Settle are good government, honest princes, and the true and honest practice of virtue and religion. Like black Moors, white Moors, when interacting with European Christians, provide a gauge with which English audiences could measure their own rulers, churchmen, values, weaknesses, and strengths. This does not mean that the representations of Moors are somehow less valid statements of popular attitudes toward Moors in this context. In fact, the contrary is true. Because playwrights could rely on a common tradition, on widely held assumptions about Moors, Moors serve as valuable examples of moral depravity in general or of specific moral vices and lapses. Just as the Spanish in times of tension between England and Spain serve as examples of Catholic duplicity, and the Irish as examples of sottish, uncivil behavior, so Moors hold a specific symbolic station, one that relies on perceived differences from Europeans and that, ironically, minimizes the actual importance of them as real people.

Conclusion

> There you shall live with honor, as becomes
> my fellow sufferers and worthy friends.
> This if we do succeed.
> —Thomas Southerne, *Oroonoko*

Perhaps the simplest thing to conclude about the representation of Moors is that it was racist. Such a conclusion, however, would be reductive and would also assert that the many playwrights were primarily concerned with rendering for their audiences the "true" nature of Africans. Most of these representations are indeed racist; to deny that would require the blindness of Celanta's husband in *The Old Wives Tale*. Yet drama as a mode of representation invokes its own demands, codes, and conventions. Characters, even the most mimetic, exist in a world of determined and overdetermined signifiers, tropes, and rhetorical constructs. Moors are created to be part of that dramatic universe and therefore never operate or interact entirely free of the greater thematic and dramatic requirements of a play. Dramatic characters exist to be more than real people.

What then do we say about Moors? As we have seen in the last chapter, white Moors, like black, are subjected to the same dramatic and thematic demands of the playwrights. We see, especially in Dryden's plays, how valuable non-Christians are as versions of the Other and as witnesses to the power and supremacy of Christianity. Of course, simultaneously the Moors helped to create an environment in which English audiences could compare and judge

Conclusion

their own government and their own mores against these non-Christian Others. Audiences could then criticize when necessary English departures from those ideals. "The Elizabethan urge to moralize was normally served most easily by presenting the foreigner in terms derived from simple nationalism," writes G. K. Hunter.[1]

Of course, as a version of the Other, white Moors attest to the greater otherness of black Moors. A few white Moors, after conversion to Christianity, appear to be freely and completely accepted into the community through marriage. Of the black men who join the community in this manner, none enters or continues free of prejudice; none maintains or increases his esteem in the community. The three most important such characters, Eleazar, Othello, and Oroonoko, receive drastically different treatments from their creators, but within their individual dramatic worlds, their blackness raises fundamental issues about their place in their communities. The exclusion of Othello and Oroonoko from their communities broaches important questions about the nature of virtue and the values on which society *ought* to be based, but their acts of revenge and violence, even as they make the audience conscious of the virtue and suffering of the Moors, remind that same audience of the danger of blackness, the danger that may accompany the inclusion of the Other. Another two black Moors, Osmin and Joffer, win acceptance from the Christians when they display a willingness to forsake their black compatriots and to embrace Christian virtue. But neither of these makes any demands for total legitimacy in Christian society. Osmin dies at the hands of Abdelazer, but this honest Moor's acknowledgment of order and hierarchy identifies him as being unlike the other Moors who seek to destroy that order or at least to ignore it. Joffer makes no demands on the community. He sues for admission because he desires only to be among the virtuous, and this is an acceptable and safe ambition.

Yet these four are rare. The great many black Moors, including those in pageants and masques, even when not evil themselves know that blackness is a signifier of evil and sin. These characters know that they do not belong and that the community that admits

---

1. G. K. Hunter, "Elizabethans and Foreigners," in *Dramatic Identities*, 15.

them struggles to be free of them. When evil black characters are viewed metaphorically, the audience learns neither to embrace nor to indulge evil, nor to become black in reputation and in spirit. Characters such as Niger's daughters and the Christian Moors in the pageants recognize this truth even as they acknowledge their own imperfections. These characters instruct the audience to live up to the blessings of being English and Christian.

The only truly happy or truly benign Moors are those who are separated from the real world. The Moors on those pastoral plantations pose no threat to the community because they are not a part of it. They live in a prelapsarian world free of malice and free of ambition. Having exchanged their labor (and probably their freedom) for the right to sing and dance, they desire nothing else. The irony of this representation, of course, reminds us of dangerous black men in other communities. Where blacks exist in a nonpastoral world, a world in which power is at stake and political and sexual intrigues are ongoing, where blacks exist in a world that is most like that postlapsarian world we know, they busy themselves with other kinds of activities.

In the end, we must remind ourselves that all of these Moors are stage Moors. While they represent ideas and attitudes about blackness and black men, they also only represent those ideas and attitudes. That there are several types and exceptions to and divergence from those types reveals some awareness in the minds of playwrights that all Africans were not a priori the same. Shakespeare has Aaron choose evil; Southerne makes Oroonoko a victim of white duplicity. What is always evident, however, is that blacks are different and that the black on their faces, when not thought to signify the Moors' kinship to the devil, reveals at the very least their separation from the community. How these assumptions and representations through the centuries have come to shape our lives and the opinions of our contemporaries about blacks is, I am afraid to say, all too easy to assess. For many, blackness still signifies evil and sin, and black people remain the Other, excluded still.

Bibliography

PLAYS

Barnet, Sylvan, ed. *The Complete Signet Classic Shakespeare.* New York, 1972.

Berkeley, William. *The Lost Lady.* London, 1638.

Bowers, Fredson, ed. *The Dramatic Works of the Beaumont and Fletcher Canon.* 4 vols. Cambridge, England, 1979.

———.*The Dramatic Works of Thomas Dekker.* 4 vols. Cambridge, England, 1961.

Brome, Richard. *The Dramatic Works of Richard Brome.* London, 1873.

Bullen, A. H., ed. *The Works of John Marston.* 3 vols. London, 1887.

Cunliffe, John W., ed. *The Supposes,* in *The Complete Works of George Gascoigne.* 1907; rpr. New York, 1969.

D'Avenant, William. *The Dramatic Works of Sir William D'Avenant.* 5 vols. London, 1873.

Dyce, Alexander, ed. *The Works of John Webster.* 4 vols. London, 1830.

Edwards, Philip, and Colin Gibson, eds. *The Plays and Poems of Philip Massinger.* 5 vols. Oxford, 1976.

Garter, Thomas. *The Commedy of the Moste Vertuous and Godlye Susanna.* 1569; rpr. Oxford, 1936.

Heywood, Thomas. *The Fair Maid of the West, Parts I and II.* Edited by Robert K. Turner, Jr. Lincoln, Neb., 1967.

Magnus, Leonard, ed. *Respublica.* London, 1905.

Bibliography

Marlowe, Christopher. *Tamburlaine the Great, Parts I and II*. Edited by John D. Jump. Lincoln, Neb., 1967.
Parrott, Thomas Marc, ed. *The Plays of George Chapman*. 4 vols. New York, 1961.
Prouty, Charles Tyler, ed. *The Life and Works of George Peele*. 3 vols. New Haven, Conn., 1961.
Ravenscroft, Edward. *Titus Andronicus, or the Rape of Lavinia*. 1687; rpr. London, 1969.
Settle, Elkanah. *The Empress of Morocco*. London, 1673.
———. *Heir of Morocco*. London, 1682.
Shakespeare, William. *Othello*. Edited by M. R. Ridley. New York, 1958.
Simpson, Richard, ed. *The Famous History of the Life and Death of Captain Thomas Stukeley*. In Vol. I of *The School of Shakespeare*. 2 vols. London, 1878.
Southerne, Thomas. *Oroonoko*. Edited by Maximillian E. Novak and David Stuart Rodes. Lincoln, Neb., 1976.
Stork, Charles Wharton, ed. *William Rowley: His All's Lost by Lust and A Shoemaker, A Gentleman*. Philadelphia, 1910.
Summers, Montague, ed. *The Works of Aphra Behn*. 6 vols. 1915; rpr. New York, 1967.
Swedenberg, H. T., Jr., et al., eds. *The Works of John Dryden*. 19 vols. Berkeley, Calif., 1956-1976.
Waller, A. R., ed. *The Works of Francis Beaumont and John Fletcher*. 10 vols. Cambridge, England, 1909.
Webster, John, *The Devil's Law-Case*. Edited by Francis A. Shirley. Lincoln, Neb., 1972.
———. *The White Devil*. Edited by J. R. Mulryne. Lincoln, Neb., 1969.

MASQUES

Buchanan, George. *Opera Omnia, Historica, Chronologica, Juridica, Politica, Satyrica an Poetica*. Leiden, 1725.
Chambers, E. K., ed. *Aurelian Townshend's Poems and Masks*. Oxford, 1912.
Davis, Walter R., ed. *The Complete Plays of Thomas Campion*. New York, 1976.
Herford, C. H., and Percy Simpson, eds. *Ben Jonson*. 10 vols. Oxford, 1925.
Maidment, James, and W. H. Logan, eds. *The Dramatic Works of John Crowne*. 4 vols. Edinburgh, 1873-74.
Orgel, Stephen, ed. *Ben Jonson: The Complete Masques*. New Haven, Conn., 1969.

PAGEANTS

Bullen, A. H., ed. *The Works of Thomas Middleton.* 8 vols. New York, 1964.
Jordan, Thomas. *The Goldsmiths Jubile, or, Londons Triumphs.* London, 1674.
———. *London in its Splendor.* London, 1673.
———. *London in Luster, Projecting Many Bright Beams of Triumph.* London, 1679.
———. *London's Glory, or, the Lord Mayor's Show.* London, 1680.
———. *London's Joy, or, the Lord Mayor's Show.* London, 1681.
———. *London Triumphant, or, The City in Jollity and Splendour.* London, 1672.
———. *The Triumphs of London.* London, 1678.
Munday, Anthony. *Chrysanaleia: The Golden Fishing, or Honour of Fishmongers.* London, 1616.
Settle, Elkanah. *The Triumphs of London.* London, 1691.
———. *The Triumphs of London.* London, 1692.
Tatham, John. *London's Tryumph, Presented by Industry and Honour: with Other Delightful Scaenes.* London, 1658.
———. *London's Tryumph.* London, 1659.
———. *Londons Tryumphs.* London, 1661.
Taubman, Matthew. *London's Yearly Jubilee.* London, 1686.

BOOKS AND ARTICLES

Augustine. *Expositions of the Book of Psalms.* New York, 1893. Translated by A. Cleveland Coxe. Edited by Philip Schaff. Vol. III of *A Select Library of the Nicene and Post Nicene Fathers of the Christian Church.* 14 vols.
Bentley, Gerald Eades. *The Jacobean and Caroline Stage.* Oxford, 1956.
Berger, Thomas L., and William C. Brandford, Jr. *An Index of Characters in English Printed Drama to the Restoration.* Englewood, Colo., 1975.
Bergeron, David M. *English Civic Pageantry, 1558-1642.* London, 1971.
Bernheimer, Richard. *Wild Men in the Middle Ages: A Study in Art, Sentiment and Demonology.* Cambridge, Mass., 1952.
Bissel, B. H. *The American Indian in English Literature of the Eighteenth Century.* New Haven, Conn., 1925.
Bloomfield, Morton W. "A Grammatical Approach to Personification Allegory." *Modern Philology,* LX (1963), 161-71.
Burton, Robert. *The Anatomy of Melancholy.* Edited by Holbrook Jackson. London, 1977.
Chambers, E. K. *The Early English Folk Play.* Oxford, 1933.
———. *The Medieval Stage.* 2 vols. Oxford, 1903.

Bibliography

Chew, Samuel. *The Cresent and the Rose.* New York, 1937.
Coleman, D. C. *The Economy of England, 1450-1750.* Oxford, 1977.
Corominas, Joan, and José A. Pascual. *Diccionario Critico Etimologico de la Lengua Castellana e Hispanico.* Madrid, 1981.
Craton, Michael. *Sinews of Empire: A Short History of British Slavery.* Garden City, N.Y., 1974.
Davies, Godfrey. *The Early Stuarts.* 2nd ed. Oxford, 1959. Vol. IX of Sir George Clark, ed., *The Oxford History of England.* 15 vols.
Davis, David Brion. *The Problem of Slavery in Western Culture.* Ithaca, N.Y., 1966.
Davis, Ralph. "English Foreign Trade, 1660-1700." In *The Growth of English Trade in the Seventeenth and Eighteenth Centuries*, edited by W. E. Minchinton. London, 1969.
Deane, Cecil V. *Dramatic Theory and the Rhymed Heroic Play.* London, 1931.
Deighton, Kenneth. *The Old Dramatists: Conjectural Readings.* Westminster, England, 1896.
Eden, Richard. *The Decades of the Newe World.* London, 1555.
Ellis-Fermor, Una. *The Jacobean Drama: An Interpretation.* London, 1936.
Empson, William. *English Pastoral Poetry.* 1938; rpr. Freeport, N.Y., 1972.
Fairholt, Frederick W. *Lord Mayors' Pageants: Being Collections Towards a History of these Annual Celebrations.* London, 1843-44.
Felperin, Howard. *Shakespearean Representation: Mimesis and Modernity in Elizabethan Tragedy.* Princeton, 1977.
Finny, Gretchen Ludke. *Musical Backgrounds for English Literature, 1580-1650.* New Brunswick, N.J., 1961.
Fletcher, Angus. *Allegory: The Theory of a Symbolic Mode.* Ithaca, N.Y., 1964.
Gardiner, Harold C., S.J. *Mysteries' End: An Investigation of the Last Days of the Medieval Religious Stage.* New Haven, Conn., 1946.
Gardner, Helen. *The Noble Moor.* London, 1955.
Godwyn, Morgan. *The Negro's + Indians Advocate, Suing for Their Admission into the Church.* London, 1680.
Gordon, Donald. "The Imagery of Ben Jonson's *Masques of Blacknesse and Beautie.*" In *The Renaissance Imagination*, Edited by Stephen Orgel. Berkeley, Calif., 1975.
Greenblatt, Stephen Jay. *Renaissance Self-Fashioning: From More to Shakespeare.* Chicago, 1980.
Greg, W. W. *Two Elizabethan Stage Abridgements: The Battle of Alcazar and Orlando Furioso.* Oxford, 1922.

Bibliography

Hakluyt, Richard. *The Principal Navigations, Voyages, Traffiques and Discoveries of the English Nation.* 8 vols. 1598-1600; rpr. London, 1927.

Hall, Edward. *Henry VIII.* Edited by Charles Whibley. London, 1904.

Harbage, Alfred, and S. Shoenbaum. *Annals of English Drama, 975-1700.* 2nd ed. Philadelphia, 1964.

Heliodorus. *An Aethiopian History.* Translated by Thomas Underdowne. Edited by Charles Whibley. 1587; rpr. London, 1895.

Hickeringill, Edmund. *Jamaica Viewed.* 2nd ed. London, 1661.

Hildburgh, W. L. "Medieval English Alabasters." *Archaelogia*, XCIII (1949), 51-101.

Horace. *Satires, Epistles, Ars Poetic.* Loeb Classical Library. 1926; rpr. Cambridge, Mass., 1970.

Hoy, Cyrus. *Introductions, Notes and Commentaries to Texts in "The Dramatic Works of Thomas Dekker,"* Edited by Fredson Bowers. Cambridge, England, 1980. 4 vols.

Huizinga, Johan. *Homo Ludens: A Study of the Play Element in Culture.* Boston, 1955.

Hume, Robert D. *The Development of English Drama in the Late Seventeenth Century.* Oxford, 1976.

Hunter, George K. *Dramatic Identities and Cultural Tradition: Studies in Shakespeare and his Contemporaries: Critical Essays.* New York, 1978.

Jerome. *Letters and Works.* New York, 1893. Translated by W. H. Fremantle. Edited by Philip Schaff. Vol. VI of *A Select Library of the Nicene and Post Nicene Fathers of the Christian Church.* 14 vols.

Johnson, Lemuel. *The Devil, the Gargoyle, and the Buffoon: The Negro as Metaphor in Western Literature.* Port Washington, N.Y., 1969.

Jones, C. M. "The Conventional Saracen of the Songs of Geste." *Speculum*, XVII (1942), 201-25.

Jones, Eldred D. *Othello's Countrymen: The African in English Renaissance Drama.* Oxford, 1965.

Jordan, Winthrop. *White over Black: American Attitudes Toward the Negro, 1550-1812.* Chapel Hill, N.C., 1968.

Las Casas, Bartolome. *Popery Truly Display'd in its Bloody Colours.* Translated anonymously. London, 1689.

———. *The Spanish Colonie.* Translated by M. M. S. London, 1583.

———. *The Tears of the Indians.* Translated by John Phillips. London, 1656.

Leo Africanus. *The History and Description of Africa.* Translated by John Pory. Edited by Robert Brown. 3 vols. New York, 1896.

———. *Ioannis Leonis Africani de Totivs Africae Descriptione.* Translated by Ioannes Florianus. Zurich, 1559.

Bibliography

———. *Il Viaggio di Giovan Leone e Le Navigazioni*. Edited by Giovanbattista Ramusio. Venezia, 1837.

Lewis, Bernard. *Race and Color in Islam*. New York, 1971.

Ligon, Richard. *A True and Exact History of the Island of Barbados*. London, 1657.

Loftis, John. *The Politics of Drama in Augustan England*. Oxford, 1963.

Machyn, Henry. *The Diary of Henry Machyn, Citizen and Merchant Taylor of London, From A.D. 1550 to A.D. 1563*. Edited by John Gough Nichols. London, 1848.

Malone Society. *Collections III: A Calendar of Dramatic Records in the Books of the Livery Companies of London*. Edited by Jean Robertson and D. J. Gordon. Oxford, England, 1954.

Mandeville, Sir John. *Travels*. London, 1953.

———. *Mandeville's Travels*. Edited by P. Hamelius. London, 1919.

Metlitzki, Dorotheé. *The Matter of Araby in Medieval England*. New Haven, Conn., 1977.

Meyer-Baer, Kathi. *Music of the Spheres and the Dance of Death: Studies in Musical Iconology*. Princeton, N.J., 1970.

Mill, Anna Jean. *Mediaeval Plays in Scotland*. New York, 1924.

Nicoll, Allardyce. *Restoration Drama, 1660-1700*. Cambridge, England, 1955. Vol. I of *A History of English Drama, 1660-1900*. 6 vols.

Novum Glossarium Mediae Latinitatis Ab Anno DCCC Usque Ad Annum MCC. Copenhagen, 1959.

Oelschlager, Victor R. B. *A Medieval Spanish Word List: A Preliminary Dated Vocabulary of First Appearances up to Berceo*. Madison, Wisc., 1940.

Oliphant, E. H. *The Plays of Beaumont and Fletcher: An Attempt to Determine Their Respective Shares and the Shares of Others*. New Haven, Conn., 1927.

Orgel, Stephen. *The Jonsonian Masque*. Cambridge, Mass., 1965.

Orgel, Stephen, and Roy Strong. *Inigo Jones: The Theatre of the Stuart Court*. 2 vols. Berkeley, Calif., 1973.

Plato. *The Symposium*, in *The Dialogues of Plato*. Translated by B. Jowett. 4th ed. 4 vols. Oxford, 1953.

Polemon, John. *The Second Part of the Book of Battailes, Fought in Our Age*. London, 1587.

Purchas, Samuel. *Purchas, His Pilgrimage*. London, 1613.

Rice, Warner G. "A Principal Source of *The Battle of Alcazar*." *Modern Language Notes*, LVIII (1943), 428-31.

Riese, Alexander, ed. *Anthologia Latina*. Leipzig, 1869. 2 vols.

Ripa, Cesare. *Iconologia*. Facsim.; New York, 1976.

———. *Iconologie*. Translated by Jean Baudouin. Facsim.; New York, 1976.

Bibliography

Roblin, M. "Mauritania." *Bulletin de la Société National des Antiquaires de France*, 1949.

"Rouland and Vernagu." In *The English Charlemagne Romances*, edited by Sidney Herrtage. London, 1882.

Rymer, Thomas. *A Short View of Tragedy*, in *The Critical Works of Thomas Rymer*. Edited by C. R. Zimansky. New Haven, Conn., 1956.

Said, Edward W. *Orientalism*. New York, 1978.

Simpson, Percy, and C. F. Bell. *Designs by Inigo Jones for Masques and Plays at Court*. Oxford, 1924.

Snowden, Frank M. *Blacks in Antiquity: Ethiopians in the Greco-Roman Experience*. Cambridge, Mass., 1970.

The Song of Roland. Translated by Howard S. Robertson. London, 1972.

Spencer, M. Lyle. *Corpus Christi Pageants in England*. New York, 1911.

Spenser, Edmund. *The Works of Edmund Spenser*. Edited by Edwin Greenlaw, et al. Baltimore, 1935.

Spivack, Bernard. *Shakespeare and the Allegory of Evil: The History of a Metaphor in Relation to His Major Villains*. New York, 1958.

Strong, Roy. *Splendor at Court, Renaissance Spectacle and the Theater of Power*. Boston, 1973.

Summers, Montague. *The Restoration Theatre*. London, 1934.

Sypher, Wylie. *Guinea's Captive Kings: British Anti-Slavery Literature of the XVIIIth Century*. New York, 1969.

Tokson, Elliot H. *The Popular Image of the Black Man in English Drama, 1550-1688*. Boston, 1982.

Tooley, Ronald Vere. *Collectors' Guide to Maps of the African Continent and Southern Africa*. London, 1969.

Tryon, Thomas. *Friendly Advice to the Gentlemen-Planters of the East and West Indies*. N.p., 1684.

Van Lennep, William. *The London Stage, 1660-1800: 1660-1700*. Carbondale, Ill., 1965. Part I of *The London Stage, 1660-1800*. 5 vols.

Vercoutter, Jean, et al. *The Image of the Black in Western Art*. 2 vols. New York, 1976.

Welsford, Enid. *The Court Masque: A Study in the Relationship between Poetry and the Revels*. Cambridge, England, 1927.

Whitney, Lois. "Did Shakespeare Know 'Leo Africanus'?" *PMLA*, XXXVII (1922), 470-83.

Wilson, F. P. *The English Drama, 1485-1585*. Edited by G. K. Hunter. Oxford, 1969.

Yoklavich, John, "Introduction to *The Battle of Alcazar*." In *The Dramatic Works of George Peele*, edited by Charles Tyler Prouty. New Haven, Conn., 1961. Vol. II of Prouty, ed., *The Life and Works of George Peele*. 3 vols.

Index

Aaron (character), x, 91-97, 148n
Abdelazer, 91, 112-17, 122-23, 176, 201
Abdelmelec (character), 77, 82
Aboan (character), 179
Aethiopian, 16
Africa: in Court Masques, 35; in pageants, 50-52; maps of, 50n; music of, 59-61; religious situation of, 15n; wealth of, 63-64
African, x, 1, 13-17
Affricani bianchi, 12, 14, 15, 182
Affricani neri, 14, 15
Africans: arrival in England, 1; bestiality of, 4-6; color of, 9, 12-16; sexuality of, 5-6, 92-93, 120-23, 145-46
Alcade (character), 147n
All's Lost by Lust, 117-19, 135
Almahide (character), 190-92
Almanzor (character), 187-93
Almeyda (character), 194-97
Alphonsus, King of Aragon, 76n
Alvara, Francisco, 15n
America (character), 68-69
American Indians. *See* Native Americans
Anastasius, 8

Anatomy of Melancholy, The, 155-56
Anne of Denmark, 20, 21, 33, 35
Arabian, 16n
Arcadia, 40
Armusia (character), 184-86
Aron (character), 97-103
Aston, Edward, 192n
Augustine, 2, 3
Avarice (character), 73

Baptism, 3, 11, 25
Barabas (character), 96
Battle of Alcazar, The, ix, 72-84, 183
Beaumont, Francis, 182-83
Beauty and blackness, 21-41
Bebritius (character), 149-50
Behn, Aphra, 91, 112-17, 122-23, 173, 174, 176
Believe as You List, 84n
Berceo, Gonzalo de, 10
Bergeron, David, 45-46
Berkeley, William, 139-42
Bestiality, 4-6, 36
Bible, 22, 32, 188
Bishop's Bible, 22
Black (color), 2-4
Black-a-moores, 7, 48n
Blackening, 20, 25-26, 47n

Index

Blackness: and beauty, 21–41; and bestiality, 4–6; and Christianity, 2–4; and evil, 2–4, 26, 72, 84, 91, 94–96, 201–202; and sin, 26, 65
Blacks: arrival in England, 1; as heroes, 180–81; morality of, 67–68; music of, 59–61; and Native Americans, 47–48; sexuality of, 5–6, 92–93, 120–23, 145–46; and slavery, 52–56, 69–71; women, 123–44
Blind Beggar of Alexandria, The, 147, 149
Bridges, Bess (character), 163–71
Brome, Richard, 142–44
Brown, Robert, 12n
Burton, Robert, 155–56

Calisto, 37–40, 173
Calisto and Melibea, 74n
Calypolis (character), 81n, 85, 124n
Campion, Thomas, 35
Candace, "the pride of Ethiopia" (character), 33
Carleton, Dudley, 26
Castle of Perseverance, The, 72, 79–80, 120
Celanta (character), 133–34
Chanson de Roland, 10–11
Chapman, George, 147
Charles I, 20
Charles II, 62
Chew, Samuel, 192n
Christian Turned Turk, A, 183
Christianity: baptism, 3, 11, 25; and blackness, 2–4; and Moors, 64–71; and superiority, 195–96
Chronographia, 8
Chrysanaleia, 46–47, 62–63
Clem (character), 164
Cleopatra (character), 148n
Coleman, D. C., 42–43
Collectors' Guide to Maps of the African Continent and Southern Africa, 50
Colonialism and masques, 42–43
Comedy of the Moste Vertuous and Godlye Susanna, 74, 120
Comprehensive Etymological Dictionary of the English Language, 8
Confession Amantis, 7
Conquest of Granada, 183, 186–93, 196–99

Corneille, Pierre, 190n
Court masque, 18–41; early masques, 19–20; exotics in, 20; personifications in, 18–19; Scottish Court, 19n; type characters, 19
Court Masque, The: A Study in the Relationship between Poetry and the Revels, 20n
Crescent and the Rose, The, 192n
Crowne, John, 37, 40, 173
Cruelty of the Spaniards, The, 171n

Daborne, Robert, 183
D'Avenant, William, 171, 173
Dekker, Thomas, 72, 91, 122
Desdemona (character), 152–54, 157–58
Destruccion de las Indias, 56–57, 63, 69, 119–20
Device of the Pageant Borne before Woolstone Dixi Lord Maior of the City of London, The, 48–49, 78, 172
Devil, the, 4, 10, 72–76
Devil's Law-Case, The, 136
Diccionario Critico Etimologico de la Lengua Castellana, 9
Dictionnaire Etymologique de la Langue Grecque, 8
Doctor Faustus, 75n
Don Sebastian, 84n, 186, 193–97
Dryden, John, 61, 84n, 183, 186, 199
Duchess of Malfi, The, 120
Duke of York, 37

Egyptian Gap, 7n
Eleazar (character), 103–12, 196, 201
Elimine (character), 149–50
Elizabeth I, 49, 53
Empress of Morocco, The, 173, 198
Empson, William, 58
English Moor, The, 142–44
Ethiopia, 9
Evil and blackness, 2–4, 26, 72, 84, 91, 94–96

Faerie Queene, The, 92
Fair Maid of the West, The, 162
Falstaff (character), 79
Famous History of the Life and Death of Captain Thomas Stukeley, The, 84–91, 183
Felperin, Howard, 79

212

Index

Fletcher, Angus, 18
Fletcher, John, 182
Florianus, Joannes, 12–14
Freigius, Thomas, 76
Friendly Advice to the Gentlemen-Planters of the East and West Indies, 57–58, 70
Fructifera (character), 67
Fulgens and Lucrece, 74n
Fydella (character), 135–36

Gascoigne, George, 35
Geneva Bible, 22
Gentleman Dancing Master, The, 173
Gentleness and Nobility, 74n
Godwyn, Morgan, 57, 70, 103
Goldsmiths Jubile, The, 44–45, 47, 51
Gordon, Donald, 29
Gower, John, 7
Gratiano (character), 159
Greene, Robert, 76n, 182
Guilds, 42–44
Gypsies Metamorphosed, The, 33–35

Hakluyt, Richard, 53, 63–64
Ham, 3, 25, 84, 92
Hamlet, 78, 199
Heir of Morocco, The, 198
Heywood, Thomas, 49, 162
Hickeringill, Edmund, 56
Hildburgh, W. L., 4
History and Description of Africa, The, 3, 5, 6, 12–15, 104n, 155n
History of Sir Francis Drake, The, 171–73
Horace, 2
Hunter, G. K., 177, 201

Iago (character), 151–62
Indian, definition of, 6, 48
Indians. *See* Native Americans
Interracial marriage, 196–97
Isabella (character), 106–108, 110
Islam, 10–12, 16–17, 192
Island Princess, The, 136n, 182–86, 197

Jamaica Viewed, 56
James II, 37, 53
Jerome, 2, 3, 170
Jew of Malta, The, 75, 78–79

Joffer (character), 169–71, 201
Jones, C. M., 11
Jones, Eldred, 14n
Jones, Inigo, 20, 36n
Jonson, Ben, 20, 21, 85, 143n
Jordan, Thomas, 42, 44–45, 47, 50, 52–55, 58–59, 61, 66–67
Jordan, Winthrop, 3, 5, 121–23, 132, 197n

Kate (character), 134
King of the Moors, 62–64
Klein, Ernest, 8
Knight of Malta, The, 128–31

Las Casas, Bartolmé, 56–57, 63, 69
Leo Africanus, 3, 5, 6, 12–15, 104n, 155n
Libya, 132
Liddell and Scott, 8
Lightness, 24, 28–33
Ligon, Richard, 55–58, 60, 70
Loftis, John, 102
Lok, John, 4–5, 132
London in its Splendor, 55
London Triumphant, 47–48, 53–54, 59, 62, 67–69
London's Joy, 47, 52–53, 67
London's Tryumph (1658), 52
London's Tryumphs (1661), 48
London's Yearly Jubilee, 51
Lord mayors' pageants, 42–71; Africa, in, 50–52; and class oppression, 58–59; and colonialism, 42–43; commercial considerations, 70–71; cost of, 43–44; and guilds, 42–44; personifications in, 46–48; publication of texts, 44
Lost Lady, The, 139–42, 144
Lust's Dominion, 72, 91, 103–20, 122–23, 162, 180, 196–97

Mahomet, 84n
Mandeville's Travels, x, 7, 9
Manners, Lawes and Customes of All Nations, The, 192n
Mαυpos, 8
Maps of Africa, 50n
Marlowe, Christopher, 48, 76, 91n
Marston, John, 124
Masque of Beauty, The, 26–30, 32, 35

213

Index

Masque of Blackness, The, 20-27, 32, 35, 39
Masque of Queens, The, 30-33, 35
Masques. *See* Court masque
Massinger, Philip, 138-39
Maura, 8
Mauretania, 7, 9
Maurus, 8-10
A Medieval Spanish Word List, 9-10
Merchant of Venice, The, 60-61, 124, 144, 147
Merchant-Taylor's Books, 45
Metlitzki, Dorotheé, 11
Middleton, Thomas, 44-46, 64
Monsieur Thomas, 134
Moor: and *African*, 1, 13-17; definition, of, 6, 7, 17; etymology of, ix-x, 1, 6-17
Moore, John, 66-67
Moors: and Christianity, 64-71; color of, 12-16; royalty, 61-62; sexuality of, 5-6, 92-93, 120-23; white Moors, 182-99; women, 123-44
Moredo, 10, 12
Moro, 9-10, 12
Morocco (character), 147-50
Mowres, 7n
Mullisheg (character), 163-71
Muly Hamet (character), 80n, 86
Muly Mahamet (character), 72, 76-84, 87-91, 96, 183
Munday, Anthony, 46-47, 62
Music of blacks and Indians, 59-61
Mystery plays, 72-76

Native Americans: bestial nature of, 36; and blacks, 47-48; music of, 59-61; as type characters, 19; and slavery, 53-55, 56-58, 69
Negro, x, 14-15, 16, 83-84
Negro's & Indians Advocate Suing for Their Admission into the Church, The, 57, 70
Netherlands, The, 68-69
Noah, 3
Novum Glossarium, 8

Old Wives Tale, The, 133-34, 200
Opulenta (character), 65-66
Orlando Furioso, 148n, 182
Oroonoko, The Royal Slave, ix, 161-62, 171, 174-81, 200-202
Osmin (character), 115, 201

Othello, x, 147, 150-62, 201
Othello's Countrymen: The African in English Renaissance Drama, 14n, 90n, 126n
Other, the, x, 17, 20, 41, 201-202
Oxford English Dictionary, 7

Pageants. *See* Lord mayors' pageants
Parliament of Love, The, 138-39
Peele, George, 48-49, 72, 76-84
Personification in Masques and pageants, 18-19, 46-48
Philip of Spain, 88-90, 105-12
Planters, 52-58, 69-71
Plato, 18
Playhouse to Be Let, The, 171n, 173
Poetaster, 85
Polemon, John, 77-78
Popery Truly display'd in its Bloody Colours, 57
Portia (character), 148-50
Porus (character), 147, 149-50
Pory, John, 12-16, 182
Presenter (character), 80-82
Prince of Darkness, 72, 91
Principal Navigations, Voyages, Traffiques and Discoveries of the English Nation, The, 4-5, 53, 63-64, 132
Prophetess, The, 131
Purchas, His Pilgrimage, 5, 16-17
Purchas, Samuel, 3, 5, 6, 16-17, 48, 55

Ravenscroft, Edward 91, 97-103, 173
Renegado, 183
Respublica, 73
Revenger's Tragedy, The, 120
Richard III, 78, 79
Rowley, William, 91, 117
Rymer, Thomas, 160-61

Scottish Court masques, 19n
Sebastian (character), 77-78, 82-83, 84n, 86, 196-97
Second Part of the Book of Battailes, Fought in Our Age, The, 76
Settle, Elkanah, 173, 198-99
Sexuality of blacks, 5-6, 92-93, 120-23, 145-46
Shakespeare, William, 60-61, 91, 147, 150, 202
Sin and blackness, 2-4, 11, 26, 65
Slavery, 52-58, 69-71

214

Index

"Song for St. Cecilia's Day, 1687," p. 61
Song of Songs, 21, 22
Southerne, Thomas, 171, 174-81, 200, 202
Spain, 69, 171
Spanish Colonie, The, 56-57, 63, 63n, 119-20
Spencer (character), 163, 165-69
Spenser, Edmund, 92
Spivack, Bernard, 73, 75
Squire's Masque, The, 35
Summer's Last Will and Testament, 75n
Supposes, The, 35
Symposium, The, 18, 21, 22, 29, 30, 40
Sypher, Wylie, 177

Tamburlaine, 48, 76
Tatham, John, 48, 49, 51
Taubman, Matthew, 51
Tawny, 33-34
Tawny moors, 53-55, 56-60, 148n, 182, 184
Tears of the Indians, The, 57
Tempe Restor'd, 19, 36-37
Thesaurus Graecae Linguae, The, 8
Thracian Wonder, The, 147n, 182-83
Tide Tarrieth No Man, The, 131
Titus Andronicus, 90, 91-99, 148n, 196n, 197
Titus Andronicus, or The Rape of Lavinia, 91, 97-103, 162
Tokson, Elliot, 90n, 126n, 147n

Tooley, Ronald Vere, 50
Towneley Plays, The, 1, 4
Townshend, Aurelian, 36-37
Townson, William, 60
Triall of Treasure, The, 131
Triumphs of London, The, 42, 50, 54-55, 59, 65-66
Triumphs of Truth, The, 44, 46, 64-65
True and Exact History of the Island of Barbados, A, 55-58, 60, 70
Type characters, 19
Tyron, Thomas, 57-58, 70, 103

Unnatural Mother, The, 173

Vice (character), 72-76, 79
Villain (character), 74-75, 79

Webster, John, 126-28, 136-38
Welsford, Enid, 20
White (color), 2-4
White Aethiopian, The, 148n
White Devil, The, 126-28, 136-37
White moors, 182-199
White Over Black, 3, 5, 121-23, 132, 197n
Whiteness, 3-4, 21-41
Winwood, Sir Ralph, 26
Wonder of Women, 124-26
Wycherly, 173

Zanche (character), 126-28
Zanthia (character), 124-26, 128-31
Zarack (character), 106-10